U.S. Depart..........
Homeland Security

United States
Coast Guard

MW00650739

Aids to Navigation Manual Administration

23 FEB 2015
COMDTINST M16500.7A

U.S. Department of Homeland Security

United States Coast Guard

Commandant
United States Coast Guard

US Coast Guard Stop 7418
2703 Martin Luther King Jr Ave, SE
Washington DC 20593-7418
Staff Symbol: CG-NAV-1
Phone: (202) 372-1551
Fax: (202) 372-8358

COMDT

CHANGENOTE 16500
23 FEB 2015

COMMANDANT CHANGE NOTICE 16500

Subj: CH-2 TO AIDS TO NAVIGATION MANUAL – ADMINISTRATION COMDTINST M16500.7A

1. <u>PURPOSE.</u> To provide changes to the Coast Guard's Aids to Navigation Manual – Administration, COMDTINST M16500.7A.

2. <u>ACTION.</u> All Coast Guard unit commanders, commanding officers, officers-in-charge, deputy/assistant commandants, and chiefs of headquarters staff elements shall comply with the provisions of this Commandant Change Notice. Internet release is authorized.

3. <u>DIRECTIVES AFFECTED.</u> With the incorporation of this Commandant Change Notice, the Coast Guard's Aids to Navigation Manual – Administration, COMDTINST M16500.7A is updated.

4. <u>DISCLAIMER.</u> This guidance is not a substitute for applicable legal requirements, nor is it itself a rule. It is intended to provide operational guidance for Coast Guard personnel and is not intended to nor does it impose legally-binding requirements on any party outside the Coast Guard.

5. <u>MAJOR CHANGES.</u> The Commandant Change Notice announces the Coast Guard will no longer print copies of the Coast Guard Light Lists. The following Coast Guard Light Lists will remain available on the Coast Guard Navigation Center (NAVCEN) website at http://www.navcen.uscg.gov/?pageName=lightLists.

   Light List Vol. 1- Atlantic Coast from St. Croix River, ME to Shrewsbury River, NJ, COMDTPUB P16502.1
   Light List Vol. 2 - Atlantic Coast from Shrewsbury River, NJ to Little River, SC, COMDTPUB P16502.2

DISTRIBUTION – SDL No. 165

	a	b	c	d	e	f	g	h	i	j	k	l	m	n	o	p	q	r	s	t	u	v	w	x	y	z
A					X		X					X	X	X	X	X	X	X	X							
B		X	X		X	X				X			X	X								X				
C					X		X																X		X	
D	X			X									X													X
E																			X							
F																										
G																										
H																										

NON-STANDARD DISTRIBUTION:

Light List Vol. 3 - Atlantic and Gulf Coasts from Little River, SC to Econfina River, FL COMDTPUB P16502.3
Light List Vol. 4 - Gulf of Mexico from Econfina River, FL to Rio Grande, TX COMDTPUB P16502.4
Light Lists Vol. 5 - Mississippi River System COMDTPUB P16502.5
Light Lists Vol. 6 - Pacific Coast and Pacific Islands COMDTPUB P16502.6
Light List Vol. 7 - Great Lakes COMDTPUB P16502.7.

6. IMPACT ASSESSMENT. This change will have no impact on personnel resources, training, or funding.

7. ENVIRONMENTAL ASPECT AND IMPACT CONSIDERATIONS. The development of this directive and the general policies contained within it have been thoroughly reviewed by the originating office and are categorically excluded under current USCG categorical exclusion (CE) 1 from further environmental analysis, in accordance with Section 2.B.2. and Figure 2-1 of the National Environmental Policy Act Implementing Procedures and Policy for Considering Environmental Impacts, COMDTINST M16475.1 (series).

8. DISTRUBUTION. No paper distribution will be made of this Commandant Change Notice. An electronic version will be located on the following Commandant (CG-612) web sites. Internet: http://www.uscg.mil/directives/, and CGPortal: https://cgportal2.uscg.mil/library/directives/SitePages/Home.aspx.

9. PROCEDURE. Remove and replace the following:

REMOVE
Pages 12-39 to-12-42

INSERT
Pages 12-39 to 12-42

10. RECORDS MANAGEMENT CONSIDERATIONS. This Commandant Change Notice has been thoroughly reviewed by the USCG, and the undersigned have determined this action requires further scheduling requirements, in accordance with Federal Records Act, 44 U.S.C. 3101 et seq., NARA requirements, and Information and Life Cycle Management Manual, COMDTINST M5212.12 (series). This policy has significant or substantial changes to existing records management requirements or inconsistencies with existing determinations relating to documentation requirements.

11. FORMS/REPORTS. None.

12. REQUEST FOR CHANGES. Submit change requests through the chain of command to Commandant (CG-NAV-1).

G. C. RASICOT /s/
Senior Executive Service, U. S. Coast Guard
Director, Marine Transportation Systems Management

U.S. Department of Homeland Security

United States Coast Guard

Commandant
United States Coast Guard

2100 Second St SW Stop 7581
Washington, DC 20593-7581
Staff Symbol: CG-54131
Phone: 202-372-1546
Fax: 202-372-1991

COMDTNOTE 16500
8 Jan 2010

COMMANDANT NOTICE 16500   CANCELLED: 07 JAN 11

Subj: CH-1 TO AIDS TO NAVIGATION MANUAL- ADMINISTRATION, COMDTINST M16500.7A

1. <u>PURPOSE</u>. This Notice promulgates Change 1 to the Aids to Navigation Manual- Administration, COMDTINST M16500.7A.

2. <u>ACTION</u>. All Coast Guard unit commanders, commanding officers, officers-in-charge, deputy/assistant commandants, and chiefs of headquarters staff elements shall comply with the provisions of this Manual. Internet release is authorized.

3. <u>DIRECTIVES AFFECTED</u>. Aids to Navigation Battery Tracking System, COMDTINST 16478.11, has been incorporated into this change, and is hereby cancelled.

4. <u>PROCEDURES</u>. No paper distribution will be made of this manual. Official distribution will be via the Coast Guard Directives System DVD. An electronic version will be located on the Information and Technology, Commandant (CG-612), CGWEB and WWW website at: http://CGCENTRAL.USCG.MIL/ (Once in CG Central, click on the "RESOURCES" Tab and then "DIRECTIVES".) http://www.uscg.mil/ccs/cit/cim/directives/welcome.htm. For personnel who keep a paper copy of the manual, remove and insert the following pages:

Remove	**Insert**
Table of Contents	Table of Contents
1-1 and 1-10	1-1 and 1-10
2-3 and 2-4	2-3 and 2-4
2-7 thru 2-12	2-7 thru 2-12
3-13 thru 3-19	3-13 thru 3-21
Chapter 4	Chapter 4
5-1 thru 5-11	5-1 thru 5-11
6-1 thru 6-8	6-1 thru 6-9
7-1 thru 7-7	7-1 thru 7-7

DISTRIBUTION – SDL No. 153

	a	b	c	d	e	f	g	h	i	j	k	l	m	n	o	p	q	r	s	t	u	v	w	x	y	z
A		1		1		1			1	1	1	1	1	1	1	1										
B		1	1		1	1			1				1	1												
C						*	1									1							1			
D	1			1									1													1
E																										
F																										
G																										
H																										

NON-STANDARD DISTRIBUTION: C:l Burlington, St. Ignace, Portage, Lorain, Muskegon, Saginaw River, Channel Islands (1)

	Remove	Insert
	8-1 thru 8-4	8-1 thru 8-4
	Chapter 9	Chapter 9
	10-1 thru 10-4	10-1 thru 10-4
	10-11and 10-12	10-11 and 10-12
	11-5 and 11-10	11-5 and 11-10
	12-3 thru 12-8	12-3 thru 12-8
	12-15 thru 12-24	12-15 thru 12-24
	12-27 thru 12-28	12-27 thru 12-28
	12-31 thru 12-53	12-31 thru 12-53
	13-5 and 13-12	13-5 and 13-12
	Chapter 14	Chapter 14

5. <u>SUMMARY OF CHANGES</u>. Numerous corrections were made throughout the manual to reflect recent organizational name changes. The following table summarizes substantive changes:

Section	Change
1.C.4	Updates objective of aids to navigation system
2.B.2.b	Clarifies policy on CG-3213 submission requirements
2.F.3	Requires use of the I-ATONIS style guide when making data entries in order to improve data consistency
2.F.9	Specifies the use of I-ATONIS for ATON battery tracking
3.C.5	Clarifies policy on temporary changes
3.E	Implements Aid Availability categories
4.B	Additions to glossary of Aids to Navigation terms
4.D.1	Clarifies definition of Major Light
4.D.7.f	Deletes "in prioritized order" in reference to methods of sound signal control
4.G.8	Clarifies policy for marking wind farms and associated structures
5.B.3	Clarifies private aid inspection/verification requirements for Coast Guard and Coast Guard Auxiliary personnel
6.A.2	Provides policy on wreck marking waiver authority
7.A	Simplified servicing unit responsibilities
7.B.6.d	Clarifies maximum penalties that may be imposed for vandalizing an aid to navigation
7.C.1	Specifies that steel hull buoy reliefs should be extended where possible
Chapter 9	Renames the "Discrepancy Response Decision Guide" as the "Discrepancy Response Factor Decision Guide"
9.A.1	Removed guidance that temporary changes exceeding 6 months will be considered as a AtoN discrepancy
9.C	Requires an I-ATONIS data entry to reflect the date and time a unit completes a temporary corrective action to an ATON discrepancy

Section	**Change**
10.A.2	Quotas for aids to navigation training are managed through the National Aids to Navigation school
12.C.5.d(5)(o)	Provides policy for publishing positions of aids to navigation that are received from the National Oceanographic Service as a chart correction
12.D	Updates information to reflect that I-ATONIS is the data source used to publish the Coast Guard Light List. Also updates guidance on publishing Light List corrections.

6. <u>ENVIRONMENTAL ASPECT AND IMPACT CONSIDERATIONS</u>. Environmental considerations under the National Environmental Policy Act (NEPA) were examined in the development of this instruction. This instruction includes preparation of guidance documents that implement, without substantive change, the applicable Commandant Instruction or other Federal agency regulations, procedures, manuals, and other guidance documents. It is categorically excluded from further NEPA analysis and documentation requirements under Categorical Exclusion (33) as published in the National Environmental Policy Act Implementing Procedures and Policy for Considering Environmental Impacts Manual, COMDTINST M16475.1D, Figure 2-1. An Environmental Checklist and Categorical Exclusion Determination (CED) are not required.

7. <u>FORMS/REPORTS</u>. The forms referenced in this Instruction are available in USCG Electronic Forms on the Standard Workstation or on the Internet: http://www.uscg.mil/forms/; CG Central at http://cgcentral.uscg.mil/; and Intranet at http://cgweb.comdt.uscg.mil/CGForms.

K. S. COOK /s/
Director of Prevention Policy

Enclosure: CH-1 to Aids to Navigation Manual- Administrative, COMDTINST M16500.7A

U.S. Department of Homeland Security

United States Coast Guard

Commandant
United States Coast Guard

2100 Second Street, S.W.
Washington, DC 20593-0001
Staff Symbol: G-OPN-2
Phone: (202) 267-0344
Fax: (202) 267-4222
Email: JArenstam@comdt.uscg.mil

COMDTINST M16500.7A
02 MAR 2005

Subj: AIDS TO NAVIGATION MANUAL – ADMINISTRATION

1. PURPOSE. To replace and update the Aids to Navigation Manual – Administration. This Manual Instruction promulgates policy and guidance for the administration of the Short Range Aids to Navigation Program.

2. ACTION. Area and District Commanders, commanders of maintenance and logistic commands, and unit Commanding Officers shall ensure that the provisions of this Manual are followed. Internet release authorized.

3. DIRECTIVES AFFECTED. Aids to Navigation Manual – Administration, COMDTINST M16500.7; Range Design Considerations, COMDTINST 16500.23; and Aids to Navigation Information System (ATONIS), COMDTINST 16500.15 are cancelled.

4. CHANGES. Recommendations for improvements to this manual shall be submitted to the Office of Aids to Navigation – Short Range Aids Division (G-OPN-2).

5. ENVIROMENTAL ASPECT AND IMPACT CONSIDERATIONS. Environmental considerations were examined in the development of this Manual and are incorporated herein. The creation of this manual is categorically excluded under Coast Guard Exclusion 33 in the National Environmental Policy Act Implementing Procedures and Policy for Considering Environmental Impacts, COMDTINST M16475.1 (series).

6. FORMS/REPORTS. All mentioned forms can be found in the USCG Forms library.

/s/
W. UNDERWOOD
Director of Operations Policy

J.

DISTRIBUTION – SDL No.

	a	b	c	d	e	f	g	h	i	j	k	l	m	n	o	p	q	r	s	t	u	v	w	x	y	z
A		1		1		1						1	1	1	1	1	1	1	1							
B		1	1	1		1				1				1	1											
C									*	1						1							1			
D	1		1										1													1
E																										
F																										
G																										
H																										

NON-STANDARD DISTRIBUTION: C:i Burlington, St. Ignace, Portage, Lorain, Muskegon, Saginaw River, Channel Islands (1)

RECORD OF CHANGES

CHANGE NUMBER	DATE OF CHANGE	DATE ENTERED	BY WHOM ENTERED
1	8 Jan 2010	11 Feb 2010	ATON ADMIN Manual Administrator
2	23 Feb 2015	26 FEB 2015	CG-NAV-1

Table of Contents

This Page Intentionally
Left Blank.

CHAPTER 1 - INTRODUCTION

A. <u>Aids to Navigation Manual</u>.

   1. <u>Purpose</u>. The Coast Guard operates and administers the United States Aids to Navigation System. The principal policy statements, administrative practices, and technical information needed to establish, operate, and maintain those parts of the system which have audio, visual, radar, or radio characteristics are presented in this manual.

   2. <u>Content</u>. This Manual contains instructions and policies governing the operation and maintenance of federally controlled visual, audio, radar, and radio aids to navigation, along with administrative instruction for field units and commands needed to support the aids to navigation system. Reference material is included where the source documents are not widely distributed. References are also made to Coast Guard and other Federal publications, various Commandant Instructions, and standard seamanship texts.

   3. <u>Use</u>. This Manual is intended only for the internal guidance of personnel involved in the administration of the Coast Guard's aids to navigation program. The high expectations of performance contained in this manual are intended to encourage public service above and beyond the minimum threshold of due care. **This guidance is not a substitute for applicable legal requirements. It is not intended to nor does it impose legally binding requirements on any party.** Any requirements or obligations created by this manual flow only from those involved in Coast Guard aids to navigation administration to the Coast Guard, and the Coast Guard retains the discretion to deviate or authorize deviation from these requirements. This Manual creates no duties or obligations to the public to comply with the procedures described herein, and no member of the public should rely upon these procedures as a representation by the Coast Guard as to the manner of performance of our aids to navigation mission. **Questions or comments from the public concerning compliance with any statutory or regulatory requirements referenced in the manual should be addressed to Commandant (CG-5413).**

   4. <u>Organization</u>.

      a. The Aids to Navigation Manual is published in six separate volumes:

         (1) Aids to Navigation Manual – Positioning, COMDTINST M16500.1 (series). Prepared and revised by Commandant **(CG-5413)**.

         (2) Aids to Navigation Manual – Technical, COMDTINST M16500.3A (series). Prepared and revised by Commandant **(CG-432)**.

         (3) Aids to Navigation Manual – Administration, COMDTINST M16500.7 (series). Prepared and revised by Commandant **(CG-5413)**.

(4) Aids to Navigation Manual – Radionavigation, COMDTINST M16500.13 (series). Prepared and revised by Commandant **(CG-5413).**

(5) Aids to Navigation Manual-Seamanship, COMDTINST M16500.21 (series). Prepared and revised by Commandant **(CG-751).**

(6) Aids to Navigation Manual - Structures, COMDTINST M16500.25 (series). Prepared and revised by Commandant **(CG-432).**

5. Additional Information Sources. Pertinent Commandant Instructions and Notices will normally be found in the following series: 10500 and 16500.

B. Short Range Aids to Navigation Systems.

1. Definition. A short range aids to navigation system is a group of interacting external reference devices intended to collectively provide sufficient and timely information with which to safely navigate within and through a waterway when used in conjunction with updated nautical charts and other commonly available material. The system includes all navigation devices within visual, audio, or radar range of the mariner. The term "aids to navigation system" is also used to refer to the particular marking scheme used by a system of aids. Most aids to navigation employ the U.S. Marking System or a variation of this standard system. Complete descriptions of each marking system are contained in Chapters 4 and 5 of this manual.

2. System Types.

a. The U. S. Aids to Navigation System. The U. S. Aids to Navigation System is a predominantly lateral system which is consistent with Region B requirements of the International Association of Marine Aids to Navigation and Lighthouse Authorities (IALA) Maritime Buoyage System, except U.S. possessions west of the International Date Line and south of 10 degrees north latitude, which follow IALA Region A.

b. The Intracoastal Waterway (ICW) Marking System. This variation of the U.S. Marking System is employed along the Atlantic and Gulf Intracoastal Waterways. It differs from the standard U. S. Marking System by displaying distinctive yellow bands, triangles, or squares to connote ICW significance.

c. The Western Rivers Marking System. This system differs from the U. S. Aids to Navigation System due to the unstable nature of the river waters and channels. Chapter 4 outlines these differences in detail. The Coast Guard operates this system on the Mississippi River, its tributaries, South Pass and Southwest Pass to the navigational demarcation lines dividing the high seas from harbors, rivers and other inland waters of the United States. It is also used on the following rivers and waterways

(1) Port Allen-Morgan City Alternate Route,

(2) That part of the Atchafalaya River above its junction with the Port Allen-Morgan City Alternate Route including Old River.

(3) The Tennessee-Tombigbee Waterway,

(4) Tombigbee River,

(5) Black Warrior River,

(6) Alabama River,

(7) Coosa River,

(8) Mobile River above Cochrane Bridge at St. Louis Point,

(9) Flint River,

(10) Chattachoochee River, and

(11) Apalachicola River above its confluence with the Jackson River.

d. <u>Private Aids to Navigation</u>. Private aids should conform to the existing system in which they are placed. Rules for establishing and inspecting private aids are contained in Chapter 5.

C. <u>Coast Guard Authority</u>.

1. <u>General Authority</u>. The Coast Guard has authority to:

a. Develop, administer, and operate Short Range Aids to Navigation Systems to serve the needs of maritime commerce and the Armed Forces.

b. Control private aids to navigation in waters subject to the jurisdiction of the United States and on the outer continental shelf, and on the high seas when the owner is subject to the jurisdiction of the United States.

c. Mark wrecks in the navigable waters of the United States or waters above the continental shelf.

d. Prescribe lights and other signals to mark obstructions to navigation located in the navigable waters of the United States or waters above the continental shelf.

e. Disseminate information to mariners concerning the operation of aids to navigation.

2. <u>Statutory Authorities</u>.

a. The Coast Guard shall develop, maintain, establish, and operate, with due regard for the requirements of national defense, aids to maritime navigation for promotion of safety on and over the high seas and waters subject to the jurisdiction of the United States (14 USC 2).

b. In order to aid navigation and prevent disasters, collisions, or wrecks, the Coast Guard may establish, maintain, and operate aids to maritime navigation required to serve the needs of the Armed Forces or of the commerce of the United States (14 USC 81).

c. Short range aids to navigation systems shall be established and operated only within the United States, the waters above the continental shelf, the territories and possessions of the United States, the Trust Territory of the Pacific Islands, and beyond the territorial jurisdiction of the United States at places where naval or military bases of the United States are or may be located (14 USC 81).

d. The Commandant of the Coast Guard shall properly mark all pierheads belonging to the United States situated on the northern and northwestern lakes, whenever he is duly notified by the department charged with the construction or repair of pierheads that the construction or repair of any such pierheads has been completed. (33 USC 735)

e. Under authority of the Outer Continental Lands Act (43 USC 1333), enacted in 1953, the Coast Guard may promulgate and enforce regulations with respect to lights and warning devices on the artificial islands, installations, and other devices on the outer continental shelf involved in the exploration, development, removal, or transportation of resources there from. See also C.2.f (1) below.

f. Other statutes authorize the Coast Guard to:

(1) Prescribe lights and other signals to be displayed on fixed and floating structures located in or over waters subject to the jurisdiction of the United States, and on the high seas when the owner or operator is subject to the jurisdiction of the United States. (14 USC 85).

(2) Issue and enforce regulations concerning lights and other warning devices in deepwater ports and their adjacent waters. (33 USC 1509)

(3) Disseminate information to mariners concerning aids to navigation under the jurisdiction of the Coast Guard, including the publication and distribution of Light Lists and Notices to Mariners (14 USC 92, 93; 44 USC 1309)

(4) Regulate the establishment, maintenance and discontinuance of private aids to navigation. (14 USC 83).

(5) The Commandant of the Coast Guard shall provide, establish, and maintain, out of the annual appropriations for the Coast Guard, buoys or other suitable marks for marking anchorage grounds for vessels in waters of the United States, when such anchorage grounds have been defined and established by proper authority in accordance with the laws of the United States. (33 USC 472)

(6) Mark wrecks or other obstructions in the navigable waters of the United States or waters above the continental shelf. Owners of wrecks and obstructions are responsible for marking and liable for the cost of marking if performed by the Coast Guard. (14 USC 86, 33 USC 409)

(7) Prescribe lights and other signals necessary for the safety of marine navigation to be displayed from bridges over the navigable waters of the United States. (33 USC 494, 14 USC 85)

(8) Enforce laws for the protection of aids to navigation maintained by or under the authority of the Coast Guard. (14 USC 84, 89, 643; 33 USC 408, 411, 412, 413)

(9) Establish, operate and maintain aids to navigation for the primary benefit of Federal agencies other than the Armed Forces. (14 USC 93(d), 141, 633)

g. The National Environmental Policy Act of January 1970 (42 USC 4321), requires that all Federal agencies assist to the fullest extent possible the Federal effort to protect and enhance the environment.

3. Regulations. Title 33, Subchapter C, Parts 60-76 contains the regulations, as provided for in the preceding statutory authorities, pertaining to aids to navigation.

4. Objective of the Aids to Navigation System.

a. Aids to navigation systems are developed, established, operated and maintained by the United States Coast Guard to accomplish the following:

(1) Assist navigators in determining their position.

(2) Assist the navigator in determining a safe course.

(3) Warn the navigator of dangers and obstructions.

(4) Promote the safe and economic movement of commercial vessel traffic.

(5) **Promote the safe and efficient movement of military vessel traffic, and cargo of strategic military importance.**

D. Short Range Aids to Navigation Organization.

1. Tasks. To effectively carry out the statutory authorities of the Coast Guard for aids to navigation, each level of the Coast Guard's organization is assigned certain tasks. Those tasks outlined in this manual apply to units specifically assigned the mission of administration, operation or maintenance of the aids to navigation system. Commanding Officers and Officers-in-Charge of units not assigned an aids to navigation mission shall inform the District Commander by message of any aid to navigation that is found to be out of order or obviously out of position, including information as to corrective action taken. The report to the District Commander shall involve any important hydrographic information or any other information of navigational interest to shipping.

2. **Commandant (CG-00). Coast Guard regulations contain the general authority of the Commandant with respect to aids to navigation. The staff components at Headquarters tasked with administering or assisting the aids to navigation program are:**

   a. Commandant **(CG-5413).** The primary tasks of the Chief, **Navigation Systems Division**, are to:

      (1) Administer and supervise the operation and routine maintenance of the aids to navigation system, including support units.

      (2) Review for approval certain District Commander recommendations regarding establishment, discontinuance, or changes in aids to navigation. (See Chapter 2.B.)

      (3) Maintain Light Lists (COMDTINST M16502.1 thru M16502.7) and oversee issuance of Local Notices to Mariners by District Commanders.

      (4) Oversee financial management of the aids to navigation system.

      (5) Plan and budget for future developments in aids to navigation.

      (6) Prepare and review various aids to navigation publications.

      (7) Coordinate the administration and training of aids to navigation personnel.

      (8) Develop and monitor ATON program measures, including aid availability.

(9) Maintain system of aids to navigation, **aid availability objectives are outlined in section 3.E of this manual**.

(10) Maintain records necessary for the proper accomplishments of the above tasks.

b. Commandant **(CG-4)**. The primary responsibilities to support the short-range aids to navigation system **for the Assistant Commandant for Engineering and Logistics** are assigned as follows:

(1) Commandant **(CG-43)**. The primary tasks of the Chief, Office of Civil Engineering is responsible for developing policy and standards for design, maintenance, construction, and inspection of all fixed and floating aids to navigation, light stations, buildings, shops, docks, antennas over 100 feet and aids to navigation signaling equipment.

(2) Commandant **(CG-432)**, The Ocean Engineering Division is the Support Manager for the Aids to Navigation (ATON) and Marine Environmental Protection (MEP) programs. Responsibilities include program oversight for the ATON and MEP engineering support missions; development and implementation of support policy and program mission requirements; engineering management for system configuration, procurement, training, evaluation, and integration of new equipment and systems into the program; sponsorship of Research and Development initiatives; and management of financial resources for the program.

(3) Commandant **(CG-45)**. The primary tasks of the Chief, **Office of Naval Engineering** are for the alteration, maintenance and repair of tender class vessels and aids to navigation boats, and for support to the Office of Acquisition Project Managers in the design and constitution of aids to navigation vessels.

c. Commandant (CG-6). The primary responsibilities to support the short-range aids to navigation system **for the Assistant Commandant of Command, Control, Communications, Computers and IT** are assigned as follows:

(1) Commandant (CG-64), Chief, **Office of Command, Control and Navigation Systems** is responsible for the acquisition, installation, improvement and maintenance of short-range electronic aids to navigation including racons and other electronic hardware.

(2) Commandant (CG-62), Chief, **Office of Communication Systems** is responsible for landline, radio communication, radio spectrum management support, and liaison with national and international radio policy-making organizations. Application for operation of all radionavigation transmitting equipment, including racons, radars, and radar transponders must be made in accordance with Radio Frequency Plan, COMDTINST M2400.1 (series) and Telecommunications Manual, COMDTINST M2000.3 (series).

(3) Commandant (CG-66), Office of Research, Development, and **Technical** Management is responsible to plan, control, and administer research and development projects in the aids to navigation mission area; provide technical advice, information and direct laboratory support in the technical areas of optics, acoustics, engineering physics, electrical engineering, materials engineering, shore electronics systems, including communications, operations research and human factors and physiology; and to plan and manage the expenditure of funds designated for research and development in short range aids to navigation under the guidance of Commandant **(CG-54131)**.

3. <u>Area Commander</u>. As defined by Coast Guard Regulations, Area Commanders are responsible for overall mission performance in their areas, and supervises the Maintenance and Logistics Commands and District Commands.

4. <u>District Commander</u>.

   a. The District Commander has the authority to administer the aids to navigation activities within the district. Coast Guard Regulations outline general responsibilities in this regard, and the Coast Guard Organization Manual, COMDTINST M5400.7 (series), gives more detailed information as to the functions of the various staff components assisting the District Commanders. Specific tasks assigned to and administrative procedures used by the District Commander, are contained throughout this manual.

   b. The Chief, **Waterways Management** Branch in a district has many responsibilities such as planning, coordinating and reviewing the operations of the district's individual field units and maintaining contact with military and civilian users of Coast Guard aids to navigation. The position is also normally the Program Manager for Domestic Ice Operations, (in those districts that are subject to ice operations,) and ADCON for DGPS and LORAN.

   c. Monitor ATON program measures to ensure proper management of the aids to navigation system.

   d. Aids to Navigation are serviced IAW guidelines as set forth in Chapter 7.

e. Maintain the system of aids to navigation, **aid availability objectives are outlined in section 3.E of this manual.**

f. Ensure the prompt and correct entry of required data into district level **Integrated Aids to Navigation Information System** (I-ATONIS).

5. Maintenance and Logistic Commander. Specific responsibilities and coordination of activities between the operational commander in the district and the support commander in the region have been issued by each Maintenance and Logistic Commander

6. Sector Commanders and Individual Unit Commanding Officers and Officers-in-Charge shall:

a. Possess a sense of ownership. Be responsible to obtain and communicate the support needed to maintain fixed and floating aids to navigation in a high standard of materiel condition.

b. Develop a close working relationship through frequent contact and by exchanging information with the users of Coast Guard aids to navigation.

c. Service aids to navigation IAW guidelines as set forth in Chapter 7.

d. Maintain the system of aids to navigation, **aid availability objectives are outlined in section 3.E of this manual.**

e. Produce a Federal Aid Information Document (FID) every time an aid is serviced. The FID is required to be signed by the CO/OIC.

f. Ensure I-ATONIS is utilized and maintained in accordance with Chapter 2.

g. Seek out methods to improve the system, forwarding suggestions to higher authority for distribution Coast Guard wide.

7. Headquarters Units. Headquarters units operate under the direction of a Headquarters Office Chief. The aids to navigation functions performed as part of their missions are as follows:

a. The Command and Control Engineering Center, Portsmouth, VA. develops, builds, and fields advanced electronic command, control and navigation systems.

b. The Research and Development Center, Groton, CT. conducts applied research and develops operational techniques, concepts, systems, equipment, and materials.

c. The Engineering Logistics Center, Baltimore, MD. performs inventory management functions, supply cycle support, and technical/quality assurance for all ATON hardware. ATON hardware includes small ATON devices, and headquarters controlled short-range ATON equipment

d. The National Aids to Navigation School, Coast Guard Training Center, Yorktown, VA. provides training in aids to navigation equipment, systems, maintenance and policy for officer, enlisted, and civilian personnel.

CHAPTER 2 - GENERAL ADMINISTRATION OF THE SHORT RANGE AIDS TO NAVIGATION SYSTEM

A. Management Principles.

1. Personnel Management.

   a. Personnel management deals with a relatively scarce and expensive resource-- the people. "Scarce" is becoming a particularly appropriate adjective for people experienced with the aids to navigation system. Therefore, the dynamic growth and development of this resource should be the prime effort of all supervisory personnel.

   b. Commanding Officers and Officers-in-Charge of aids to navigation units must ensure proper assignments of Enlisted Qualification Codes to members of their command. The procedure for qualification and assignment of such codes is explained fully in the Enlisted Qualification Codes Manual, COMDTINST M1414.9 (series). Failure to fulfill all service record and reporting requirements for Qualification Codes may result in an inaccurate record of a person's qualifications being made available to Coast Guard Personnel Command. When this happens, qualified aids to navigation personnel may be unintentionally rotated out of aids to navigation duty or fail selection for responsible duty assignments for which they are actually qualified.

2. Unit Management.

   a. As the keystone of personnel management is interest in and concern for the individual; management of aids to navigation units should reflect this same philosophy. Frequent visits should be made to every operating unit by chain of command representatives. Since aids to navigation work lacks the glamour and action of other Coast Guard mission areas, those other areas may demand and receive more of the administrator's attention. However, aids to navigation work requires great precision and thoroughly professional competence, which only result from proper training and motivation.

   b. Sector Commanders will conform to the following policy: Primary assignment of aids to navigation officers will be given only to experienced, mature officers with a sound background in aids to navigation. Should there be no one available who meets these requirements, consult with your district's aids to navigation branch chief to arrive at a resolution.

c. Secondly, Sector Aids to Navigation Officers with subordinate units will schedule the maximum possible number of visits to these units, either by themselves or by a carefully selected conscientious representative. The purpose of these visits should be two-fold. They should insure that field units are operating in a professional manner, and they should appraise their material and personnel needs, with requests for action to meet these needs promptly addressed to cognizant superiors.

B. Administrative Procedures.

1. Introduction. Considerations that affect changes in individual aids vary widely between different types of aids. Costs may vary from a few dollars for a daybeacon to millions of dollars for a day-night range. General policies concerning additions to, or changes in, the aids to navigation system and the related operational and administrative policies are outlined in this section.

2. Aids to Navigation Operation Request (Form CG-3213) and Aids to Navigation Operation Request Supplement (Form CG-3213A).

    a. Purpose.

        (1) The Aids to Navigation Operation Request (Form CG-3213) is used to justify and authorize proposed changes in the Coast Guard aids to navigation system, and to record those changes. The submission of this form serves to:

            (a) Ensure the proposals conform to existing regulations concerning the aids to navigation system of the United States.

            (b) Provide justification for the proposed changes in terms of usage, environmental conditions, and other factors.

            (c) Obtain approval for the operating characteristics of the aid.

            (d) Provide a brief summary of the technical details of the aids, including type of equipment to be used and cost estimates.

            (e) Obtain authority to expend funds for specific projects.

(f) Provide an official record of certain data appearing in the Light List and Notice to Mariners.

(g) Ensure buoy hull type inventories are accurate so the correct numbers of maintenance relief hulls are maintained in inventory. See Chapter 14, Buoy Inventory Management, for detailed information on buoy body management.

(2) The Aids to Navigation Operation Request Supplement (Form CG-3213A) is used to provide technical information on aids to navigation projects.

b. Criteria and Approving Authority.

(1) Submission of Form CG-3213 is not required in the following cases, provided that an appropriate Notice to Mariners is issued, and a request for funds is not involved:

(a) The temporary establishment, relocation, change, or discontinuance of any short range aid to navigation.

(b) Discontinuance of any temporary aid which has served its purpose.

(c) Installation of approved types of visual reflectors or reflective material.

(d) Routine marking of channels in the Western Rivers.

(e) The permanent minor relocation of buoys and minor structures to better mark a channel, reduce the aid destruction rate, or facilitate aid construction provided that service to the mariner is not reduced.

(f) Restoration of damaged, destroyed, or missing aids to their previous operating status as shown in the Light List, **provided that the restoration efforts do not exceed the (OE) fund limits set in the Financial Resource Management Manual (FRMM), COMDTINST M7100.3 (series).**

(2) All other permanent changes to the Coast Guard aids to navigation system necessitating a Light List or chart correction must be authorized by approval of Form CG-3213. District commanders or their designated representatives are authorized to approve the Form CG-3213 form except for the following instances that require submission to the Commandant **(CG-5413)** for approval:

(a) Any project requiring expenditure of Acquisition, Construction and Improvement (AC&I) Waterways funds.

(b) Any project requiring expenditure of operating expense (OE) funds in excess of $25,000.

(c) Any project involving changes in the staffing level of a manned aid to navigation.

(d) Any project requiring submission of a Project Development Submittal (PDS).

(e) Any project proposing use of unauthorized or non-standard equipment or characteristics.

(f) Any project proposing establishment of aids in waters not already marked by the Coast Guard.

(g) Any project involving cooperation and/or coordination with state, Federal, foreign, or international agencies.

(h) Any project which proposes to eliminate, or decrease the range of, the primary light or sound signal **of** a major aid.

(i) Any projects to establish daytime ranges. Commandant **(CG-432)** will provide input for range design and equipment selection.

(j) Any project of an unusual nature, e.g., significant public interest which should be brought to the attention of the Commandant.

c. Preparation and Format.

(1) Form CG-3213 may be prepared to include more than one aid and more than one action when all are part of the same current project and are in the same geographic area. The form shall be completed in accordance with the instruction on the reverse side.

(2) Marking of major Corps of Engineers river and harbor projects, or extensive revisions in types and placement of existing aids to navigation, in terms of time and geography, should be the subject of a Waterways Analysis and Management (WAMS) study. Although the entire waterway will be studied, it may be desirable to treat the actual work as a series of smaller projects rather than as a single project. This will facilitate the review and administration of the projects in both the district and headquarters, and will minimize the need to change or amend projects.

(3) CG-3213 prepared for approval at the district level should contain the same background information required for those projects submitted to Commandant for approval. Item 14 should be signed by an individual authorized by the aids to navigation branch chief and item 16 should be signed by the aids to navigation branch chief. This is the minimum amount of administrative action necessary to ensure proper control within the district.

(4) The following should be included in each Form CG-3213 and Form CG-3213A:

(a) Adequate justification in terms of the type of vessels, cargo number of transits, how the aids would be used, etc.

(b) Accurate charting data.

  i. The position of the aid shall be given in latitude and longitude, conforming with the precision standards listed in the Aids to Navigation Manual – Positioning, COMDTINST M16500.1 (series).

  ii. If an existing aid is moved (assigned position changed), the new latitude and longitude conforming with the precision standards listed in the Aids to Navigation Manual – Positioning, COMDTINST M16500.1 (series) should be given. It shall NOT be described as "moved to a new position 50 yards, 047 degrees from its old position."

(c) A section of the largest scale chart on which the proposed changes are indicated shall be enclosed with Form CG-3213 when submitted to the Commandant. The following information must appear on the chart section:

    i. Chart number (NOS, NGA, or other).

    ii. Latitude and longitude reference marks.

    iii. Action proposed for each aid. Avoid obscuring the aid symbol and related information appearing on the chart which indicates the status of the aid before the change is made.

(d) Reasons for rejecting other obvious or more economical solutions to the problem that might be indicated from an examination of the chart.

(e) Required operational range of lights and sound signals, and other pertinent information used in the procedures for selecting an optic for an aid to navigation as outlined in Chapter 3 of Aids to Navigation Visual Signal Design Manual, COMDTINST M16510.2 (series).

(f) Light color and phase characteristics (CG-3213A).

(g) All range Design/Range Analyses and solarcalcs.

d. <u>Project Numbers</u>.

(1) Each Form CG-3213 shall be assigned a six or seven-digit project number, derived as follows:

(a) The first two digits indicate the district originating the request.

(b) The second set of two digits indicates the fiscal year in which submitted.

(c) The last two or three digits indicate the consecutive number of the project for that fiscal year. Projects approved at the district level will be identified by the suffix "D."

(2) Project numbers should be assigned in sequence without skipping numbers.

e. <u>Buoy Allowance Changes</u>. When buoy allowances are affected by district-approved projects, submit a copy of the approved CG-3213 without cover letter to Commandant **(CG-54131)**. Form CG-3213 should contain full justification for any proposed increase in the maintenance relief hull allowance.

f. <u>Changes to Approved Projects</u>.

(1) Changes to previously approved projects may be necessary to bring them into conformance with the actual work done by the Corps of Engineers or to provide the type and location of aids that will be of greatest benefit to the mariner. A much clearer understanding of the proposed changes will result if the following guidelines are observed:

(a) If few or no items on the original project have actually been accomplished in the field, cancel the previously approved project in its entirety and submit a new project. Any changes in aids actually made should be included in the new project and noted as already accomplished. A new project number must be assigned and a statement included in Box 7, "Summary of Action Proposed" that "Project _____ is canceled in its entirety."

(b) If most of the previously authorized changes in aids have been made in the field, cancel only the unaccomplished items of the original project and submit a new project (new number), referencing the original project.

(c) Minor changes. Minor changes that become necessary between project approval and accomplishment may be authorized by the District Commander. Such changes might include a change in the position, name, number, or characteristic of an aid.

3. <u>Project Funding</u>. Most routine aids to navigation projects, including replacement or restoration of aids, are completed using OE funds, regardless of whether the approving authority is the District Commander or the Commandant. Chapter 5 of Financial Resource Management Manual, COMDTINST M7100.3 (series) summarizes the thresholds where projects should be considered AC&I or OE.

C. <u>Supplementary Instructions by District Commanders</u>.

1. <u>General.</u> The District Commander shall issue such instructions as necessary to supplement this manual and ensure efficient operation of the aids to navigation systems. Such instructions should normally be incorporated in the district SOP, but may be issued as District Commander's instructions or in another appropriate format. These supplementary instructions shall include, but are not limited to, the subjects listed in this section.

2. <u>Assignment of Sector/Unit Responsibility</u>. The District Commander shall assign responsibility for the following to the appropriate Sector or Unit Commander:

   a. Periodic inspection of manned and unmanned aids to navigation and servicing facilities

   b. Monitoring of unmanned aids to navigation.

   c. Inspection, servicing, maintenance, and relief of unmanned aids to navigation.

   d. Inspection of private aids to navigation.

3. <u>Instructions to Lamplighters</u>. The District Commander shall issue the necessary detailed instructions to lamplighters to guide them in the performance of their duties. The times and conditions under which the aids are to be operated, reports required, inspection and maintenance requirements, etc., should be specified.

4. <u>Wartime Operation of Aids to Navigation</u>. District Commanders shall prepare and issue appropriate instructions concerning the operation of lighted aids to navigation when so directed by wartime operational commanders. Appropriate contingency plans for the allocation of aids to navigation resources under wartime conditions shall be prepared as required by the Coast Guard Capabilities and Mobilization Plan.

D. <u>Administrative Reports by the District Commander</u>.

1. Certain reports are necessary to enable the Commandant to administer the aids to navigation mission of the Coast Guard. As a basic premise, the number of reports required will be the minimum consistent with the requirements of law and regulation and the need for information on which to base requests for funds, make policy decisions, and establish service-wide standards of performance. Recommendations concerning the usefulness of, or change to required reports are encouraged. The following reports are required:

2. <u>Approved Corps of Engineers River and Harbor Improvement Projects - CG-3740</u>

   a. This report summarizes for the Commandant each "New Work" River and Harbor Improvement Project upon which the Corps of Engineers plans to expend Federal funds during the next three fiscal years. The report is of primary importance to Headquarters in preparing the aids to navigation budget and in justifying requests for AC&I funds for the next several years. The following comments are applicable to the completion of this report:

      (1) The title of the project shall be that assigned by the Corps of Engineers. (Any aids to navigation established later, however, would not necessarily be given names related to the project.)

(2) Indicate the district AC&I project number immediately after the project title. If none, so state.

(3) Indicate the Corps of Engineers district in which the project is located.

(4) The chart number shall be that of the largest scale chart showing the location of the project.

(5) Description of the project shall be that written by the Corps of Engineers.

(6) Estimate date of commencement of Corps of Engineers work.

(7) Estimate date of completion of Corps of Engineers work.

(8) Include an itemized list of aids to navigation that will be required to mark the project and the fiscal year the aids will be required.

(9) Estimate the cost of new aids to navigation by fiscal year.

(10) Add any additional comments as necessary.

(11) Copies of pertinent correspondence with the Corps of Engineers should also be enclosed with the report. Chart sections or copies of Corps of Engineers project maps shall be enclosed with Form CG-3740 for each project.

(12) Include the type and cost of any additional support facilities that may be required.

  b. Submit original to Commandant **(CG-54131)** on CG-3740 annually by 1 October.

3. Waterways ATON Project Schedule, CG-3739.

  a. This schedule lists all Waterways aids to navigation projects which are proposed for accomplishment during the current and next two fiscal years.

  b. The projects shall be arranged by fiscal year in which funds are estimated to be obligated and by priority within each year. If a project is expected to extend over the fiscal year, fund requirements should be shown in different columns of the Funds Obligation Schedule.

  c. All reports shall indicate the date of signature.

d. Form CG-3213 covering projects listed on the Project Schedule must be submitted as soon as practicable after the requirement for aids to navigation has been determined.

e. Submit original to Commandant **(CG-54131)** on 15 August and 15 February.

E. Charges for Coast Guard Aids to Navigation Work.

1. General. When the Coast Guard performs aids to navigation work for any other agency, person, or corporation, including the marking of sunken wrecks or other obstructions such as artificial reefs, charges for such work shall be invoiced to the person(s) responsible in accordance with 33 CFR Part 74. District **(dpw)** shall prepare a memorandum and forward it to FINCEN (OGR) in accordance with Chapter 9 of the Finance Center Standard Operating Procedures Manual, FINCENSTFINST M7000.1 (series).

2. Charges for Wreck/Obstruction Marking.

    a. Charges for the establishment, maintenance, and discontinuance of markings for a sunken wreck or other obstruction shall be invoiced to the owner from the date of marking until the date of abandonment as established by the provisions in Chapter 6.

    b. In situations where the owner can not be determined, the cost of establishing and maintaining aids to navigation to mark abandoned sunken wrecks or other obstructions is absorbed by the Coast Guard. The Corps of Engineers shall not be billed for any charges incident to such work.

    c. In those cases where reimbursement is to be made to the Coast Guard, charges shall be billed as directed by 33 CFR Part 74. If the work is performed by contract, the actual cost to the Coast Guard shall be billed. Charges for aids to navigation and vessel time are published in Standard Rates Instruction, COMDTINST 7310.1 (series). The procedures to follow if the owner refuses to pay are outlined in Coast Guard Claims and Litigation Manual, COMDTINST M5890.9 (series).

3. Charges for Destroyed or Damaged Aids. Claims against persons responsible for damaging or destroying Coast Guard Aids to Navigation are explained in 33 CFR Part 70. Charges for aids to navigation and vessel time are published in the Standard Rates Instruction, COMDTINST 7310.1 (series).

F. Integrated Aids to Navigation Information System (I-ATONIS).

1. I-ATONIS is the official system used by the Coast Guard to store pertinent information relating to short range aids to navigation. Its use is mandatory. The information used within the database is used **to generate the** Local Notice to

Mariners, Light List, **navigational charts**, and **inform** program management decisions. Therefore, it is incumbent upon everyone associated with the ATON mission to ensure data accuracy and data integrity.

2. I- ATONIS acts as a centralized database system with District, as well as unit users accessing it on-line. OSC Martinsburg houses and maintains the I-ATONIS central database for the entire Coast Guard. Authorized users may access the central database using the Coast Guard Data Network (CGDN+). It provides a history of what has happened to the record, but when the user "saves" a record, there is no way to return to the previous state of the record except by re-entry of the data.

3. Data Entry Requirements. All aids to navigation that are to be listed in the Light List and/or aids that are charted shall be stored within I-ATONIS. This includes, but is not limited to, Federal aids maintained by the Coast Guard, Federal aids maintained by other U.S. government agencies, private aids, and Canadian aids listed in the U.S. Light List. **Commandant (CG-54131) will maintain the I-ATONIS Style Guide as a reference tool for data entry. Units should utilize the Style Guide to minimize data entry inconsistencies.**

4. ATON units shall verify the information contained in I-ATONIS every time an aid to navigation is serviced. A statement stating such shall be included on the remarks section of every APR and FID. Any corrections needed to the data that are not within the direct control of the unit shall be forwarded to the district **waterways management** office for verification and correction.

5. District **(dpw)** and Commandant **(CG-54131)** shall conduct periodic spot checks, at least semi-annually, of the data and make necessary corrections.

6. I-ATONIS data serves many purposes such as planning ATON service work, tracking program performance measures, tracking hardware configuration, and historical recordkeeping. To serve these purposes, I-ATONIS data must be accurate, timely, and consistent within Districts and across the Coast Guard. I-ATONIS data serves two important purposes:

   a. It provides information necessary to inform the public of the status of aids to navigation.

   b. It provides information necessary for budget and management decisions.

7. Some potential uses of I-ATONIS data include:

   a. Breaking aid availability down into a useable management indicator,

   b. Statistically tracking equipment failures,

c. Justifying "quality" versus "low cost" equipment procurements,

d. Statistically tracking weather and knockdown failures,

e. Justifying mission requirements for ATON assets,

f. Justifying AC&I and AFC 43 funding,

g. Adjusting the AFC 30 budget model.

8. <u>Recordkeeping</u>. I-ATONIS provides the ability to store ATON data for historical purposes. While I-ATONIS generates an electronic Aid Positioning Record (APR) and Federal Aid Information Document (FID), the official aid record continues to be in a paper format and remains at the primary servicing unit. The secondary servicing unit will utilize the electronic records in I-ATONIS.

9. <u>Battery tracking</u>. **All batteries shall be tracked using I-ATONIS. Batteries will be identified through the use of Coast Guard generated serial numbers. Specific procedures for entering data into I-ATONIS are listed in the I-ATONIS Batteries tutorial.**

a. Entries will be made when:

(1) **Batteries** are received at the servicing unit **and assigned serial numbers**. For self contained LEDs, all batteries shall be marked as one battery.

(2) Batteries are stored, installed, recovered, removed, stolen, or lost.

(3) Disposing of batteries in accordance with the Hazardous Waste Management Manual, COMDTINST M16478.1 (series).

b. Battery serial numbers shall be recorded on receipt or transfer documents to facilitate cross-checking. Likewise, transfer document numbers shall be entered in the appropriate field in I-ATONIS.

c. For Federal aids maintained by the Coast Guard, every battery must have a designated unit "OWNER" who is ultimately responsible for that battery.

BATTERY TRACKING FLOWCHART

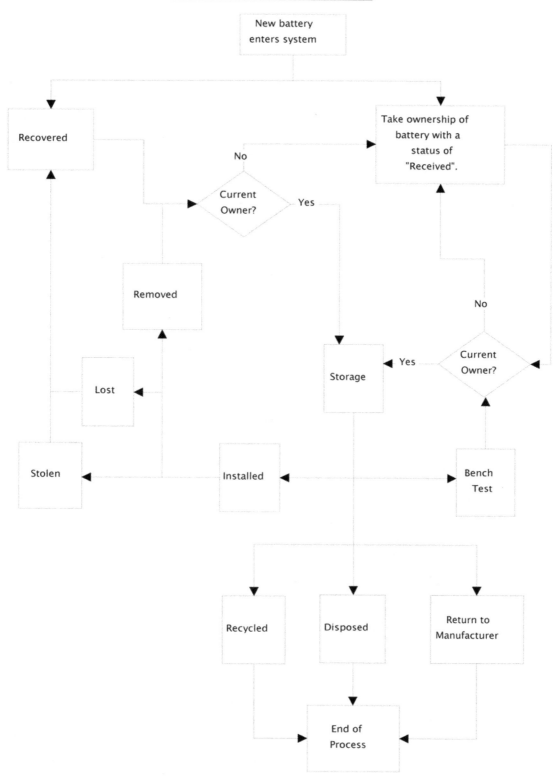

Revision Date: 29 September 2004

This Page Intentionally
Left Blank

CHAPTER 3 - ESTABLISHMENT, REVIEW, AND MODIFICATION OF COAST GUARD AIDS TO NAVIGATION SYSTEMS

A. General.

1. Primary Responsibility. The District Commander has the primary responsibility for the establishment, review, and modification of aids to navigation systems. Requests for aids or aid systems may be initiated by user groups, field units or the District Commander as a result of an analysis of the need for aids to navigation within the district. The following discussion, policies, and procedures apply equally to the establishment, review, or modification of an aid to navigation system or of individual aids within a system.

2. Governing Policies.

   a. Overview.

      (1) Coast Guard aids to navigation are established, insofar as is practicable within the limitations of the lateral system, to mark channels and other areas of "safe water." In those areas, which have rocks and shoals scattered throughout, the marking of safe water may be of necessity by the marking of the dangers. Where several channels, equally accessible and of similar size and depth, exist in the same area, special care must be exercised to avoid the placement of aids where they might mislead the mariner.

      (2) Coast Guard aids are used to mark pier heads belonging to the United States on the Great Lakes.

      (3) Coast Guard aids to navigation are used to mark hazards to navigation, wrecks and obstructions.

      (4) Aids may be established on the Outer Continental Shelf, if the benefits to be derived warrant the expenditure involved.

      (5) The following situations should be avoided unless specifically warranted by unusual circumstances:

         (a) Mixing Federal and private aids. This applies primarily to the marking of channels and should not be construed to prohibit the establishment of private aids necessary to mark bridges, pier-heads, structures, marine sites, submerged structures, wrecks, marinas, etc.

         (b) Serving the interest of only one party or small group.

(c) Establishing aids in areas not properly charted or where they would invite the inexperienced to attempt a passage, which would still be dangerous in spite of the aids.

(d) Marking shallow, trustable waterways used only for convenience rather than necessity, unless they are maintained by the Corps of Engineers. If such a waterway has only a small amount of traffic, private aids may be more appropriate.

(e) Marking narrow or shallow channels where a well-defined channel existing nearby is already marked by Coast Guard aids.

(f) Showing the location of fishing grounds in which no menace to the mariner exists.

(g) Indicating a bifurcation unless both channels are marked by Coast Guard aids or the unmarked channel is a safe, natural channel. A junction is usually not indicated if one channel is marked by the Coast Guard and the other by private aids.

(h) Marking areas that are not charted.

b.   Aids for The Armed Forces.

(1) Requests from the other Armed Forces for aids to navigation are considered along with requests from other parties with priorities among projects assigned on the basis of individual justifications.

(2) Coast Guard funds will not be expended for aids to navigation projects simply because they have been requested by the other Armed Forces. However, every effort will be made to budget for such aids once a need is established.

(3) In every case, the requesting agency will be advised of the estimated date of establishment or such other action proposed.

c.   Aids for Other Federal Agencies.

(1) The Coast Guard marks areas for special purposes, including properly designated anchorage, quarantine, danger, restricted, and prohibited areas upon request of the agency having jurisdiction for establishing the limits of those areas.

(2) No aids shall be established until areas are specifically designated for such purposes by the Coast Guard, the Center for Disease Control, or the Secretary of the Army, as appropriate.

d. Aids for Regattas and Marine Parades.

    (1) The Coast Guard may establish aids to navigation to mark marine parades and regattas which are regulated by the Coast Guard under 33 CFR 100 for the purpose of protecting life and property, or to assist in the observance and enforcement of special regulations.

    (2) Aids to navigation established in connection with regattas and marine parades are provided for the safety of navigation. These aids shall be established only for the duration of water events, which are regulated by the Coast Guard. (See 33 CFR 100.45 and 33 CFR 62.01-35).

    (3) Aids, that delineate a race course solely for the convenience of such parties, shall be treated as temporary private aids to navigation. Guidelines for exercising effective control over regattas and marine parades as required under 33 CFR 100 can be found in Regattas and Marine Parades, COMDTINST 16751.3(series).

e. Marking of Marine Construction Sites.

    (1) The Coast Guard regulates the marking of channel approaches and restricted areas caused by tunnel or bridge construction. The type and number of aids used to mark such areas are to be determined by the District Commander on the basis of operational need.

    (2) In no case should federal aids substitute for private aids which can be established on the bridge and/or tunnel structures.

f. Privately Dredged And Maintained Channels Marked By Federal Aids.

    (1) Federal aids, if the public benefit in terms of safety and economic gain to the community warrants the expenditure involved, may mark privately dredged and maintained channels.

    (2) Federal aids marking private channels must be justified using the criteria set forth in the following sections of this chapter.

    (3) Aids should be discontinued if the channel becomes unstable or inadequately maintained or when marking costs become disproportionate to user benefits.

(4) Where available funds do not permit marking of all qualified channels, preference shall be given to those maintained by public agencies (including states, cities, port authorities, etc.).

(5) Channels leading to areas open to general commerce such as port authority or commercial terminals, marinas, etc., may be eligible for Coast Guard marking. The imposition of dockage charges or other fees will not disqualify an otherwise eligible channel from Federal marking.

B. Processes Governing Establishment of an Aid to Navigation System.

1. General. An aid to navigation system must remain within the policies set forth in Section A-2 while accomplishing the program objective of providing for safe and economic movement of commercial traffic. Therefore, the establishment of an aid to navigation system requires and is greatly aided by review of criteria in three critical areas. These areas are:

   a. Initial justification.

   b. System benefit analysis.

   c. System type selection.

2. Initial Justification. Initial justification of an aid to navigation system involves identification of authority to establish an aid system and an evaluation of criteria.

   a. Basic Authority.

      (1) In the act establishing the Department of Homeland Security (Pub L.107-296,166 Stat.2135), the mission of the Department is stated as: "... Mission.-- (1) In general.--The primary mission of the Department is to-- (A) prevent terrorist attacks within the United States; (B) reduce the vulnerability of the United States to terrorism; (C) minimize the damage, and assist in the recovery, from terrorist attacks that do occur within the United States; (D) carry out all functions of entities transferred to the Department, including by acting as a focal point regarding natural and manmade crises and emergency planning; (E) ensure that the functions of the agencies and subdivisions within the Department that are not related directly to securing the homeland are not diminished or neglected except by a specific explicit Act of Congress; (F) ensure that the overall economic security of the United States is not diminished by efforts, activities, and programs aimed at securing the homeland; and (G) monitor connections between illegal drug trafficking and terrorism, coordinate efforts to sever such connections, and otherwise contribute to efforts to interdict illegal drug trafficking.

(2) The Coast Guard has authority (14 USC 81) to establish aids to navigation in the following areas:

    (a) The United States of America.

    (b) The waters above the continental shelf.

    (c) The territories and possessions of the United States of America.

    (d) Beyond the territorial jurisdiction of the United States at places where naval or military bases of the United States are or may be located.

b.   Establishment Criteria. The basic criteria for the establishment of aids to navigation are primarily directed toward facilitation of marine transportation. Provisions for safety, speed, efficiency and convenience are the areas to be considered. Specific criteria for the development, establishment, maintenance and operation of aids to navigation must consider the following:

(1) promotion of safety.

(2) requirement of National Defense.

(3) aiding navigation.

(4) prevention of disasters.

(5) prevention of collisions.

(6) prevention of wrecks.

(7) serving the needs of commerce.

(8) amount and nature of the traffic.

(9) justification in terms of public benefit.

(10) preservation of natural resources.

3. System Benefit Analysis.

   a. Response to User Needs.

     (1) In order to justify the establishment of an aid to navigation system it must be shown that the system will result in benefits that will justify the costs involved in establishing, operating, and maintaining the system. It must be shown that there is a valid need for this system and that the establishment of the system will satisfy these needs.

     (2) Aids to navigation are established specifically to enable the mariner to transit an area safely and efficiently, while avoiding groundings, obstructions to navigation, and collisions with other vessels. Therefore, to satisfy the information requirement of the user, a system of aids to navigation must:

       (a) Be available to the mariner at the time it is needed.

       (b) Provide the mariner with information that will:

         i. furnish timely warning of danger from channel limits and fixed obstructions to navigation.

         ii. enable the mariner to determine their location within the channel, relative to fixed obstructions to navigation, and relative to other vessels.

         iii. enable a safe course for the vessel to be determined.

   b. Validation of User Needs.

     (1) The necessity (or justification) for a system of aids to navigation must be validated. This requirement is closely related to the benefits to be derived from responding to the need. If the expression of need cannot be justified by benefit analysis it must be concluded that a requirement to respond to an expressed need does not exist.

(2) The first step in evaluating expressed user needs for aids to navigation is to identify the characteristics of the user. To prevent undue proliferation of different types of subsystems, each directed toward satisfying the needs of a specific group, it is necessary to clearly define all categories of users who will employ the system. To minimize unnecessary duplication of response, the needs of the entire spectrum of users must be considered at the same time. In this analysis the needs of the following groups must be considered:

   (a) International shipping.

   (b) Coast-wise trade.

   (c) Inland waterway trade.

   (d) Intra-harbor traffic (tugs, ferries, small commercial craft, etc.).

   (e) Fishing industry.

   (f) Recreational boating.

   (g) Special operations (survey, oceanographic, search and rescue, etc.).

   (h) Vessels of very large size.

   (i) High speed vessels.

   (j) Submersibles.

(3) The operations in which the above user groups engage can usually be categorized into the following types:

   (a) Transoceanic.

   (b) Coastal (port to port).

   (c) Transit of harbors, internal waters, and canals.

   (d) Intra-harbor.

   (e) Lake navigation.

   (f) Casual and essentially undirected activities, such as pleasure boating, sport fishing, etc.

   (g) Special operations.

(4) Needs of the user must also be defined in light of the various environments in which the user will be operating, i.e.:

(a) Varying weather and visibility.

(b) Varying channel lengths, widths and configurations.

(c) Nature of the hazards beyond the channel limits.

(d) Traffic density.

(e) Traffic mix.

(f) Traffic patterns.

(g) Ice conditions.

(h) Channel stability.

(5) Viewing needs in terms of the individual types of users, the categories of operations in which they are involved, and the environmental conditions under which they operate, will ensure that all aspects of the situation are thoroughly investigated. Needs for specific services however, vary widely among users in terms of user capabilities. These needs must be clearly defined within the following areas:

(a) The position accuracy needed in different environments and under different types of operations.

(b) The time intervals between acquisition of position information.

(c) The amount of time required from receipt of information until the user can determine this position.

(d) The method of presentation of position information to the user.

(e) Geographic coverage needed.

(f) The size, height, sensitivity, and power required of any receiving equipment.

(g) The cost of required receiving equipment.

(h) The navigation skills of user personnel.

(i) The reliability of the system.

(j) The maneuvering capabilities of the user in regard to vessel responsiveness and channel constraints.

(6) It must be recognized that there is an expected level of navigation expertise that has a bearing on user needs for aids to navigation. Unless these levels are observed, even the most extensive system that could be developed would be unable to provide assurance of avoiding accidents and disasters. Some of these are:

(a) Conformance to accepted navigation procedures.

(b) Conformance to the rules of the road.

(c) Conformance to local regulations and operating practices.

(d) Basic knowledge of the use of charts and navigation publications.

(e) Basic knowledge of the meaning of aids to navigation signals (color, shape, etc.).

c. Types of Benefits.

(1) Economic benefits: Assist a user's being able to proceed on a personal schedule without delay caused by hydrographic or weather conditions and traffic congestion.

(2) Safe benefits: Ensure a user will be able to operate with minimum danger of grounding and collision with obstructions and other vessels.

(3) Convenience benefits: Ensure that the above users, as well as users that are not engaged in economic endeavors, will be able to proceed without unnecessary inconvenience or delays and inability to operate due to hydrographic or weather conditions.

d. Evaluation of Benefits.

(1) Identification and, where possible, quantification of the above and additional benefits must consider such factors as:

(a) Number of vessels transiting an area per unit of time.

(b) Size of vessels transiting the area.

(c) Value of the cargo transiting the area.

(d) Nature of the cargo transiting the area.

(e) Level of economic activity in an area.

(f) The number of routes through and within an area.

(g) Pleasure boating activity.

(h) Fishing activity.

(i) Permanence of the traffic.

(j) Environmental impact.

(2) The benefits will not be considered for aids to navigation that solely serve the needs of the armed forces, other Federal agencies, or the marking of quarantine and restricted areas. Law defines the established criteria for aids in these categories.

(3) When evaluating the benefits to be derived from an aid to navigation system, answers to the following questions must be obtained:

(a) In the absence of an aid to navigation system, what specific limitations are imposed on maritime traffic; what are their causes and their impacts?

(b) Is the limitation generally applicable to all users in all areas or is it purely a local problem confined to a specific geographic area or particular category of users?

(c) How would response to this need reduce user costs?

(d) What would be the result if a means of satisfying the need were not provided by the Federal government?

(e) What are the alternatives to Coast Guard response?

e. <u>Benefits Difficult to Quantify</u>. When evaluating the benefits that would accrue from an aid to navigation system or improvements thereto, many benefits may be described in quantitative terms such as those directly relating to economic improvement, increase in speed, and reduction of delay for vessels engaged in commerce. However, there are many other benefits, which are difficult, if not impossible to quantify. Benefits such as safety, prevention of pollution, avoidance of delay caused by blocking of harbors, and benefits to recreation are examples of these. Such benefits may, in many cases, be the primary reason for the establishment of aids to navigation systems or changes thereto. These benefits should be given consideration along with those that can be readily quantified.

f. Weighing Benefits vs. Costs.

(1) Before making a final decision on the establishment of an aid or an aids to navigation system, the system costs must be balanced against the estimated benefits to be gained. (See Planning and Programming Manual – Volume II, COMDTINST M16010.6(series), Appendix N).

(2) Costs to be considered in this evaluation are as follows:

(a) Whenever possible, annualized life cycle costs should be used, including all costs associated with research, development, testing and evaluation (RDT&E): initial investment, and annual operation and maintenance.

(b) The total life cycle costs should be divided by the expected life of the components of the system to develop an annualized life cycle cost basis for comparison of various alternatives.

g. User-Suggested Changes. 33 CFR62.63 provides guidelines for making recommendations and requests about aids to navigation. These guidelines, which should be published quarterly in the Local Notice to Mariners, should be helpful to users by identifying the information required for a complete evaluation of the request. Refer to Chapter 11 of this manual for guidance on user participation in aids to navigation system design.

4. System Type Selection.

a. Capabilities of the System.

(1) All available systems should be reviewed and those that have the capability of satisfying user needs should be considered for implementation. Candidate systems which might be considered are:

(a) Audio-visual piloting systems consisting of buoys, lights, daybeacons, sound signals, retro-reflective signals, etc.

(b) Radar piloting systems including radar reflectors and racons (coastal piloting only).

(c) Precision navigation systems including piloting devices using radionavigation signals as external references.

(d) Vessel Traffic Service systems.

(2) In order to provide information needed by the mariner, informational signals must have specific capabilities. Either alone or in conjunction with other system signals they must be:

    (a) available when needed by the mariner,

    (b) readily identifiable, having distinctive, unambiguous characteristics.

(3) The source of the signal should be located in a clearly defined position, which must be indicated on reference charts.

(4) Technically it is feasible to provide all required information through the use of radio navigation systems or radar systems or a combination of these. Constraints such as cost, space, and power requirements on the user vessel, place limitations on the use of these systems by certain categories of users. The existence of these constraints requires that the system providing audio-visual information be available to all users regardless of the availability of a radio navigation system. (Details on Radionavigation Aids can be found in Volume 4 of this manual.)

(5) The primary limitation on the visual system is diminished effectiveness imposed by low visibility. To some extent the audio system can supplement the visual under low visibility conditions. However because of the lack of accurate directional capabilities, the audio system is effective only as a warning device indicating proximity to navigational dangers.

(6) The use of radar aboard vessels offers additional navigation capabilities without resorting to the use of other electronic systems. This is accomplished either through the use of reflected radar signals (primary radar system) or signals transmitted (secondary radar system) from the aid.

b. Characteristics of the System.

    (1) Types of visual, audio and radar signals:

        (a) Visual.

            i. Daymarks.

            ii. Retro reflective signals.

            iii. Lights.

        (b) Audio: Various non-directional sound producing devices.

(c) Radar.

    i.   Reflectors.

    ii. Radar beacon transponders (racons).

    iii. Shore based radar systems.

(2) The characteristics of these types of aids in terms of availability are shown in Table 3-1, which also indicates the user equipment needed to make effective use of these aids.

(3) A basic requirement of an effective aid to navigation is that it be readily identifiable. Table 3-1 indicates the methods by which various aids to navigation can present unique identification signals to the mariner. To obtain optimum use from these aids to navigation, the mariner must have:

(a) Up to date charts and proper Light Lists for areas being transited.

(b) Basic knowledge of the meaning of the various signal characteristics.

(4) Chapter 4 presents criteria for employment of various types of aids and should be consulted to ensure that the individual aids intended for a system under consideration will be:

(a) Standardized, insofar as is practicable.

(b) Established in sufficient numbers and spacing to provide desired system capabilities.

(c) Not unnecessarily duplicated.

(5) From the capabilities listed in the previous paragraphs, a type of signal that will satisfy the needs of the mariner can be identified. Having identified the proper signal, the next step is to design the system so that the information is provided to the mariner at the time, and in the place required.

C. Review and Modification of Aids to Navigation Systems.

   1. District Review.

      a. District commanders shall conduct an initial Waterway Analysis and Management System (WAMS) analysis for all critical waterways, which have not had one completed. Once the initial analysis is completed, each critical waterway will be scheduled for review at least once every five years. Waterways which need more frequent review due to significant user changes, waterway configuration changes, or marine accidents may be reviewed on a more frequent basis at the discretion of the District Commander. Non-critical waterways will be scheduled for review at the discretion of the District Commander; but the scope of the documentation required should only be enough to validate the non-critical designation. District commanders shall approve all WAMS analysis. Forward a copy of all critical analyses and reviews to Commandant **(CG-54131)** and include a brief executive summary. Each review will ensure that:

         (1) The aids are required as necessary elements in an aids to navigation system.

         (2) Changes to augment and/or reduce aids are made when needed to conform to changes in hydrographic and marine traffic.

         (3) The aids conform to the criteria set forth in the foregoing sections of this chapter.

         (4) Individual aids as well as entire aid systems provide required operational characteristics as specified in Chapter 4.

         (5) Waterways are categorized into one *or more* of the following:

            (a) Militarily Critical Waterways: Militarily critical waterways include those that serve military or militarily essential facilities.

            (b) Environmentally Critical Waterways: **Virtually all waterways are considered environmentally sensitive. Environmentally critical waterways pose higher environmental risk levels, where a degradation of the aids to navigation system would present an unacceptable level of risk to general public safety or to the environment. For example, waterways that traverse densely populated areas and are used to transport hazardous materials or dangerous cargoes as defined in Titles 46 and 49 of the CFR.**

(c) <u>Navigationally Critical Waterways</u>: Waterways where degradation of the aids to navigation system would result in an unacceptable level of risk of a marine accident, due to the physical characteristics of a waterway, difficult navigation conditions, aid establishment difficulties, or high aid discrepancy rates.

(d) <u>Non-Critical Waterways</u>: Waterways serving commercial and recreational interests, where the disruption or degradation of an aids system, beyond the normal level of discrepancies, will not increase the risk of a marine accident to an unacceptable level.

b. Should it appear that there are aids or aid systems that do not conform to the standards required by this chapter or Chapter 4, a project will be initiated for modifying these systems. Each project will be assigned a priority for accomplishment of required modifications.

c. The District Commander shall encourage district aids to navigation units to submit reports of unnecessary aids or aids which should be changed.

2. <u>Public Reaction to Changes</u>. Changes must not be withheld, or needless aids perpetuated, because of concern over possible public reaction. Proposed discontinuances or a reduction in numbers of aids which might be controversial should be discussed with interested user groups and the Coast Guard's position carefully presented.

3. <u>Commandant Support</u>.

a. The Commandant will strongly support all justified, reasonable requests to improve, add, change or remove aids to improve the effectiveness and overall operating economy of the aids to navigation system.

b. The Commandant will particularly support requests for reduction in number or replacement with more effective aids in cases of:

(1) Aids previously established to meet requirements which no longer exist.

(2) Too many aids in the same area having the effect of confusing the mariner.

4. Defining the Need for Increasing the Number of Aids.

   a. The basic consideration in recommending or authorizing additional aids to navigation is to only furnish aids in areas where user needs are justified as necessary for safe navigation.

   b. Justification for changes must follow the same criteria review outlined earlier in this chapter for establishing aids to navigation systems.

5. Temporary Changes.

   a. District commanders are authorized to temporarily change, establish, or discontinue an aid to navigation. The temporary modification should be announced in the Local Notice to Mariners.

   b. **Temporary changes are intentional short term changes to the authorized aid station. For example, a buoy must be repositioned to facilitate dredging operations and will be reset on its Assigned Position after dredging is complete. Temporary changes do not include temporary responses to a discrepancy, such as setting a temporary buoy to mark the position of a destroyed light.**

   c. To prevent temporary aids from becoming unintentionally permanent, with possible reduction of service to the user, the need for each temporary aid shall be reviewed each quarter.

   d. No temporary aid should remain on station longer than six months except for infrequent cases as justified by the District Commander. In such cases, the District Commander shall take action to:

      (1) Restore the original aid; or

      (2) Make the temporary **change** permanent; or

      (3) Discontinue both the temporary and permanent aid.

   e. District commanders will maintain a record of all temporary changes in effect. A tabulation of all temporary changes shall be published each week in the Local Notice to Mariners along with a tabulation of temporary changes corrected since the last published list.

f. Temporary changes may be made for:

(1) dredging

(2) testing or evaluating new aids

(3) marking an obstruction or wreck

(4) other reasons within the definition of temporary change

g. Do not classify aids as temporary if they are only awaiting completion of a Form CG-3213 to become permanent.

h. An Aid to Navigation Operation Request, Form CG-3213, is not necessary for a temporary change.

D. Survey Requirements for Fixed Aids to Navigation.

1. The following survey requirements for the Aids to Navigation Program have been identified:

a. High level accuracy fixed aids (fixed aids used as reference landmarks to position other aids to navigation, and range structures) shall be surveyed IAW current standards as published by **National Geodetic Survey** (NGS).

b. The surveying requirements for a new high level of accuracy fixed aid shall be listed on the Aids to Navigation Operation Request (Form CG-3213). Any Form CG-3213 for these aids that does not specifically state the requirement for surveying will not be approved.

c. When it is feasible and economical, surveys financed by Federal funds shall contribute to the **National Geodetic Reference System** (NGRS) in accordance with the Office of Management and Budget Circular No. A16.

2. Listed below are the avenues most commonly used to satisfy survey requirements:

a. Federal Agency Cooperation. District aids to navigation office shall specify local procedures for interaction with other government agencies for their survey needs. Other government agencies which have provided surveying assistance include USACE and NOAA.

b. Private Contracting. Surveys have been conducted by private contractors to determine positions of newly constructed aids. Private survey contracts shall meet the standards of accuracy and procedure specifications as defined in FGCC publication "Standards and Specifications for Geodetic Control Networks".

c. In-House Surveying. A limited amount of Coast Guard in-house surveying has been undertaken to satisfy survey requirements. Professional training is available to develop survey skills, but it should be emphasized that surveying is a technical field and proper training requires an extensive commitment. Classroom training must be supplemented with field experience. The hands-on, practical experience can be acquired through one or more of the following means:

(1) Training courses which include a field workshop.

(2) Field demonstrations conducted by equipment manufacturers.

(3) Participating in a geodetic survey party.

E. Aid Availability.

1. **Definition. Aid Availability is the probability that an aid to navigation or system is performing its specified function at any random chosen time. Basically, aid availability is a measure of the health of an aids to navigation system in a given waterway. It is not a measure of unit, sector, or district effectiveness.**

2. **Aid Availability Categories. Waterways have a variety of traffic patterns and risk levels. Therefore, aid availability objectives for each aid to navigation or system is categorized according to their level of criticality. All Coast Guard maintained aids to navigation are assigned to one of the following aid availability categories:**

   a. **Category 1: An Aid to Navigation (ATON) or system of ATON that is considered by the Coast Guard to be of vital navigational significance.**

   b. **Category 2: An ATON or system of ATON that is considered by the Coast Guard to be of important navigational significance.**

   c. **Category 3: An ATON or system of ATON that is considered by the Coast Guard to be of necessary navigational significance.**

3. **Aid Availability Category Determining Factors.** The aid availability category for a particular aid to navigation is determined from information derived from Part I of the Discrepancy Response Factor Decision Guide (DRF1) for the aid and the WAMS criticality category of its associated waterway.

   a. As described in Chapter 9, the value derived from the completed DRF1 form places an aid to navigation into one of five categories numbered 1 - 5. The DRF1 form is completed in I-ATONIS, which automatically assigns the Part I category for the aid.

   b. During the WAMS process waterways are assessed and categorized per paragraph 3.C.1.a(5). Critical waterways are those in which a degradation of the ATON system would present an unacceptable level of risk from a Military, Environmental, or Navigational standpoint. This information is entered into I-ATONIS by filling in the appropriate criticality flag(s) for that WAMS segment. A WAMS criticality group value (1 – 5) is then automatically assigned to that portion of waterway represented in the WAMS segment using the following order of precedence:

      (1) CM: Critical Military, Environmental, and Navigation (CMEN), Critical Military and Environmental (CME), Critical Military and Navigation (CMN), or Critical Military (CM).

      (2) CEN: Critical Environmental Navigation (CEN)

      (3) CE: Critical Environmental (CE)

      (4) CN: Critical Navigation (CN)

      (5) NN: Non-Critical (NN)

4. **Calculating Aid Availability Categories.** Aid availability categories are automatically calculated in I-ATONIS by combining the values of Part I of the Discrepancy Response Factor Decision Guide (DRF1) and the WAMS Criticality Group. The following table provides the mechanics for calculating aid availability categories:

Aid Availability Categories

WAMS Criticality Group Value		DRF1 Value				
		1	2	3	4	5
1	CM	1	1	1	2	2
2	CEN	1	1	2	2	3
3	CE	1	2	2	3	3
4	CN	2	2	3	3	3
5	NN	2	3	3	3	3

5. **Aid Availability Objectives.** The aid availability objectives for each category are calculated over a period of three continuous years. The objective for each aid availability category is as follows:

a. Category 1   99.8%

b. Category 2   99.0%

c. Category 3   97.0%

6. **Calculating Aid Availability.** The following formula is used to calculate aid availability:

$$Availability = \frac{(MTBF)}{(MTBF + MTTR)} \quad or \quad \frac{Up\ time}{Total\ Time} \quad or \quad \frac{(Total\ time - Down\ Time)}{Total\ Time}$$

MTBF = Mean Time Between Failures
MTTR = Mean Time To Repair

	DAY	NIGHT	GOOD VISIBILITY	POOR VISIBILITY	USER EQUIPMENT	COLOR	SHAPE	CODED	NUMBERED
DAYMARK	X		X			X	X		X
RETRO- REFLECTOR	X	X	X		LIGHT	X	X		X
LIGHT	X	X	X	X		X		X	
SOUND	X	X	X	X				X	
RADAR REFLECTOR	X	X	X	X	RADAR- Must relate to surroundings			X	
RADAR TRANSPONDER	X	X	X	X	RADAR			X	
RADAR Advisory	X	X	X	X	RADIO- Vessel Identification by shore station				

Aid Signal Availability and Identification

Table 3-1

This Page Intentionally
Left Blank

CHAPTER 4 - SHORT RANGE AIDS TO NAVIGATION SYSTEMS – DESCRIPTION AND DESIGN GUIDELINES.

A. Introduction.

1. This chapter provides guidance on how to analyze a waterway's marking requirements and the configuration of its aids to navigation.

2. The guidelines presented here should not be considered strict rules but flexible constraints. The physical diversity of waterways dictates the need to temper any systematic analysis with plenty of common sense and on-scene evaluation. WAMS studies should be consulted and used as part of the analysis and evaluation process in making waterway aid design decisions.

3. Remember that aids only supplement natural and man-made landmarks and those other environmental features that provide the mariner with the cues needed to navigate. Consequently, existing geographic composition must be considered throughout the design process.

4. An additional source for design guidelines is the SRA System Design Manual for Restricted Waterways. It applies in narrow channels navigated by deep draft vessels. The design manual differs from this chapter in that it produces a quantitative measure of system quality, valuable for assessing the relative merits of competing aids to navigation configurations.

B. Glossary of Aids to Navigation Terms.

1. Adrift - Afloat and unattached in any way to the shore or seabed.

2. Aid to Navigation - Any device external to a vessel or aircraft specifically intended to assist navigators in determining their position or safe course, or to warn them of dangers or obstructions to navigation.

3. Assigned Position - The latitude and longitude position for an aid to navigation.

4. Availability (also technical availability) - The probability an aid or system of aids performs its required functions under stated conditions at any randomly chosen instant in time. Often expressed as a percentage.

5. Availability Standard - The minimum operational availability goal.

6. Bifurcation - The point where a channel divides when proceeding from seaward, the place where two tributaries meet.

7. <u>Broadcast Notice to Mariners</u> - A radio broadcast designed to provide important marine information.

8. <u>Commissioned</u> - The action of placing a previously discontinued aid to navigation back in operation.

9. <u>Conventional Direction of Buoyage</u> - Some reference direction for defining the lateral and numbering significance of an aid system. In U.S. waters, the direction of flood current provides the most common indication. For coastal marking, the conventional direction of buoyage is southerly along the East coast, northerly and westerly along the Gulf coast and northerly along the West coast.

10. <u>Cutoff Turn</u> - A type of dredged channel configuration where the triangular area formed by slicing off the inside corner or apex of a turn is incorporated into the channel, thus effectively increasing the available maneuvering room.

11. **<u>Daymark</u>- Daytime characteristic of an aid to navigation.**

12. <u>Dead Weight Tonnage</u> (DWT) - The capacity in long tons of cargo, passengers, fuel stores, etc. of a vessel. The difference between loaded and light displacement tonnage.

13. <u>Direct Monitoring</u> - A person assigned to keep watch over an aid's performance; requires a 24 hour watch within sight of the major aid.

14. <u>Discontinue</u> - To remove from operation (permanently or temporarily) a previously authorized aid to navigation.

15. <u>Discrepancy</u> - Failure of an aid to navigation to maintain its position or function as prescribed in the Light List.

16. <u>Establish</u> - To place an authorized aid to navigation for the first time.

17. <u>Exposed Locations</u> - Offshore areas which are not sheltered by adjacent land and thus may be exposed to extreme weather and sea conditions.

18. <u>Extinguished</u> - A lighted aid to navigation which fails to show a light characteristic.

19. **<u>Focal Plane Height</u> - Height above water from the focal plane of the fixed light to mean high water (low water datum for Great Lakes), in feet.**

20. <u>Fog Detector</u> - An electronic device used to automatically determine conditions of visibility which warrant the activation of a sound signal or additional light signals.

21. Highest Astronomical Tide (HAT) - The highest tide level that can be predicted to occur under average meteorological conditions and any combination of astronomical conditions.

22. Inoperative - Sound signal or electronic aid to navigation out of service due to a malfunction.

23. Junction - The point where a channel divides when proceeding seaward. The place where a tributary departs from the main stream.

24. Link Monitoring - Remote monitoring by means of electronic data gathering and reported via radio and/or landline to a master monitor location.

25. Local Notice to Mariner - A written document issued by each U.S. Coast Guard district to disseminate important information affecting aids to navigation, dredging, marine construction, special marine activities, and bridge construction on waterways within the district.

26. Luminous Range - The distance at which a light is visible based on the visibility of the area.

27. Mariner Monitoring - Passing ships' masters or pilots report aid failures when observed.

28. Mark - An artificial or natural object of easily recognizable shape or color, or both, situated in such a position that it may be identified on a chart. (An aid to navigation.)

29. Nominal Range - The nominal range is the luminous range of a light when the meteorological visibility is 10 nautical miles, and a threshold of illuminance of 0.67 sea-mile candela is used.

30. Off Station - A floating aid to navigation not on its assigned position.

31. Operational Availability - The availability, to a mariner with at least a fifteen foot height of eye, of a specific aid at a specific distance. Example: The operational availability of a certain light, viewed from a distance of two miles, might be 65%. That is to say, based on historical visibility data, a mariner can see that aid at least two miles away 65% of the time.

32. Operational Range - The distance at which a light is required to be seen to meet the user requirements.

33. Protected Locations - Inshore areas that are not exposed to extremes of weather and sea conditions.

34. Quarterline - A line parallel to the channel centerline, equidistant from the centerline and the channel edge.

35. Redundancy - A desirable attribute of an aid system intended to prevent the failure of one aid from significantly degrading the effectiveness of the entire system.

36. Reliability - The probability an aid or system of aids performs its required functions under stated conditions for a specified period of time. Often expressed as a percentage.

37. Relighted - An extinguished aid to navigation returned to its advertised light characteristics.

38. Replaced - An aid to navigation previously off station, adrift, or missing, restored by another aid to navigation different type and/or characteristic.

39. Reset - A floating aid to navigation previously off station, adrift, or missing, returned to its assigned position (station).

40. Semi-Exposed Locations - Offshore or inshore areas that may be sheltered by adjacent land and are exposed to lesser extremes of weather and sea conditions.

41. Sound Signal - A device which transmits sound intended to provide information to mariners during periods of restricted visibility and foul weather.

42. Structure Height - Height from terra firma or sea bed to the highest point on the structure, excluding the uppermost optic.

43. System of Aids - A group of interacting aids to navigation intended to collectively provide sufficient and timely information with which to safely navigate vessels within and through a waterway. For example, systems may range in size from all the Western Rivers to the waters serving a small fishing port; i.e., Sitka Harbor System.

44. Temporary Change - An USCG approved, intentional change to the authorized characteristics of an aid to navigation. This does not include temporary responses to a discrepancy, such as setting a TRUB in lieu of a destroyed DBN.

45. Temporary Response – The date and time at which a unit completes temporary corrective action to a discrepancy but does not completely restore the aid to watching properly status. This information is to be entered in I-ATONIS in the Temp Response DTG field.

46. <u>Watching properly</u> - An aid to navigation on its assigned position exhibiting the advertised characteristics in all respects.

47. <u>Waterway</u> - A water area providing a means of transportation from one place to another, principally a water area providing a regular route for water traffic, such as a bay, channel, passage, river, or the regularly traveled parts of the open sea.

48. <u>Withdrawn</u> - The discontinuance of a floating aid to navigation during severe ice conditions or for the winter season.

C. <u>Short Range Aid Marking Systems</u>.

1. <u>The U.S. Marking System</u>. The U.S. marking system is a predominantly lateral system which conforms to the Region B requirements of the IALA Maritime Buoyage System. The color schemes referred to in this manual apply to IALA Region B. Marks located in IALA Region A exhibit reversed color significance: port hand marks will be red when following the Conventional Direction of Buoyage, and starboard hand marks will be green. The meaning of daymark and buoy shapes is identical in both regions. Specific marking and signal requirements can be found in the Aids to Navigation Manual - Technical, COMDTINST M16500.3 (series) and Section **F**.3. of this chapter.

   a. <u>Types of Marks</u>.

      (1) <u>Lateral</u>. Lateral marks define the port and starboard sides of a route to be followed. Their most frequent use is to mark the sides of channels; however, they may be used individually to mark obstructions outside of clearly defined channels. Lateral marks include sidemarks and preferred channel marks. Sidemarks are not always placed directly on a channel edge and may be positioned outside the channel as indicated on charts and nautical publications.

         (a) Port hand marks indicate the left side of channels when proceeding in the conventional direction of buoyage. Beacons have green square daymarks, while buoys are green can or pillar buoys. Green lights of various rhythms are used on port hand marks.

         (b) Starboard hand marks indicate the right side of channels when proceeding in the Conventional Direction of Buoyage. Beacons have red triangular daymarks, while buoys are red nun or pillar buoys. Red lights of various rhythms are used on starboard hand marks.

(c) Preferred channel marks indicate channel junctions or bifurcations and may also mark wrecks or obstructions. Preferred channel marks have red and green horizontal bands with the color of the topmost band indicating the preferred channel. Buoy or daybeacon shape and the color of the light are determined by the color of the uppermost band. Preferred channel marks display a composite group flashing light rhythm.

(2) <u>Isolated Danger</u>. These marks are erected on, moored over, or placed immediately adjacent to an isolated danger that may be passed on all sides by system users. They are black with one or more broad horizontal red bands and will be equipped with a topmark of two black spheres, one above the other. If lighted, they display a white group flashing two lights with a period of five seconds.

(3) <u>Safe Water Marks</u>. Safe water marks indicate that there is navigable water all around the mark. They mark fairways, mid-channels, and offshore approach points. Safe water marks have red and white vertical stripes. Beacons have an octagonal daymark; buoys display a red spherical topmark. They can be used by a mariner transiting offshore waters to identify the proximity of an intended landfall. When lighted, safe water marks show a white Morse Code "A" rhythm.

(4) <u>Special</u>. Special marks are not primarily intended to assist safe navigation, but to indicate special areas or features referred to in charts or other nautical publications. They may be used, for example, to mark anchorages, cable or pipeline areas, traffic separation schemes, military exercise zones, ocean data acquisition systems, etc. Special marks are colored solid yellow, and show yellow lights with a slow-flashing rhythm preferred. They may not show a quick-flashing rhythm.

(5) <u>Information and Regulatory</u>. Information and Regulatory Marks are used to alert the mariner to various warnings or regulatory matters. These marks have orange geometric shapes against a white background. When lighted, these marks display a white light with any rhythm not reserved for other types of aids. The meanings associated with the orange shapes are as follows:

(a) A vertical open-faced diamond signifies danger.

(b) A vertical diamond shape having a cross centered within indicates that vessels are excluded from the marked area.

(c) A circular shape indicates that certain operating restrictions are in effect within the marked area.

(d) Warnings, instructions or explanations may be shown within the shapes.

(6) <u>Mooring Buoys</u>. Mooring buoys are white with a blue horizontal band. This distinctive color scheme facilitates identification and avoids confusion with other aids to navigation. When lighted, these marks display a white light with any rhythm not reserved for other types of aids. Federal mooring buoys and those private mooring buoys permitted through the PATON application process, that are charted or included in the Light List, shall be listed in I-ATONIS.

(7) <u>Inland Waters Obstruction Mark</u>. On inland waters designated by the Commandant as State waters in accordance with 33 CFR 66.05-5 (33 CFR 66.05-100 provides the specific listing of navigable waters designated as State waters) and on non-navigable internal waters of a State which have no defined head of navigation, a buoy showing alternate vertical black and white stripes may be used to indicate to a vessel operator that an obstruction to navigation extends from the nearest shore to the buoy. The black and white buoy's meaning is ``do not pass between the buoy and the shore". The number of white and black stripes is discretionary, provided that the white stripes are twice the width of the black stripes.

(8) <u>Cardinal Marks</u>. These marks indicate, in the cardinal points of the compass, the direction of good water from the aid. They are not used in the U.S. marking system but may be encountered in Canadian waters.

(9) <u>Other</u>. Lighthouses (substantial structures, and/or structures in prominent positions), ranges, sector lights, and crossing marks do not fall under the IALA agreement. While their signal characteristics are largely discretionary, these aids should be marked to provide maximum information to the mariner while avoiding conflicts with nearby aids displaying IALA markings.

2. <u>Intracoastal Waterway (ICW) Identification</u>. This aid system is used along the Atlantic and Gulf Intracoastal waterways. The Aids to Navigation Manual – Technical, COMDTINST M16500.3 (series) details marking specifications. Procedures for using this system are outlined in paragraph **F.3.f.(3)** of this chapter. In addition to the conventional signals, aids marking the ICW differ from the U.S. Aids to Navigation System in that:

a. ICW aids display a distinctive yellow symbol according to aid type and function.

b. Distance Markers may be used. Distance indicated is from a designated point established by each district.

3. <u>Western Rivers Marking System</u>. The marking system used on the Western Rivers differs from the U.S. system in that:

   a. Buoys are not numbered and shore structures are not numbered laterally.

   b. Numbers on shore structures indicate mileage from a designated point.

   c. Diamond-shaped non-lateral daymarks, red/white or green/white as appropriate, are used instead of triangular or square lateral daymarks where the river channel crosses from one bank to the other.

   d. The conventional direction of buoyage, for the purpose of installing the proper aid signals, is upstream. Local terminology, however, refers to the "left" and "right" banks viewed from a vessel proceeding downstream.

   e. Lights on the right descending bank show single flashing rhythms and may be green or white. Lights on the left descending bank show "group-flashing-two" rhythms and may be red or white. When clear lenses are replaced due to age, floods or other reasons they should be replaced with a green or red lens as appropriate.

   f. In pooled waters (behind dams), buoys should mark the nine-foot contour for normal pool elevations.

   g. In unstable waters (free-flowing rivers), buoys should mark the project depth for the prevailing river stage. Buoys may be set in deeper water when a drop in water level is predicted. Buoys should not normally be set, however, in water depths less than the project depth when a rise in water level is predicted. Constantly changing river conditions prevent strict design guidelines. Unit Commanding Officers and Officers-in-Charge must use their best judgment concerning the number and placement of aids.

   h. Isolated danger marks are not used.

4. <u>Private Aids to Navigation</u>.

   a. The District Commander authorizes private aids to navigation. Where required, inspection of private aids are accomplished by the Coast Guard for Class I aids. Class I, Class II, and Class III private aids are inspected/verified by the Coast Guard, Coast Guard Auxiliary or the owner. More information about the private aid process is contained in Chapter 5 of this manual.

   b. Private aids may, in some instances, comprise an entire aid system. Taconite Harbor on Lake Superior and Delaware City in the Delaware River are two examples of private aid systems.

c. A more common use of private aids, however, is as an extension to the Federal aid system. Private aids are used to extend a particular Federal aid system to mark obstructions, pierheads, and channels that may be of use to a single owner or a small user group.

d. The characteristics of a private aid to navigation shall conform to the U.S. Aids to Navigation System (33 CFR 66.01-10).

D. Aid to Navigation System Elements and Their Use.

1. Major Lights. A major light is a light of moderate to high candlepower and reliability that is exhibited from a fixed structure. It may or may not have colored sectors with higher intensities. Major lights have a **nominal range 10 nautical miles (10 statute miles on the Great Lakes) or greater, and are visible over their usable range 90% of the nights of the year when local visibility conditions are considered**, and fall into two broad categories:

    a. Coastal or seacoast lights assist vessels either during coastal navigation or when making a landfall. The following standards apply to major lights:

        (1) Their operational range should, based on local visibility conditions, supply needed navigation information 90% of the time for the transition into waters marked by the short range system.

        (2) In those situations where an operational range has not been determined, a minimum standard is to provide a luminous range equal to the geographic range of the light for a mariner with a 15-foot height of eye. This standard is not intended to require modifications to existing optical equipment, but is a threshold for future modifications and design of major lights where the operational range has not been determined. In some areas attaining this standard may not be possible because of poor visibility or severe background lighting. In such cases, attaining the highest operational availability with current equipment is acceptable.

        (3) In all cases, the operational range, as determined through a WAMS analysis, will provide information for selecting the proper equipment.

    b. Inland major lights are found in bays, sounds, and coastal approaches. They can serve a variety of functions including use as a leading light, range light, obstruction mark, sector light, or simply a reference mark from which to obtain a needed visual bearing or radar range. They too should have sufficient intensity so they are visible over their usable range 90% of the nights of the year when local visibility conditions are considered.

c. Major aids may be remotely monitored and controlled for two reasons:

    (1) To inform the mariner of a change in the advertised characteristic of an aid

    (2) To promptly dispatch repair personnel to correct a discrepancy.

d. The following items are to be considered in each decision to monitor a major aid to navigation:

    (1) The criticality of the aid, and the need to notify the mariner promptly of any discrepancy;

    (2) The availability of other short range aids in the vicinity;

    (3) The frequency of transits and the nature of cargoes;

    (4) The mariner's ability, or inability, to communicate information concerning the discrepancy;

    (5) The electronic navigation equipment in general use by the mariner using the aid;

    (6) The reliability of the installed signal equipment and power systems;

    (7) The remoteness and accessibility of the aid.

e. The operational decision to monitor should first resolve the availability of direct and mariner monitoring. The proximity of an aid to an established Coast Guard operational unit will generally decrease the need for link monitoring equipment. If either direct or mariner monitoring are not sufficient, link monitoring should be considered. The Category Selection Aid, Figure 1-1 of the Automation Technical Guidelines COMDTINST M16500.8 (series), integrates the Waterways Analysis and Management System (WAMS) into the monitor decision.

f. The link monitor master unit shall be located in a space continuously staffed by a live watch. The master unit may be located in another space if a remote alarm is maintained to a watched space. A link monitor system that does not directly interface with a live watch defeats the purpose of monitoring. Furthermore, no watch shall be established to directly monitor an aid or link monitor system.

g. The Aid Control and Monitor System (ACMS), is the service-wide standard monitor and control equipment and is the only equipment which is centrally supported.

2. Ranges. Ranges are pairs of beacons commonly located to define a line down the center of a channel. They are usually, but need not be, lighted. Range design is discussed in detail in the Range Design Manual, COMDTINST M16500.4 (series).

a. When possible, within the constraints imposed by the Range Design Manual, select range sites to:

(1) Use existing structures such as lights, or daybeacons.

(2) Exploit shoal areas where shallow water depths will decrease structure construction costs.

(3) Access available commercial power.

b. Each range provides a mariner with a given lateral sensitivity at a given distance from the near end of the channel. Lateral sensitivity is expressed as Cross-Track Factor and lends a more physical feel to the performance of the range. The cross-track factor, is a measure of effectiveness for finding and maintaining track on the range axis. A cross-track factor of 25% means that a mariner may be as far as 25% of the distance from the channel centerline to the edge of the channel before determining the vessel is off the centerline. A high cross-track factor implies low sensitivity.

c. The following general guidelines are provided for range usage:

(1) Construction of a range for a track keeping region of a channel may permit increased aid spacing. See section **F.3.e.** on channel regions and aid spacing.

(2) Determination of an acceptable cross-track factor must take into account the maximum beam of vessels transiting the waterway.

(3) If maintaining a track on the quarterline is necessary due to a great deal of two-way traffic, upbound and downbound ranges may be needed.

(4) Traditionally the lights on ranges, particularly those powered by batteries, were secured during daylight. The daytime signal was provided by dayboards. Recent efficiency improvements in optics combined with solar power has allowed us to expand the use of daytime ranges even when commercial power is not available.

(a) Dayboards are not necessary when daytime lights are provided.

(b) Distances less than 2 nautical miles, as measured from the rear structure to the far end of the channel, are best marked by dayboards. The nighttime signal can usually be provided with standard omnidirectional lanterns and associated equipment. In this situation daytime range lights should only be considered in areas prone to poor meteorological visibilities.

(c) Distances greater than 4 nautical miles are best marked by daytime lights provided there is an operational requirement to mark the entire channel.

(d) Distances between 2 and 4 nautical miles should be marked as operationally required or as economically as possible. It may be that a lighted daytime range is not required but the system lifecycle cost of a lighted range might be lower than using dayboards.

(e) Range project documentation requirements are outlined in Automation Technical Guidelines, COMDTINST M16500.8(series), Chapter 1.

3. Directional or Sector Lights. Directional lights, also known as sector lights, are devices that generate two or more defined regions displaying different light color characteristics. In practice those aids that have two sectors (usually white and red) have been called sector lights while those with three sectors have been called directional lights.

   a. Sector Lights. Sector lights are usually used to provide mariners with a warning that they are in an area where navigation may be impaired by a shoal, rock, etc. The mariner will have to use other aids or navigational tools to determine position relative to the danger.

   b. Directional Lights. Directional lights usually have red and green sectors separated by a white sector. They are usually used to give an indication of a vessel's position with respect to the center of a waterway. Because there is only one light source, the mariner has no indication of how fast a vessel is moving across a given sector nor how far into a sector has a vessel moved. Therefore, the following guidelines apply:

   (1) Directional lights should be avoided when an aid is needed to initiate a turn and the turn must be started an appropriate distance before the intersection of the channel centerlines.

   (2) Directional lights should be avoided in channels used by larger vessels unless there is considerable room to maneuver outside the white sector. This rules out the use of a sector light in narrow channels used by large vessels. The problems with large vessels and direction lights are compounded by the presence of a cross-channel set.

(3) Direction lights should be avoided in channels where vessels meet and an aid is needed to help them pass.

(4) When choosing a directional light, the angle of the white sector should generally be chosen so that the sector will cover 40 to 50% of the width of the channel at the far end.

(5) A directional light should show the red sector on the side of the channel with the red buoys and the green sector on the side of the channel with the green buoys.

(6) A directional light, although not as good as a 2-station range, is better than nothing if it is impossible to build a 2-station range.

(7) Projects to establish directional lights shall be submitted to Commandant **(CG-5413)** for approval.

4. <u>Beacons</u>. Strictly defined, a beacon is any fixed aid to navigation. For our purposes, however, we take beacons to mean all minor lights of relatively low candlepower and daybeacons.

   a. Fixed aids provide immobile, stable signals. Floating aids do not. Beacons, therefore, are superior to floating aids in the signal quality they provide to the mariner.

   b. Beacons may be set back from the channel edge to protect them from damage. The utility of a beacon decreases as its distance from the channel edge increases. When beacons must be set back, the distance from the channel edge should remain constant within a waterway.

   c. The risk that a mariner will allide with a daybeacon during periods of reduced visibility should be considered when determining whether or not to light a fixed aid to navigation.

   d. Fixed aids are generally cheaper to maintain than floating aids with comparable signals.

   e. Lights or daybeacons are normally preferable to buoys when:

      (1) Annualized life cycle cost for the fixed aid is less than that for the floating aid. Structure costs become competitive when reasonably shallow depths border the channel.

      (2) Severe ice conditions do not routinely threaten the structure.

(3) The aid station is not one frequently involved in marine collisions.

(4) We have assurance of channel stability or continued maintenance from the Army Corps of Engineers.

(5) Lack of horizontal control and alternate positioning methods make positioning the buoy difficult.

    f.   Buoyant Beacons. Buoyant beacons appear to be fixed, but in actuality are moored to the bottom by a sinker. They remain afloat through use of a buoyant collar attached below the waterline. Buoyant beacons are deployed only in unusual situations where their high cost is offset by the requirement for a reduced watch circle.

5. Buoys. Buoys are unmanned, floating aids to navigation moored to the seabed. They may be lighted or unlighted.

    a.   Use whatever size buoy is necessary to meet user needs. Consult the ATON Manual - Technical COMDTINST M16500.3 (series), Chapter 2, for the operational characteristics of all standard buoy types.

    b.   Ensure buoy types correspond to the environmental location of the aid station; i.e., exposed, semi-exposed, or protected.

    c.   Place buoys inside the channel toe, as near the channel toe as possible. For buoys marking obstructions, place buoys on the channel or navigable side of the obstruction. Input from user groups may necessitate placement of buoys a set distance away from the channel toe, on the shoulder of the channel.

6. RACON. A RACON is a radar transponder which produces a coded response, or radar paint, when triggered by a surface search radar signal. They are normally operated in the frequency ranges of the X-band and S-band marine radars.

    a.   Application. RACONS provide radar enhancement, help improve aid identification, and help during the transition from ocean to inland navigation. This is accomplished by:

(1) Placing a RACON on a prominent point of land to allow the mariner to make a positive identification of the point for a landfall.

(2) Placing a RACON on an aid to assist the mariner in distinguishing that aid from other aids and vessels in areas where many echoes appear on the radar screen.

(3) Temporarily placing a RACON on an aid that marks a new danger. Such a racon should be coded Delta (-..).

b. Locating.

(1) Whenever possible a RACON should be collocated with another aid that will itself present a reasonable radar echo at short ranges to eliminate or reduce the range error introduced by the RACON's response delay.

(2) A RACON should be located such that the area "behind" it, as viewed from a ship, will present as little primary echo response as possible so as not to obscure the RACON response on the radar screen.

(3) Where acquisition at maximum range is required, a RACON should be located so that vessels cannot pass close aboard. This will reduce side-lobe interference.

(4) As a general rule RACONS should not be placed within 4 to 5 miles of each other. Proliferation of RACONS could result in contacts being masked by racon returns.

(5) RACONS should not be installed on buoys that have a history of dragging or broken moorings.

c. Coding.

(1) RACONS are coded with Morse-code letters that begin with a dash and contain no more than four elements.

(2) Where possible RACONS should be coded to be consistent with the name or location of the aid (i.e., "G" for Galveston, "M" for Midway Islands, etc.).

(3) The length of the coded response is adjustable from approximately 350 yards to 2.5 miles. In practice, the length is set to provide the best presentation on the most likely used radar scale.

(4) RACONS located on buoys are usually set for a 50% duty cycle. Those on structures are usually set for a 75% duty cycle.

(5) The Morse-code letter "D" is reserved for RACONS marking new, uncharted dangers.

d. Possible problems that may cause mariners to report the racon as discrepant.

    (1) Side-lobe triggering. This is caused by close proximity radars triggering the RACON by the transmitted power contained in the radar side lobes. This type of interference causes the RACON signal to appear over an extended arc. It can be reduced in certain cases by setting the RACON receiver sensitivity to a level consistent with the maximum range at which it is desired to first paint the RACON signal on the radar screen. Locating the RACON a short distance from the main traffic flow will also reduce the probability of side-lobe interference.

    (2) Loss of RACON signal in sea return. With a RACON installed on a buoy, it is possible that the RACON signal will be painted but will be lost in the sea return or clutter on the radar screen. The use of the Sensitivity Time Control (STC) on the radar receiver will probably not correct this problem. While the STC control will reduce the sea return, the RACON signal will also be reduced to the point where it may be lost. Operation of the anti-clutter or Fast Time Constant (FTC) will also reduce or eliminate the RACON paint.

    (3) Loss of RACON signal in land return. RACON responses will be lost in strong land return or ground clutter.

    (4) Loss or reduction of signal due to multipath effects. Radar signals are often reflected irregularly (e.g., multipath) due to a combination of antenna height, sea state, and propagation conditions which cause reduction of signal return to the radar antenna. This will cause coarse variations in the maximum range that a RACON response will be received. It is also the reason that RACON signals will disappear for a time and then reappear again at a shorter or longer range than was previously experienced.

    (5) Loss of signal due to receiver interference rejection. Modern radars employ "interference reject" circuits. Unfortunately these circuits will also inhibit the display of valid racon signals. Generally, interference circuits should be shut off to observe racon returns on the PPI display. Increasing the racon on time beyond 12 seconds will also help.

7. Sound Signals.

a. A sound signal (fog signal) is a device which transmits sound, intended to provide information to mariners during periods of restricted visibility. The term also applies to the sound emitted by the device.

b. Due to the inability of the human ear to accurately judge the direction of a sound source, these signals are limited to only one general use: the signal serves to warn mariners of the proximity of an obstruction.

c. Although sound signals are valuable, mariners should not implicitly rely on them when navigating. They should be considered supplements to radar and radio-navigation aids for reduced visibility navigation.

d. There is no longer a general requirement for sound signals with a range greater than two nautical miles. Any signals of greater range are considered non-standard and are not centrally supported.

e. Sound signals are a source of noise pollution to non-mariners. Therefore, the provisions for considering the environmental impact of a proposed establishment or change, contained in National Environmental Policy Act Implementing Procedures and Policy for Considering Environmental Impacts, COMDTINST M16475.1 (series), must be followed.

f. Continuously operating sound signals are preferable when the location is remote and the signal doesn't create a nuisance to nearby residents. The following methods of sound signal control have application where noise pollution is an issue:

(1) Fog Detector. Fog detectors are very convenient devices for controlling sound signal operation. They are particularly useful where a live watch could be reduced or a radio link to a remote station could be eliminated.

(a) Fog detectors only sample a small portion of the air directly in front of the detector. Therefore they are usually calibrated to energize the sound signal when the visibility drops below 3 miles. This provides a margin of safety should the visibility vary in the vicinity of the detector.

(b) In noise complaint areas it may be necessary to reduce the visibility setting to a lesser range that will not compromise the operational requirement.

(2) Remote Control. Remote control systems may be used for sound control. They may use radio links or telephone lines. The disadvantage of this type of control is the signal may be very remote from the person controlling it. Consequently, that person may be uncertain of weather conditions at the sound signal site.

(3) Manual Control. Manual control by Coast Guard personnel or by personnel of a Federal, state, or local agency is acceptable, but only where an existing live watch is available to activate the device when necessitated

by reduced visibility. Personnel from a state or local agency may control sound signals under an agreement for gratuitous services, worded to relieve the agency from liability. Live watches should not be maintained solely to control sound signals.

(4) <u>User Activated</u>. User activated sound signals must be approved by Commandant **(CG-5413).**

g. <u>Baffles</u>. Baffles may be used to reduce the sound pressure level (SPL) on the back side of fixed aids equipped with pure-tone signals. Commandant **(CG-432)** can assist in determining the need for a baffle at a particular location.

h. Standard sound signal characteristics listed in the Aids to Navigation Manual - Technical COMDTINST M16500.3(series), Chapter 7, should be used. The rhythm of one two-second blast every twenty seconds is reserved for private aid use.

i. Sound signals available for use on floating aids consist of four basic types. These are gong, bell, whistle, and electronic horns. The first three are wave actuated and are consequently useful in exposed or semi-exposed environments. Electronic horns, being battery powered, are suitable for any environment. When using sound signals on buoys, the following guidelines apply:

(1) Wave actuated signals should be used where environmental conditions permit.

(2) When two or more channels are in the same general area, such as near a junction or bifurcation, use a different signal type for each waterway to aid in identification.

(3) Historically, mid-channels, fairways, and approaches have been marked with whistles. This marking should continue if a wave actuated whistle is available for the buoy body in use. If not, an electronic horn may be used.

(4) Previous guidance issued on sound signals attached lateral significance to the bell and gong signals. Since we discourage mariners from relying implicitly on sound signals, we should not encourage the use of sound signals as lateral aids. Placing gongs to port and bells to starboard may be a convenient method of waterway design, just as marking adjoining waterways with different signal types may be. However, placing reliance on the necessity to always leave a gong or bell to port or starboard should be discouraged.

E. General Design Considerations.

1. Until recently, mariners have used the radio aids to navigation systems and the short range systems in two distinct geographic areas. The short range system was needed and used close to shore and in restricted waterways. An offshore vessel was able to use the less accurate radio aids system. However, with the low cost, high precision Loran C and GPS/DGPS receivers and electronic charting programs available today, these two areas are beginning to overlap. This is especially evident in those transitional areas where the mariner shifts from the low accuracy requirements of ocean navigation to the high accuracy needs of coastal and inshore piloting. As electronic aids continue to improve, their use will increase in areas where previously only short range aids afforded the necessary accuracy. This evolutionary change must be recognized and accounted for when conducting waterway analyses.

2. User Interface.

    a. Meeting and riding with the users of a waterway is one of the most important steps in waterway analysis and should be done prior to any decision to establish or modify an aid system. Viewing the waterway from the user's perspective is critical. Glaring deficiencies and redundancies may be apparent from a user's viewpoint that is not readily apparent from the viewpoint of the Coast Guard servicing unit.

    b. The "wants" of the users must be carefully considered and evaluated by the waterway analyst and then translated into user "needs".

3. Shoreside Property.

    a. Before establishing an aid, an easement or purchase must be obtained to ensure subsequent access.

    b. Restrictions should be placed on the future use of property disposed of as excess to the needs of the Coast Guard if necessary to preserve the arc of visibility of an aid or the minimum distance at which it should be seen. Restrictions may also be needed if a fog signal's sound pressure levels might be offensive to prospective occupants.

4. Conditions.

    a. The physical and environmental condition of a waterway, as well as the size of the vessels using the waterway, must be considered. The design of the waterway's aid system should deal with, but not necessarily be driven by, the worst conditions the largest vessel might encounter.

b. Vessel traffic data can be obtained from several sources. The local pilots and/or harbormaster may be able to provide it or the data may be obtained from a local VTS. The Army Corps of Engineers Waterborne Commerce of the United States Reports contain transit, tonnage, and commodity information. The four parameters of vessel size that need to be considered are length, beam, draft, and dead weight tonnage. Of these, research has shown dead weight tonnage to be the best predictor of vessel controllability.

c. The goal is to design aid systems for the largest vessel using the waterway. There may be cases where the largest vessel is significantly larger than the majority of the vessel population using the waterway. Such a large vessel may also make infrequent transits of the waterway. In this situation, consideration should be given to other methods, besides aids to navigation, for helping ensure the safety of this vessel. Speed and visibility restrictions, escort vessels, and one-way traffic are some options that the COTP could invoke to reduce risk to an acceptable level without significantly altering the aid system when exceptionally large vessels transit the waterway.

d. Physical conditions of the waterway must also be considered. When channels are narrow compared to the beam of the user, ranges may be essential for safe navigation. The bottom conditions and clearances may also mandate the use of particular aids.

e. Environmental conditions are more difficult to address. The decision to mark for average or worst conditions, or something in between, cannot always be easily made. The following guidelines may be helpful:

   (1) The design should accommodate the maximum or worst case tidal current in the waterway.

   (2) Reduced visibility due to haze and fog must be considered. Designing for worst case visibility is not practical. The goal, or availability standard, for minor aids is to provide a system based on a meteorological visibility that is met or exceeded 80% of the time. The system of major lights should be designed for a visibility that is met or exceeded 90% of the time. Following the constraints in section **D. of this chapter**, these availability standards will help describe the necessary hardware combinations.

   (3) In some areas attaining these availability standards may not be possible because of very poor visibility or severe background lighting. These occurrences should be infrequent. In such cases, attaining the highest operational availability with current equipment is acceptable.

(4) Selected aid types should be appropriate for the existing environmental category (exposed, semi-exposed, or protected). The Aids to Navigation Manual - Technical, COMDTINST M16500.3(series), lists the design environment for all standard aid types. Section **B**. of this chapter defines the environmental category terms.

(5) The effects of ice during the winter and frequent heavy rain squalls during the summer also dictate aid mix. Unlighted buoys, which have a tendency to surface through the ice, may be necessary in the former case. Racons might prove useful in the latter case when all but the strongest of radar signals might be covered by return from a heavy squall.

f. Due to the significant potential for loss of life caused by bridge allisions, approaches to bridges over the water must receive careful attention. This includes highway and railroad bridges over waterways marked with aids to navigation and over adjoining waters. The following guidelines may be helpful:

(1) Coordinate ATON system design with district bridge administration officials. Considerations include existing bridge marking (e.g. lighting, retro reflective panels, racons), physical characteristics of the bridge (e.g. height, span width), extent of fendering systems, and types of waterway traffic. ATON systems should facilitate safe transit of vessels on the centerline of main channels approaching bridges.

(2) Where bridges cross over waters adjoining waterways marked with aids to navigation, consideration must be given to the accessibility of these waters from the marked waterways and the impact of their use by traffic as alternate routes or as staging areas. The use of Information Marks may be appropriate in those areas where bridges may pose a hazard to vessel activity.

5. Simulators. Using simulators to analyze aid configurations will be more common in the future. At the very least, simulators can provide a good overview of aid effectiveness in a waterway during daytime and for a clear night.

F. Short Range Aid System Configuration and Design.

1. General. The short range aid system consists of four sub-systems. They are daytime visual, nighttime visual, radar or reduced visibility, and sound systems. Characteristics of each sub-system are:

a. The daytime visual system consists of the daymarks of beacons and buoys and daytime range lights.

b. The nighttime visual system consists of lights and retro reflective signals.

c. The radar system consists of radar reflectors, racons, and shore-based radar systems.

d. Sound systems consist of various non-directional sound producing devices.

2. Since the above systems are collocated, they must be designed or evaluated concurrently. Guidelines for the use of major lights, ranges, racons, and sound signals have been provided earlier in Section D of this chapter. The following more specific guidelines should help determine the needs for the two largest categories of short range aids: beacons and buoys.

3. Procedure for Marking. Whether designing a new **aid** system or evaluating an existing one there are many factors to be considered. The following procedure is intended to promote a systematic review of each of these factors, resulting in a thorough treatment of even the most complex situation. These steps parallel those presented in the SRA Systems Design Manual for Restricted Waterways (USCG R&D Report Nr CG-D-18-85).

   a. Determine the Conventional Direction of Buoyage (CDB): Direction of flood and ebb currents throughout U.S. waters have been determined by NOAA and are usually available in current charts and tide tables. This information, as well as coastwise and Great Lake conventions provided in Title 33 of the CFR, defines our conventional direction of buoyage for assigning lateral markings. The designer should indicate the direction of buoyage on the working chart, paying particular attention to intersections, islands, and headwaters where currents meet and part.

   b. Mark the Approaches: The approach to any restricted waterway is usually classified as a bay, sound, channel, inlet, or strait. The aid systems in these regions consist of mixtures of radio aids and short range aids. Several procedures are used for marking in this area:

      (1) Short range aids in this region conform to the conventional direction of buoyage and usually mark good water.

      (2) Traffic separation schemes (TSS) may be found in this area. Aids marking a TSS are usually special purpose, with the most seaward aid usually being a safewater mark. For a TSS to be internationally **recognized** the International Maritime Organization (IMO) must approve the layout and ATON provided to ensure that vessels can determine their position within the TSS. Commandant **(CG-5413)** and **(CG-543)** will make the notification. This approval will take a minimum of 24 months.

      (3) Wrecks and obstructions should be marked if the traffic situation so dictates.

(4) Prioritize Channels: When more than one channel needs marking they should be ranked by order of importance. This ranking is usually based on width, depth, and predominant traffic flow. Draw a continuous line, numbered "1", down the center of the primary channel in the direction of buoyage, as in Figure 4-1. Continue with each subsequent channel, leaving short gaps where a subordinate waterway crosses or intersects one of a higher priority, until all are drawn and numbered. With one exception, you should prioritize the ICW based on its importance relative to other proximate waterways, and not necessarily downgrade it to the lowest ranking. For example, there may be places where the ICW is deeper or supports a higher volume of traffic than a nearby non-ICW waterway. The exception arises when the conventional direction of buoyage for the ICW runs opposite to that of the normal waterway. In that case, the normal waterway must have a higher priority than the ICW.

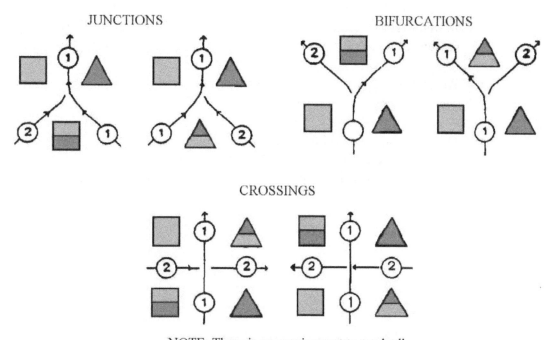

JUNCTIONS

BIFURCATIONS

CROSSINGS

NOTE: There is no requirement to mark all three or four corners of the intersections.

Prioritized Channels

Figure 4-1

c. <u>Channel Subdivision</u>. When conducting an aid system design or evaluation, it is helpful to divide the channel or waterway into regions according to the unique requirements of the maneuvering tasks for each. These descriptive maneuvering tasks are: turn, recovery (from a turn), and track keeping.

(1) A turn region should generally extend a half mile either side of the apex of the turn. Different turn types, such as cutoff, non-cutoff, or bends, require that the designer use discretion when establishing region boundaries. The constraining consideration should be the desire to enclose the area in which the navigator is actually executing the turn.

(2) The recovery region, as the name implies, should enclose the area, immediately following a turn, which is needed to regain a steady heading. Research has shown this distance to be approximately three quarters to one and one-half miles. A shallow turn, 15 degrees or less, would require the shorter distance for recovery, while a larger turn, up to 35 degrees or more, would require a greater distance to regain track. Vessel size is also an important variable in delineating recovery region distances, with larger vessels, 50K DWT or greater, needing greater distances to regain track.

(3) The remaining portion of the waterway necessarily becomes the track keeping region.

(4) These regions should be plotted directly on the chart showing the channel under consideration. Figure 4-2 illustrates the technique. This is especially useful when evaluating the interaction between regions later.

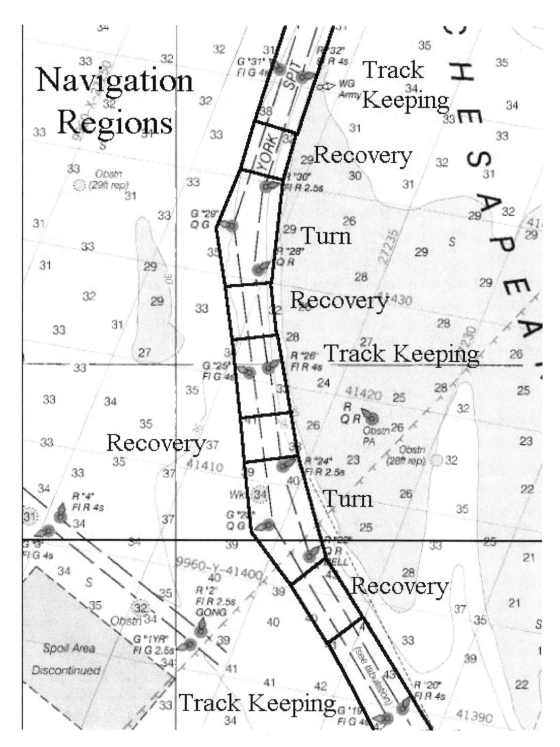

Navigation Regions

Figure 4-2

d. <u>Region Marking</u>. The next logical step is to determine the number and location of aids within each region. By later analyzing the entire waterway as a system, the designer can identify excessive redundancy or apparent marking voids at common boundaries, and make necessary adjustments. Some general guidelines for marking each region are listed below:

(1) The turn is the most difficult task in the navigation process, so logically the turn region should contain the highest aid density. The most important need in this region is to mark the inside of the turn. This translates to one lateral mark at the inside apex of a non-cutoff turn and two lateral marks at the inside corners of a cutoff turn. Bends should be treated as cutoffs. Complicating factors such as two-way traffic, narrow channel width, large ship size, frequently reduced visibility, and excessive cross-currents will suggest the need for additional turning aids. The exact number and configuration are subject to the designer's discretion. In general, the goal when marking a turn region is to outline the available maneuvering space. Figure 4-3 illustrates some possible arrangements.

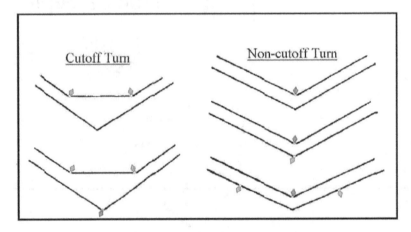

Figure 4-3

(2) When executing a turn, there is a tendency for a vessel to be displaced radially toward the outside of the turn. Given this fact, the first consideration in the recovery region should be to provide a side mark to help the vessel pullout from the turn. This translates to one aid along the outboard channel edge, usually within a half mile from the turn apex. After the pullout, gated configurations promote the most precise navigation performance, followed by staggered and one-sided configurations, respectively. Figure 4-4 illustrates each type. Your choice should be based on the operational conditions discussed in section E.4. of this chapter. ATON spacing along the track usually falls between 1/2 and 1 1/2 miles. Maximum spacing should be governed by the criteria in the following paragraph.

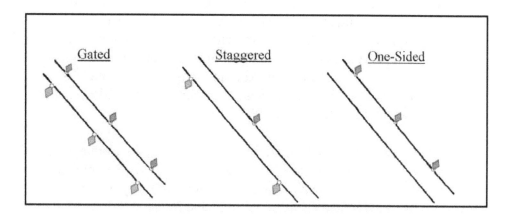

Figure 4-4

(3) Track keeping, being the simplest of the three tasks mentioned, requires the sparsest aid density. Ranges have been shown to promote the best performance in straight channel segments. Even with ranges, however, side marks will nearly always be needed to promote safe navigation when environmental conditions preclude using the visual range or in passing or meeting situations. The following paragraph lists possible arrangements in order of their effectiveness. Maximum aid spacing is constrained by the following criteria. The standards stated assume use by a mariner with a fifteen foot height of eye or greater.

(a) During nighttime, a mariner aboard a vessel constrained to the channel by her draft should see at least two lighted aids forward, on at least one side of the channel, from any position in the waterway, 80% of the nights of the year. Vessels not so constrained, such as small boats or vessels transiting open bays or sounds, need see only one lighted aid forward. Consult the Visual Signal Design Manual, COMDTINST M16510.2 (series) to obtain the 80% visibility value for the appropriate geographic area. The Allards Law program, available from Commandant **(CG-432)** can be used to determine optic/lamp combinations to meet minimum candela requirements.

(b) During daytime, a mariner aboard a vessel constrained to the channel by her draft should see at least two aids forward, on at least one side of the channel, from any position in the waterway, at least 80% of the days of the year. Mariners not constrained to the channel need see only one aid forward. Next enter Table 2-4, Change in Visual Range of Buoy Types Versus Change in Visibility (NM), in the Aids to Navigation Manual – Technical, COMDTINST M16500.3 (series) with the buoy type and the visibility to get visual range. For dayboards, simply use the nominal range listed in the ATON Manual-Technical as the visual range.

(c) Research has shown navigation performance deteriorates with increased aid spacing, especially for vessels larger than 50,000 DWT. Consequently, when marking channels where vessels are constrained by their draft, no range lights are present, or natural or man-made landmarks are limited, maximum along-track spacing should normally not exceed 1.5 miles for vessels larger than 50K DWT and 2.0 miles for those less than 50K DWT.

(d) By using the smallest aid spacing which results from applying these three criteria, each constraint will be satisfied. Remember, this is only an upper limit on aid spacing. Peculiarities of your waterway and its users may dictate shorter spacing and higher aid density.

(4) Once each region is evaluated for proper marking, the region boundaries must be examined to ensure a smooth transition. Adjust the initial design to eliminate excessive redundancy or fill in the gaps.

e. Assign Signals. With the aids in place, the appropriate signals may now be assigned. Detailed specifications for all signals are contained in the following paragraphs and in the Aids to Navigation Manual – Technical, COMDTINST M16500.3 (series). FIGURE 4-5 provides a quick reference for the most common signals assigned on aids in the U.S. and Western Rivers Marking Systems.

Type of Mark	LIGHT		DAYMARK				Top Mark
	Color	Rhythm	Color	LB	ULB	Beacon	
Lateral Starboard	Red	Fl 2.5s Fl 4s Fl 6s Fl (2) 5s Fl (2) 6s Q Oc Iso	Red				None
Preferred Channel to Port	Red	Fl (2+1) 6s	RGR Bands				None
Lateral Port	Green	Fl 2.5s Fl 4s Fl 6s Fl (2) 5s Fl (2) 6s Q Oc Iso	Green				None
Preferred Channel to Starboard	Green	Fl (2+1) 6s	GRG Bands				None
Special	Yellow	Fl 2.5s Fl 4s Fl 6s	Yellow	Standard buoy body as appropriate, not to conflict			None

TYPE OF MARK	LIGHT		DAYMARK				TOP MARK
	COLOR	RHYTHM	COLOR	LB	ULB	BEACON	
Safewater	White	Mo(A)	Red and White Striped	Standard Lighted Buoy with Topmark	Pillar With Topmark or Sphere		Red
Isolated Danger	White	Fl (2) 5s	Black and Red Bands	Standard Buoy Body with two Black Spherical Topmarks		None	Black
Range	Red Green White Yellow	See Chap 6, COMDTIST M16500.3 and Range Design Manual	Green Black Red White	None	None	Contrasting Stripes	None
Left Descending Bank (LDB)	Red	Fl (2) 5s Fl (2) 6s Iso	Red				None
Right Descending Bank (RDB)	Green	Fl 4s Iso	Green				None
Crossing (CNR)	Red or White	Fl (2) 5s Fl (2) 6s Iso	Red and White	None	None		None
Crossing (CNG)	Green or White	Fl 4s Iso	Green and White	None	None		None

INFORMATION AND REGULATORY MARKERS		ILLUSTRATION
Boat exclusion areas	Explanation may be placed outside the crossed diamond shape, such as DAM, RAPIDS, SWIM AREA, etc.	
Danger	The nature of the danger may be indicated inside the diamond shape, such as ROCK, SHOAL, DAM, PIPELINE, etc.	
Controlled	The type of control is indicated in the circle, such as SLOW, NO WAKE, ANCHORING, SPEED, etc.	
Information	Used for displaying information such as directions, distances, locations, etc.	
Mooring Buoy	This distictive color scheme facilitates identification, avoids confusion with other aids to navigation.	

Figure 4-5

(1) <u>Daymarks</u>: The daymark is characterized by its color, shape, and number or letter.

    (a) <u>Color</u>: Since most of our aids are lateral marks, assigning the proper shape and color is usually clear. When looking in the direction of buoyage, aids to the right are red; those to the left are green. For those aids alongside two channels (junction, bifurcation, intersection), preferred channel marks are required. The higher priority channel dictates the dominant or uppermost color, while the lower priority channel dictates the auxiliary or lowermost color. Figure 4-6 shows an example of this application. Safewater marks are painted with red and white vertical stripes. Isolated Danger marks are black with a wide red, horizontal band. Special marks are yellow. Ranges can show any two of the colors red, green, black, white or yellow. Certain non-lateral aids, such as lighthouses, leading lights, crossing, or sector lights may carry NB, NG, or NR dayboards. Information daymarks are white with orange bands and orange geometric shapes.

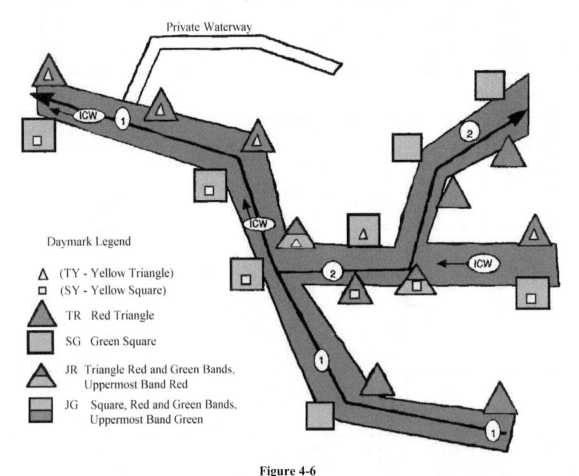

Figure 4-6

(b) <u>Shape</u>: For fixed aids, the dayboard shape carries significance. Lateral aids colored red are triangular; those colored green are square. Preferred Channel marks are shaped according to the uppermost or dominant color. Safewater marks are octagonal. Special marks, crossing and other non-lateral marks are diamond shaped. For large lighted buoys, shape is insignificant, except for the safewater mark and the isolated danger mark. The safewater mark must carry a single red sphere as a topmark and the isolated danger mark must carry two black spheres as a topmark. Five and three foot lighted buoys have shape significance. For unlighted buoys, red aids are nuns, green aids are cans, and red and white striped aids are cans or pillars with a red spherical topmark. Yellow aids may use various hulls. As with dayboards, unlighted Preferred Channel buoys are shaped according to the uppermost color.

(c) <u>Numbers and Letters</u>: Channels should be numbered and lettered sequentially. Lateral aids are numbered or lettered as consecutively as possible, beginning at the seaward end of the waterway, and increasing in the previously defined direction of buoyage. Use even numbers on red aids and odd numbers on green aids. In addition to a number, the first aid in a waterway may be suffixed with an identifying letter(s). This provides positive identification where two or more buoys in an area have the same number (e.g. Buoy 2A). Preferred Channel, Safewater, Isolated Danger, and Special marks shall be lettered. On the Western Rivers, numbers displayed on distance markers, or suspended from lateral and crossing dayboards, indicate the mileage from a designated point. Buoys on the Western Rivers are not numbered. More guidance on numbering and lettering can be found later in the section on Aid Names.

(2) <u>Lights</u>.

(a) <u>Terminology</u>: An aid's light <u>characteristic</u> consists of its <u>color</u> and <u>rhythm</u>. Authorized colors are red, green, white, and yellow. Authorized rhythms are <u>fixed,</u> <u>flashing</u> (duration of light clearly less than duration of darkness), <u>isophase</u> (light and darkness equal in duration), and <u>occulting</u> (duration of light clearly longer than duration of darkness). Flashing lights may be <u>single flashing</u> (one flash per period) or <u>group flashing</u> (flashes combined in groups with darkness between groups clearly longer than darkness between flashes). Single flashing lights may be <u>slow flashing</u> (less than 30 flashes per minute; the adjective "slow" is usually omitted) or <u>quick flashing</u> (60 or more flashes per minute). A <u>Morse code</u> light groups flashes (long and short) to form Morse characters.

(b) Authorized characteristics: A light's characteristic is determined by the aid's function. Authorized characteristics for most aids are contained in Figure 4-5. The quick rhythm is the most conspicuous, and should be used on important lateral aids. Some examples are aids in turns, marking shoals, and marking wrecks. Because a single fixed light can be mistaken for a vessel, use of fixed rhythm lights as lateral aids to navigation is not authorized. Those non-lateral aids not subject to the IALA agreement (lighthouses, range lights, leading lights, sector and direction lights) are not constrained to particular characteristics. The choice of characteristic should reflect a desire to provide the best conspicuity while avoiding conflicts with other aids which might mislead the mariner. An example of such a conflict would be a major seacoast light showing a Morse Alpha rhythm, since, as shown in Figure 4-5, Morse Alpha indicates a safewater mark. Common sense should eliminate any confusion.

(3) ICW Markings. Yellow symbols indicate that an aid marks the Intracoastal Waterway. Yellow triangles indicate starboard hand aids, and yellow squares indicate port hand aids when following the ICW's conventional direction of buoyage: southerly along the East coast, westerly along the Okeechobee waterway, and westerly along the Gulf coast. Non-lateral aids such as safe water, isolated danger, and front range boards are marked with a horizontal yellow band. Rear range boards do not display the yellow band because of the inconspicuity of the symbol. At a junction with a federally maintained waterway, the preferred channel mark will display a yellow triangle or square as appropriate for the conventional direction of buoyage of the ICW. Junctions with the ICW and privately maintained waterways are not marked with preferred channel buoys.

f. Other Marks and Considerations. The designer must bear in mind the discussions presented thus far apply mainly to the relatively small portion of our total aid population marking dredged channels and restricted waterways. Most aids simply delineate safe water or mark wrecks, obstructions, isolated dangers, etc. These must be marked as the prevailing traffic situation dictates. Common sense, experience, and user preference will provide the basis for their location and configuration.

(1) <u>Marking of Coaxial Waterways</u>: Occasionally, it may be necessary to
mark the deep draft channel within a wider waterway while marking the
wider boundaries for shallow draft traffic. Begin by considering the limits
of each traffic route independently. Then refine the system to eliminate
unnecessary aids where close spacing results. Large potential for
confusion to the mariner exists in naming and numbering the aids in this
area. The aids marking the deep draft route should be named and
numbered first. Included in the name should be a noun indicating a
feature of that route, probably channel, traffic lane, cut, or canal. An
example would be Black River Channel Lighted Buoy 3 (see Figure 4-7).
The other aids that mark the broader expanse of water should then be
named and numbered. The name should not include the word "Channel"
unless, by chance, it does lie on the channel edge. For example, an aid
between Black River Channel Buoys 3 and 5, but not lying on the channel,
could reasonably be named Black River Buoy 3A. It should not be
numbered in pure numerical sequence with the channel. In a narrow river,
the use of alpha-numerics, as in the above example, may be the most
obvious solution. But, on a very wide river, the auxiliary lateral markings
could be numbered totally independent of the channel numbering system.
The application of common sense toward the goal of creating simplicity
and minimizing confusion should prevail.

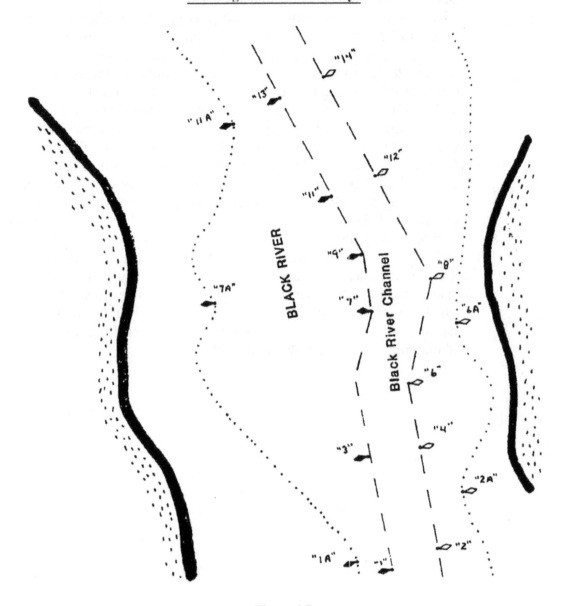

Figure 4-7

(2) <u>Variations on Direction of Buoyage</u>: At times, strict adherence to using the direction of flood to determine the conventional direction of buoyage may cause confusion and result in an inconsistent marking scheme. This situation is most likely to arise near islands or river mouths. A little ingenuity and common sense should suggest the proper deviation from the rules. The goal should be to design the simplest, most straightforward waterway while keeping exceptions to the rules to a minimum. In Figure 4-8, an apparent confusing situation exists between points "B" and "C". This can be eliminated by deviating from the rules and changing the direction of buoyage to go from point "B" to point "C".

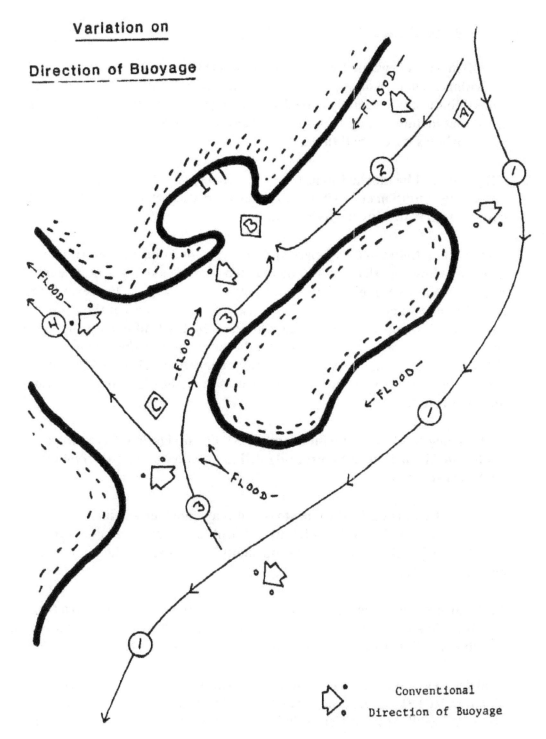

Variation on Direction of Buoyage

Conventional Direction of Buoyage

Figure 4-8

G. **Offshore Renewable Energy Installation**.

1. **An Offshore Renewable Energy Installation (OREI) is a facility, an individual structure or apparatus placed in the navigable waters of the United States that creates electricity by using sources other than oil or gas. Examples include wind farms and hydrokinetic apparatus such as buoys, wave turbines, or current turbines.**

2. **OREIs should be marked so as to be conspicuous by day and night, given to prevailing conditions of visibility and vessel traffic. OREIs shall be marked with/or as private aids to navigation.**

3. **Consultation between developers and district aids to navigation staffs to determine how an OREI should be marked should take place at an early stage in the development of the renewable energy project. However, these consultations do not imply that the Coast Guard approves of the project. Approval of the project is a function handled by the lead permitting agency. In general, development of OREIs should not prejudice the safe use of Tships' routing measures such as Traffic Separation Schemes (TSS) or two-way routes, for example, and the safe access to anchorages, harbors and places of refuge.**

4. **Preliminary Notices to Mariners and/or Radio Navigational Warnings [Notice to Airmen] must be promulgated in advance of, and during any OREI construction.**

5. **On a case-by-case basis, the Coast Guard may consider establishing Limited Access Areas, 33 CFR 165, which would prohibit or restrict vessels from entering an OREI. Such information should be shown on the appropriate navigation charts.**

6. **At the discretion of the Coast Guard, appropriate routing measures through the OREI to enhance mariner safety may be authorized. Ideally, individual structures within an OREI would not be utilized as lateral marks.**

7. **In order to avoid confusion from a proliferation of Aids to Navigation in a high density OREI, full consideration should be given to the use of synchronized lighting, different light characteristics and varied light ranges.**

8. **Mariners should be warned on the navigational chart by way of a legend or note that the OREI and associated seabed electric cables may cause propagation problems and electro-magnetic interference to onboard navigation equipment.**

9. <u>Wind farms</u>. Wind farms should be marked as a single unit or as a block as follows:

a. The tower of every wind generator should be painted yellow all around from the level of Highest Astronomical Tide (HAT) to 50 feet (15 meters) or at least the height of the Aid to Navigation, if fitted, whichever is greater. Retro reflective material must also be used.

b. Due to the increased danger posed by an isolated structure, it should be lighted as an Offshore Structure, in accordance with 33 CFR 67.

c. A Significant Peripheral Structure (SPS) is the "corner" or other significant point on the periphery of the wind farm. Every individual SPS should be marked by sufficient lights so as to be visible to the mariner from all relevant directions in the horizontal plane. Such lights should display the character of a special mark with an operational range of not less than four nautical miles. As a minimum, lights on individual SPSs should be synchronized, but District Commanders may require all SPSs to be synchronized.

d. In the case of a large or extended wind farm, the distance between SPSs should not normally exceed 3 nautical miles.

e. Selected intermediate structures on the periphery of a wind farm other than the SPSs in (c) and (d) above, should be marked with flashing yellow lights which are visible to the mariner from all relevant directions in the horizontal plane. The flash character of such lights should be distinctly different from those displayed on the SPSs with an operational range of not less than two (2) nautical miles. The lateral distance between such lighted structures or the nearest SPS should not exceed two (2) nautical miles.

f. Depending on the lateral separation of individual turbines, the District Commander may require each turbine within a wind farm to be lighted. Depending on the marking and lighting of the peripheral structures, the additional marking of the individual structures within a wind farm should be considered as follows:

(1) Unlit.

(2) Unlit with retro-reflective areas.

(3) Down lighting floodlights on ladders and access platforms.

(4) Flashing yellow lights with an operational range of not less than 2 nautical miles.

(5) Lit/unlit identifying numbers or names for each unit.

g. The Aids to Navigation on the structure of a wind generator should be mounted below the lowest point of the arc of the rotor blades. They should be exhibited at a height above the level of the Highest Astronomical Tide (HAT) of not less than 20 ft (6 meters) nor more than 50 feet (15 meters).

h. The Aids to Navigation described herein should have an availability of not less than 99.0 %.

i. A wind farm may be additionally marked by Racon(s).

j. Consideration should be given to the additional use of radar reflectors and radar target enhancers.

k. Consideration should be given to the provision of sound signals where appropriate, given prevailing conditions of visibility, topography and vessel traffic.

l. An electrical transformer station or a meteorological or wind measuring mast, if considered to be a composite part of the wind farm, should be included as part of the overall wind farm marking. If not considered to be within the wind farm block it should be marked as an offshore structure, in accordance with 33 CFR 67.

m. As far as practicable, Aeronautical obstruction lights fitted to the tops of wind turbines should not be visible below the horizontal plane of these lights. Aviation authorities should be consulted regarding the specification of such lights.

10. **Hydrokinetic projects:** Marking of hydrokinetic projects will be determined on a case-by-case basis.

H. Aid Names.

1. General.

a. The U.S. Board on Geographic Names (BGN) is a Federal body created to establish and maintain uniform geographic name usage throughout the Federal Government. An official name is one that has been approved by the BGN or appropriate administrative agency. It is the policy of the Federal Government that only official domestic geographic names are to be used on Federal maps and in other publications. An official name is one in which the written form of that name and its application to the appropriate place, feature, or area are approved by the U.S. Board on Geographic Names or the appropriate administrative agency. The naming of aids to navigation is generally not subject to BGN decisions. As such, the Coast Guard is the administrative agency with authority to name aids to navigation.

b. Names of aids to navigation assist mariners in verifying they are in or near a particular geographic area and in referencing that area on nautical charts. Naming aids to navigation after individuals should be avoided.

c. Assign an appropriate name, as brief as possible, to each aid to navigation. Names should include the following:

(1) A geographic place name, preferably one shown in the latest edition of the nautical chart of the area. If no such name is shown in the immediate area of a proposed aid, the name assigned should conform to the local usage. Duplication of place names within the same or adjacent Coast Guard Districts should be avoided.

(2) When not included in the geographic place name, a noun indicating the waterway feature being marked, such as Approach Channel, Entrance Channel, Rock, Shoal, Reef, Junction, Traffic Lane, Wreck, etc. This noun may be omitted when not necessary for clarity.

(3) A noun indicating the type of aid such as Light, Daybeacon, Buoy, etc. The type of buoy must be fully described, i.e., Lighted Whistle Buoy.

(4) An identifying number or letter(s), assigned as previously discussed. Numbers should be limited to two digits. Aids required to be numbered may, when needed, have a letter after the number. In channel marking, it is highly desirable to apply the same geographic name to a series of aids using numbers and/or letters to distinguish among them.

Examples of proper aid names:

Cashes Ledge Whistle Buoy CL
Sugar Point Lighted Gong Buoy 3
Calcasieu Channel Range A Front Light
Mendocino Bay Whistle Buoy M
Rogue River North Jetty Light 3
Southwest Spit Junction Lighted Gong Buoy SP

2. Collocated Aids.

    a. An aid to navigation is composed of all needed signals required by operational considerations for the safety of navigation. An aid may be composed of a daymark and light, sound signal, and racon or any combination of the above. All of these components, at a location, are described in the remarks section of the Light List as an aid to navigation. In some cases similar aid types are collocated at the same facility or structure.

    b. Sometimes a structure may serve as a support for two different aid functions. Perhaps the most common example is a range structure that displays an omnidirectional light shown from the range lantern or a separate lantern.

    c. If, because of the location of the range structure at or near the channel edge, the omnidirectional light serves as a lateral aid, the structure should be equipped with a range daymark and one or more lateral daymarks. The range daymark is required only if a daytime optic is not used for the range.

    d. If the aid uses the same lantern for both range light and lateral aid purposes, it should be considered one aid, with the name of the range light suffixed with an appropriate number to indicate the dual function of the aid. For example, such an aid could be named Sacramento Channel Range B Front Light 75.

    e. If separate lanterns are used for the two functions, the structure should be considered as two aids. For example, Sacramento Channel Range B Front Light and Sacramento Channel Light 75 would be treated as separate aid stations for Light List, Notice to Mariners, and I-ATONIS purposes.

    f. A range light may be so arranged that it produces, in addition to the beam on the channel axis, an all-around light of lower intensity. If separate lanterns with the same synchronous characteristic are used and the lanterns are atop one another, the structure should be considered a single aid. Such a light is considered an additional feature of the range as long as the characteristic is the same as the range light.

    g. If the two lanterns have different characteristics, then the omnidirectional light is described as a "passing light" and the aids should be assigned two different names where one is the range light and the other is the passing light.

        Morgans Point Approach Range Front Light
        Morgans Point Approach Range Front Passing Light

    h. A similar procedure is followed when two range light functions are accomplished on one structure. For example, a single lantern, double purpose range structure could be named Houston Ship Channel Ranges S and X Front Light or Houston Ship Channel Range E Front and Range H Rear Light. If separate lanterns were used, two separate aid stations would be considered to exist at the same location

3. Additional Guidelines.

   a. The words "Special Purpose" should not be included in the name of an aid, i.e. Cape Cod Special Purpose Lighted Buoy D. Instead, the reason the buoy is a special purpose buoy should be included in the name, i.e., Bolivar Roads Anchorage Buoy A. If necessary, additional special purpose information should be listed in the "Remarks" column of the Light List.

   b. When the structure of a discontinued light is retained as a daybeacon, the aid should be designated "Daybeacon", as in Timbalier Daybeacon.

   c. To preclude confusion with numerals, the letters "I" and "O" are not normally used on aids. However, they may be used when considered necessary, such as:

      Oregon Inlet Approach Lighted Whistle Buoy OI
      Outer Shoal Daybeacon OS

   d. Aids marking a dredged channel in a river need not have "Channel" in their names unless necessary for clarity. Hackensack River Channel Buoy 2 could be named Hackensack River Buoy 2.

   e. All solid color buoys or daybeacons marking sunken or partially sunken wrecks, obstructions or wreckage should be numbered in proper sequence with the other aids to navigation in the same channel or waterway. The letters "WR" should be used on all wreck markings, and should prefix the regular number or letter, if any. Los Angeles Entrance Channel Lighted Wreck Buoy WR2A is an example.

   f. The words "preferred channel", "bifurcation" and "safe water" should not normally be used in aid names.

   g. Temporary additional aids, not relocations, are marked with a number and a letter designation. Example: A channel marked by two aids 12 and 14 has experienced shoaling between the aids. The aid between 12 and 14 would be designated 12A. If more shoaling occurs between the permanent aids, the next aid is numbered 12B.

This Page Intentionally
Left Blank

CHAPTER 5 - NON COAST GUARD MAINTAINED AIDS

A. General.

1. There are categories of aids to navigation which are not maintained by the Coast Guard. These aids, in many areas of the navigable waters subject to federal jurisdiction, are maintained by various entities including other federal agencies, the States, other Armed Forces, private corporations and private individuals. These aids are not maintained by the Coast Guard because marking by the Coast Guard would:

    a. Relieve the owner of a wreck, of his responsibility to warn others of its existence and location.

    b. Place upon the Coast Guard the burden of marking structures or other hazards which have been established for the benefit of only the owner.

    c. Require the expenditure of federal funds far exceeding the expected benefits that would be derived.

    d. Benefit only a limited number of users.

2. 33 USC 409 requires that wrecks of vessels, constituting a hazard in the navigable waters of the United States, must be marked for the protection of marine traffic. The law requires that the owner of such a wreck mark it with a "buoy or beacon during the day and unless otherwise granted a waiver by the Commandant of the Coast Guard, a light."

3. No person, public body or instrumentality not under the control of the Commandant, exclusive of the Armed Forces, shall establish and maintain, discontinue, change or transfer ownership of any aid to maritime navigation, without first obtaining permission to do so from the Commandant (33 CFR 66.01).

B. Private Aids to Navigation.

1. Classification of Private Aids.

    a. Private aids include both those which are legally required, and those which are merely desired by the owner. There are three classifications of private aids:

        (1) Class I private aids are those aids to navigation on marine structures or other works which the owners are legally obligated to establish, maintain, and operate as prescribed by the Coast Guard. This obligation is contained in 33 CFR Parts 64, 66, and 67. The owner of a structure is

required by law (14 USC 85, 33 CFR 64.21) to establish the aids to navigation required by the District Commander.

   (2) Class II private aids to navigation are those, exclusive of Class I aids, that are located in waters used by general navigation.

   (3) Class III private aids to navigation are those, exclusive of Class I aids and Class II aids, that are located in waters not ordinarily used by general navigation.

b. Authorization for the establishment of a Class II or III private aid by the Coast Guard imposes no legal obligation that the aid actually be established and operated. It only specifies the location and operational characteristics of the aid for which the authorization was requested. Once the aid is established, however, the owner is legally obligated to maintain it in good working order and properly painted. The owner must also give the Coast Guard 30 days notice before discontinuing the aid in accordance with 33 CFR 66.01-25.

c. All private aids must be approved by the appropriate District Commander before the aid is established.

2. <u>District Administration of the Private Aids Program</u>.

a. Requests for authority to establish, discontinue or change private aids to navigation are made on Forms CG-2554 and CG-4143 IAW 33 CFR 66. These forms are available in the CG-Forms library and the Internet. These forms, executed by the person, company, corporation, or municipality at whose expense the aid is to be maintained, are submitted to the appropriate District Commander who shall:

   (1) Review the form for compliance with aids to navigation regulations; all applicable environmental regulations, including National Environmental Protection Act and Coastal Zone Management Act; accuracy of plotting; and correctness.

   (2) Ensure that all positions are given by latitude and longitude as obtained from a GPS/DGPS receiver or from a licensed surveyor.

   (3) In unusual situations, cases involving electronic aids, or examples not covered by directives, the application will be sent to Commandant **(CG-5413)** for approval.

b. After determining the class of the aid/obstruction marking, the District Commander shall recommend to the National Ocean Service, through publication in the Local Notice to Mariners, for charting all permanent:

   (1) Class I private aids.

   (2) Class II fixed private aids, **other than information/regulatory marks.**

   (3) Class II floating private aids equivalent in size to, or larger than a 6NR/6CR.

   (4) Class III private aids shall not be recommended for charting except in special circumstances.

c. All private aids included in sub-paragraphs b(1), b(2), and b(3) above shall be reported in Local Notices to Mariners upon establishment, change or discontinuance.

d. When a private aid is established that needs to be charted, it shall be listed in the Local Notice to Mariners in the same manner as a Federal aid, with the notation ("Private Aid" or in the case of a **lighthouse** "Structure and Daymark Privately Maintained"). Refer to Chapter 13 for more detail.

e. Markers which cause an obstruction to navigation, especially those in or adjacent to fairways or navigational channels, must be of appropriate size, shape, and color to warn traffic of their existence and purpose and shall be listed in the Light List.

f. Small private aids which mark fishing reefs and race courses may be excluded from the Light List when:

   (1) The fishing reefs do not cause an obstruction to navigation.

   (2) The markers are not located in or adjacent to fairways, navigational channels, or traffic separation schemes customarily used by craft in approaching or leaving harbors.

g. Previously charted private aids no longer meeting the requirements above will be removed from charts and the Light List.

h. Aids submitted for removal from charts will be removed from the Light List and applicable charts. Removal of these private aids from the Light List requires notification in Local Notices to Mariners.

i. Any private aid to navigation that is published in the Light List will be entered into I-ATONIS.

j. In conjunction with the district review of federal aids to navigation specified in Chapter 3, charted private aids will also be reviewed to identify those with changed classification.

k. Queries regarding private aids should be directed to the District Commander. All correspondence between the Coast Guard and the maintainer of private aids should normally be through the District Commander.

l. All approved private aid permits that are not acted on within one year of the approval are nullified. If the private aid is established within one year the permit is valid until discontinued or changed as outlined in this chapter.

m. All private aids not maintained and repaired, are susceptible to prosecution under 14 USC 83. Proceedings under 14 USC 83 should be instituted only in cases of persistent neglect or refusal to comply with regulations.

n. Coast Guard units discovering unauthorized private aids shall make every effort to identify the persons responsible for their establishment. A report shall be made to the District Commander describing the unauthorized aid and the action taken to ascertain the owner. The report shall include the name and address of the owner, if known. Auxiliary units discovering such aids shall report them to the District Commander who will ascertain ownership. The District Commander's action will then depend on the circumstances of the individual case. If the owner makes reasonable effort to comply with regulations, the application should be processed without prejudice. Proceedings under 14 USC 83 should be instituted only in cases of persistent neglect or refusal to comply with the regulations.

o. U.S. Army Corps of Engineers' Approval. As outlined in 33 CFR 66.01-30

    (1) Before any private aid to navigation consisting of a fixed structure is placed in the navigable waters of the United States, authorization to erect such structure shall first be obtained from the District Engineer, U.S. Army Corps of Engineers in whose district the aid will be located.

    (2) The application to establish any private aid to navigation consisting of a fixed structure shall show evidence of the required permit having been issued by the Corps of Engineers.

3. Inspection and Verification of Private Aids to Navigation.

  a. Private aids to navigation are authorized by the U.S. Coast Guard in accordance with law, and are to be maintained by, and at the expense of, the responsible parties. Inspections and verifications are to ensure that private aids are in compliance with the conditions of the private aid application.

    (1) Inspection: An inspection is defined as Coast Guard personnel or Coast Guard Auxiliary performing a hands-on check of an aid to ensure the authorized hardware is installed as approved in the private aid application and that the aid is operating properly.

    (2) Verification: A verification is a self-verification where the owner provides a written report to the Coast Guard stating that the aid is operating properly. It can also be Coast Guard or Coast Guard Auxiliary personnel viewing the aid from a distance and determining if the aid **operates** as advertised.

  b. District Commanders shall ensure that all private aids to navigation in their areas of responsibility are inspected or verified on a periodic basis as outlined below.

    (1) New Class I private aids should be verified by Coast Guard or Coast Guard Auxiliary personnel as soon after their establishment as possible.

    (2) Class I private aids will be verified annually.

    (3) Class II private aids will be verified every three years.

    (4) Class III aids will be verified every five years.

    (5) Districts should conduct spot check inspections **on a representative sample of** Class I private aids to ensure self-verifications are being properly conducted. Inspections should focus on those aids that are frequently discrepant or generate complaints. **Inspections/verifications by Coast Guard or Coast Guard Auxiliary members are not required for private aids except as noted in paragraph 5.B.3.b(1).**

  c. When notification has been received that a private aid has been discontinued, the site should be inspected to ensure that the aid has been removed.

  d. Report of inspections and verifications should be made through an approved computer program.

e. Inspections of private aids to navigation should, whenever possible, be made in the presence of the owner or the owner's agent. If present, the owner or agent shall be advised of any discrepancies noted. No repair, change, repositioning, or servicing of private aids is authorized by Coast Guard personnel; however, friendly advice is encouraged. **Until establishment of a National Auxiliary ATON PQS, the Order Issuing Authority is responsible for ensuring that CG Auxiliary Members utilized to inspect or verify private aids as described above are qualified and acting within the scope of employment.**

4. Use of the Coast Guard Auxiliary

   a. District Commanders are encouraged to use the Coast Guard Auxiliary for the verification or inspection of private aids to navigation to the extent that funds are available from current budgets.

   b. When using the Auxiliary, District Commanders shall ensure that Auxiliarists receive training and maintain qualifications necessary to carry out the mission.

   c. District Commanders are encouraged to use the Auxiliary to assist with the administration and review of private aid to navigation application forms and other duties that may arise from their verification/inspection of private aids.

C. State Aids to Navigation.

   1. General. 33 CFR 66.05 permits the Commandant to designate navigable waters of the United States as "State Waters for private Aids to Navigation." These are waters not marked by the Federal government on which a State government may regulate the establishment, operation, and maintenance of marine aids to navigation. All private aids operated in "State Waters", whether owned or operated by a State, political subdivision thereof, or by individuals, corporations, or organizations are "State Aids to Navigation."

   2. Action by District Commander.

      a. District Commanders shall establish close liaison with the State officials having responsibility for enforcement of the boating laws of the states within the district's boundaries. They shall consult with State officials on any matters involving aids to navigation, particularly where the waters involved are contiguous to Federal waters. Those states which show interest in aids to navigation agreements shall be given the utmost cooperation and assistance.

b. The provisions of 33 CFR 66.05 concerning "State Waters" agreements shall be followed. Specification of standards for minimum size and shape, etc., in 66.05-20(c) should be required by the Coast Guard. If a State cannot accept the minimum size and shape standards because acceptance would result in costly replacement of present aids, then a statement of intent to manufacture or purchase future aids meeting the standards will suffice. Such a statement shall be attached as an appendix to the basic agreement. Aids throughout the State must show the specified color and light characteristics required by 33 CFR 62.

3. <u>Negotiations and Conditions</u>.

   a. All agreements shall contain a clause whereby the Coast Guard agrees to furnish to the State a description of all private aids to navigation which have been authorized by the Coast Guard in the affected waters prior to the effective date of the agreement. The agreements shall also contain a clause whereby the State, if it should desire to withdraw from the agreement, agrees to furnish the Coast Guard with a description of all State Aids to Navigation in the affected waters prior to the resumption of exclusive supervision of the aids by the Coast Guard.

   b. The agreements will remain in effect until canceled, with no requirement for periodic renewals.

   c. All agreements shall contain a clause whereby each State agrees to notify the District Commander by letter of all aids being administered in "State Waters for Private Aids to Navigation" as of 30 June each year. The report should detail the quantity of each type of aid.

   d. 33 CFR 66.05-20 requires inclusion of a clause in the agreement, reserving to the District Commander, the right to inspect aids without prior notice. Normally such examinations will be undertaken only when complaints have been made to the Coast Guard concerning the condition of aids in a specific area.

   e. Examinations deemed necessary by the Coast Guard should be made jointly by representatives of the State and the District Commander exercising responsibility over the area of the aids in question. The Coast Guard Auxiliary should not be used to inspect state aids to navigation.

   f. The following are geographical considerations:

      (1) Normally agreements will be executed with only one State. Under unusual circumstances a body of water common to two states may have a single administrator representing both states. Such an administrator would be an acceptable agent to execute an agreement.

(2) Those states which have waters lying within two or more Coast Guard districts will be required to execute only one agreement, that one being with the Coast Guard district in which the State Capital is located. Vermont and Minnesota, however, will continue to be the responsibility of the 1st and 9th Coast Guard Districts respectively. Non-Signatory District Commanders must be kept informed of agreements being negotiated and given opportunity to comment. Unresolved conflicts should be brought to the attention of Commandant (CG-5413). A clause will be inserted in such agreements to furnish the addresses of the other district aids to navigation branches to which marine information must be supplied when the area involved lies within their district boundaries.

4. Designation of State Waters.

   a. Normally a State would not be expected to request an agreement until it intended to take action in a specific area. Therefore, a request from a State for designation of "State Waters" should be forwarded to the Commandant (CG-5413) when negotiations on an agreement commence to facilitate review. Specific designation of waterways should not be included in the basic agreement. Separate submission of the designation requests will allow later inclusion of other waters without rewriting the basic agreement. Once an agreement is finalized, forward it to Commandant (CG-5413) for approval and publishing in 33 CFR 66.05-100.

   b. Designations will normally be one of two types:

      (1) Specific waters such as "Lake X" or "The Jones River from the _____ boundary upstream to the Midville City Limit."

      (2) All-inclusive such as "all navigable waters within the State of _____ not marked by the U.S. Coast Guard on the effective date of the agreement." This type of wording requires that an agreement be consummated prior to designation of waters. This should not present a problem since a state would not normally want a designation made unless it intended to install aids, which would then come under the agreement. There is no preference for one type of designation over the other, since situations vary. The choice should be based on whichever wording best meets the needs of the state.

   c. Requests for amendments to designations are to be submitted in the same manner as the original request.

d. If a body of water has been designated as "State Waters for private Aids to Navigation", and the volume of traffic indicates that federal marking should be established, or if the Corps of Engineers executes a River and Harbor Improvement Project throughout the body, the Commandant will revoke such designation upon request of the District Commander, in order that federal aids may then be established in the area. At least 30 days advance notice shall be given to the State(s) concerned.

e. Infrequently, a state might request that waters presently marked by the Coast Guard be designated as "State Waters." Approval of such a request will be based on the District Commander's investigation of the waters in question, proximity to other "State Waters; type and number of Coast Guard aids involved; use and types of users of the waterway; and possible benefit through monetary savings to Coast Guard versus potential degradation of service to mariners. Should the District Commander recommend that a State be allowed to assume responsibility for waters which are presently federally marked, the Commandant may authorize discontinuance of all Coast Guard aids, allowing the State to mark the area with state aids in accordance with the agreement.

f. State and Coast Guard aids cannot exist in the same area.

5. <u>U.S. Army Corps of Engineers</u>. Regardless of a designation by the Commandant of waters as "State Waters for private Aids to Navigation", and in accordance with 33 CFR 66.05-40, the State must obtain permission for the installation of aids from the Corps of Engineers prior to their establishment. District Commanders may assist State authorities in initiating discussions between these parties. However, the District Commander should avoid acting as intermediary in such matters or interceding for either party.

6. <u>Information on Aid Changes</u>. Upon receipt of information concerning changes of aids to navigation in "State Waters" the District Commander shall publish the information in the Local Notice to Mariners if appropriate.

7. <u>Exclusion from Light Lists</u>. Aids maintained in "State Waters are not listed in the Light List."

8. <u>Sample Agreement</u>. District Commanders may sign agreements conforming to the sample at the end of this chapter, forwarding a copy to Commandant **(CG-5413)**. Should a State raise a major objection to the agreement, all possible alternatives in reducing the objection should be pursued on the district level. If the District Commander cannot reach a compromise with the State over the objection, a letter outlining the matter shall be forwarded to Commandant **(CG-5413)**. Commandant **(CG-5413)** will then review the state's objection along with the District Commander's comments and recommendations and advise the District Commander of the Commandant's final determination.

D. Aids Maintained by Armed Forces.

1. General. The Armed Forces of the United States are exempt from Private Aid to Navigation Regulations. In cases when other armed forces request information on marking requirements, they should be advised not only of their exemption, but also what the appropriate requirements would be if they were not exempted. In so doing, they should be requested to comply, if possible, with the U.S. Marking System which is intended to provide standardized signals to the mariner. In particular, they should be advised of the preference for incandescent light or LED sources in those cases where they indicate a preference for flashtube or "strobe" light source, indicating that this requirement is based on the perceptual problems encountered in observing flashtube light sources at night.

E. Private Radionavigation Aids.

1. General. Coast Guard regulations allow radar beacons (racons) and shore-based radar stations to be operated as private aids to navigation (33 CFR 66.01-1). Federal Communication Commission (FCC) regulations require all operators of private maritime radionavigation systems to obtain written permission from the cognizant Coast Guard District Commander prior to applying for an FCC radionavigation station license. All private and State owners of radionavigation stations must have an FCC license to operate. Operators of federal radionavigation stations are exempt from these provisions, but they must obtain approval to operate with the National Telecommunications and Information Administration (NTIA). Private surveillance radar coast stations do not require U.S. Coast Guard approval. (47 CFR 80.605(a))

2. Radar Beacons (Racons). Private and state applicants can operate a racon. The equipment must have FCC authorization. Upon approval, the District Commander shall notify the applicant in writing and follow other relevant procedures outlined in section B of this chapter. The applicant must submit the following information to the Coast Guard District Commander in accordance with 33 CFR 66.01-5 and 47 CFR 80.605:

   a. The proposed position of the racon;

   b. The name and address of the person at whose expense the racon will be maintained;

   c. The name and address of the person who will maintain the racon;

   d. The time and dates during which it is proposed to operate the aid;

   e. The necessity for the racon;

   f. The manufacturer and model number of racon;

g. The height above water of the desired installation;

h. The requested coding characteristic;

i. The maximum racon transmitted power (**Effective Isotropic Radiated Power**), only if it exceeds 5 watts.

3. <u>Radars, Radar Safety Transponders and other Radionavigation Aids</u>. Applications for surveillance radar coast stations submitted to District Commanders, should be returned with a statement saying, in accordance with 47 CFR 80.605(a), no Coast Guard approval is required. Applications for other non surveillance radar coast stations should be reviewed in accordance with section B of this chapter. In addition, all applications for radar safety transponders should be sent to Commandant **(CG-5413)** for approval in accordance with 47 CFR 80.605(d).

This Page Intentionally
Left Blank

SAMPLE AGREEMENT
(See Section B.8.)
AGREEMENT
between
THE UNITED STATES COAST GUARD
and
THE STATE OF _____

WHEREAS, THE STATE OF _____, through its Department of _____, an agency under the Laws of _____ authority to regulate, establish, operate and maintain maritime aids to navigation on waters over which _____ has jurisdiction (hereinafter referred to as _____), has requested that certain navigable waters of the United States in the State of _____ be designated "State Waters for Private Aids to Navigation" (hereinafter "State Waters") to facilitate regulation by _____ of maritime aids to navigation, including regulatory markers;

WHEREAS the Commandant, U.S. Coast Guard, has determined: That _____ has the capability to regulate certain maritime aids to navigation, including regulatory markers, so as to improve the safety of navigation maritime aids to navigation, including regulatory markers, so as to improve the safety of navigation; and That it would be in the public interest to promote regulation of such maritime aids to navigation by _____ .

NOW THEREFORE, in order to facilitate cooperative regulation of maritime aids to navigation on the waters where there is concurrent jurisdiction under the sovereign, governmental, and policy powers of the State of _____ and of the United States as contemplated by Title 33, Code of Federal Regulations, Subpart 66.05;

IT IS AGREED AS FOLLOWS:

(1) Neither party cedes by this agreement any of its powers and responsibilities to the other.

(2) is hereby permitted to regulate maritime aids to navigation, including regulatory markers, on "State Waters" on the condition that the aids conform to the Uniform State Waterway Marking System specified by Title 33, Code of Federal Regulations, Subpart 66.10 or the United States' Lateral system of buoyage, subpart 62.25.

(3) This agreement shall constitute a general permit in lieu of individual permits as prescribed in Title 33, Code of Federal Regulations, 66.01-5, for all maritime aids to navigation, including regulatory markers, which are in conformity with this agreement and the regulations in Title 33, Code of Federal Regulations, Subparts

Enclosure 5 – 1

1

62.25, 66.05 and 66.10, heretofore established or to be established in_____ "State Waters" as previously designated or hereafter designated by the Commandant. The extent of "State Waters" may be modified from time to time as provided in paragraph 9.

(4) _____ will modify or remove, or cause to be removed, maritime aids to navigation, including regulatory markers, established under the authority of _____ , without expense to the United States when so directed by the Commander, _____ Coast Guard District (hereinafter "COAST GUARD") subject to the right of _____ to appeal any such order to the Commandant, whose decision shall be final.

* Some states may attach other legal significance to the term "State Waters," in which case the term "State Waters for Private Aids to Navigation" should be used throughout the agreement.

(5) COAST GUARD shall have the right to inspect the maritime aids to navigation authorized by this agreement at any time. Whenever possible prior notice shall be given by the Coast Guard to the State of _____ to allow for joint inspection.

(6) _____ shall furnish COAST GUARD (mail address: Commander, _____ Coast Guard District, _____ a listing of the location and type of aids to navigation under the authority of _____ prior to the effective date of this Agreement. COAST GUARD shall furnish a list of all private aids to navigation under COAST GUARD jurisdiction in the "State Waters" of _____ in existence prior to the effective date of this Agreement, which are to be transferred to the administration of _____.

The list shall include the information referred to in 33 CFR 66.01-5 except for the chart or sketch noted in paragraph (a) of that section.

(7) _____ shall inform the COAST GUARD of the nature and the extent of any change in _____ maritime aids to navigation as soon as possible, preferably not less than 30 days in advance of making the changes.

(8) a. In each instance in which a regulatory marker is to be established in "State Waters," _____ shall require the agency or political subdivision of the State establishing or authorizing the marker to obtain prior permission from the District Engineer. U.S. Army Corps of Engineers, having jurisdiction to regulate the waters involved, or a statement that there is no objection to the proposed regulation of the water area. A copy of the Corps of Engineers permit or letter of authority shall be provided by _____ to COAST GUARD upon request.

Enclosure 5-1

b. When a fixed or floating aid to navigation, or a mooring buoy is to be established in "State Waters," _____ shall require the private party, agency or political subdivision establishing or authorizing the aid or mooring buoy to obtain prior permission or a statement of no objection from the District Engineer concerned.

(9) The Commandant may upon his own initiative or upon request, revoke or revise any designation of "State Waters" previously made by him. Written notice will be given (mail address: _____) of any such action contemplated by the Commandant. Except in an emergency, _____ will be afforded a period of not less than 30 days from the date of the notice in which to inform the Commandant of _____ view in the matter before final action is taken to revoke or revise such designation.

(10) At any time after this Agreement has been in effect for one year _____ may draw from this Agreement upon giving 90 days written notice to COAST GUARD. In this event, prior to withdrawal _____ will furnish to COAST GUARD data such as that described in paragraph 6 in order to facilitate resumption of exclusive COAST GUARD supervision of maritime aids to navigation in navigable waters of the UNITED STATES within the State of _____ ("State Waters").

(11) By 1 September annually, _____ will provide COAST GUARD a listing of all aids being administered in "State Waters" as of 30 June of that year. This listing will indicate the number of each type of aid but need not include the detailed information required under paragraph 6 above.

(12) The parties hereby designate the _____ State of _____ , and the Chief, _____ Branch, _____ Coast Guard District, as liaisons officers to facilitate the cooperation and assistance contemplated by this Agreement.

_____

FOR THE UNITED STATES COAST GUARD

_____

DATE

_____

FOR THE STATE OF

_____

DATE

This Page Intentionally
Left Blank

CHAPTER 6 - MARKING OF WRECKS

A. Marking Policy.

1. <u>General</u>.

    a. 33 USC 409 requires that **whenever a vessel, raft, or other craft is wrecked and sunk in navigable waters** of the United States, **it** must be marked for the protection of marine traffic. The law requires that the owner, **lessee, or operator** of such a wreck "**immediately** mark it with a buoy or beacon during the day and, unless otherwise granted a waiver by the Commandant of the Coast Guard, a light at **night.**" 14 USC 86 authorizes the Secretary of Homeland Security to mark for the protection of navigation any sunken vessel or other obstruction existing on the navigable waters or waters above the continental shelf of the United States for as long as required to meet the needs of maritime navigation. As a matter of policy therefore, wreck markings established by the Coast Guard, whether for an agency of the Federal Government or in response to a request of the owner, shall provide no lesser degree of service and protection to the mariner than that required of the owner.

    b. Wreck markings established and maintained by the United States Coast Guard (USCG) shall have at least one lighted aid in all cases, unless specifically exempted by the **District Commander**. The waiver request must clearly indicate that placing a light would be impractical and granting such a waiver would not create an undue hazard to navigation. It is recognized, however, that circumstances may not permit the establishment of a lighted buoy immediately. In such cases, unlighted aids may serve temporarily until such time as a lighted aid can be established. Alternate means to satisfy this marking requirement include the presence of a manned vessel while the hazardous condition remains.

    c. Radar beacons (racons) may also be used to mark wrecks **in addition to the aforementioned requirements**.

2. **Waiver Authority.**

    a. **The District Commander may waive the requirement to mark a wreck with a light at night if they determine that establishing a mark with a light would be impractical and granting such a waiver would not create an undue hazard to navigation. This authority may not be delegated.**

    b. **The following concerns may be considered by the District Commander when determining if establishing a light is impractical:**

(1) **Fast Moving Currents: Areas where historically fast current would preclude an adequate lighted mark from being established. For example, an unlighted mark may be submerged in periods of high water and resurface undamaged. However, if a lighted mark is submerged, the light will most likely be inoperable when the mark resurfaces.**

(2) **Excessive Debris in Water: Areas where consistent flotsam or debris would preclude an adequate lighted mark from being established. For example, damage sustained on an unlighted mark from debris probably would not render that signal ineffective. However, the damage to the light signal would likely render it inoperable.**

(3) **Economic Concern: The establishment of a lighted mark would prove an unreasonable economic hardship to the owner of the wreck. For example, a mark capable of supporting a lighted signal would be unaffordable for the party(ies) responsible for marking the wreck.**

(4) **Environmental Concern: Environmental conditions preclude the establishment of a lighted mark. For example, ice damage sustained on an unlighted mark probably would not render that signal ineffective. However, the damage to the lighted signal would likely render it inoperable.**

(5) **Lack of Equipment/Capability: An adequate lighted mark, or the capability to establish such a mark, is unavailable. For example, a mark necessary to support a lighted signal would exceed the capabilities of the party(ies) responsible for marking the wreck to deploy and/or maintain the mark.**

c. **Waiver requests shall be submitted to the District Commander via the responsible CG Sector as appropriate. Consistent with 33 CFR 1.01-1, District Commanders are authorized to review and grant waivers based on written documentation provided by the party(ies) responsible for the wreck's mark.**

3. Marking Characteristics.

a. The color, numbering, shape and light characteristics of aids marking wrecks and other obstructions must conform to the U.S. marking system and the IALA System **(33 CFR Part 62)** in use in the geographical area. The use of lateral marks shall be the first consideration when establishing a wreck marking, but the use of isolated danger marks is authorized.

b. Lateral Marks.

   (1) If a wreck may be safely passed on one side only, it shall be marked by a solid red or green buoy or corresponding dayboard on a fixed structure. If a wreck may be safely passed on either side it may be marked by a red and green horizontally banded buoy or corresponding dayboard, the color of the uppermost band denoting the preferred side.

   (2) The light color shall be red on solid red buoys and structures with TR dayboards and green on solid green buoys and structures with SG dayboards, and either red or green, depending on the color of the uppermost band, on horizontally banded buoys and structures with JG or JR dayboards.

   (3) The light rhythm shall be quick flashing on solid color buoys and structures with TR and SG dayboards. The rhythm shall be composite group flashing on horizontally banded buoys and structures with JR and JG dayboards.

   (4) Buoys and structures marking wrecks and other obstructions shall be numbered in proper sequence with other aids to navigation in the same channel or waterway. The letters WR shall be used and shall prefix the regular number.

   (5) Wreck markings shall be located near the wreck and on the channel or seaward side of the wreck. More than one aid may be used if necessary to minimize possible confusion as to the actual location of the wreck. The net effect of the wreck markings shall be such that a vessel may pass the markings with safety.

   (6) In addition to the use of buoys and structures, lights and/or daymarks may be exhibited from an exposed portion of a wreck.

   (7) Racons used to mark uncharted wrecks shall be coded with the Morse letter "D".

c. Isolated Danger Mark. If, at the discretion of the District Commander, a lateral aid to navigation is not appropriate to mark the wreck an Isolated Danger Mark may be used.

4. Regulations.

    a. Regulations issued by the Coast Guard concerning the marking of sunken vessels or other obstructions are contained in 33 CFR 64.

    b. Regulations issued by the U.S. Army Corps of Engineers (**USACE**) concerning the marking, abandonment and removal of wrecks are contained in 33 CFR 209.170.

B. Authority of and Liaison with the U.S. Army Corps of Engineers.

    1. General Policy.

        a. The Corps of Engineers, under the Secretary of the Army, is the agency charged with the protection and preservation of the navigable waters of the United States, and as such, is authorized to remove or to destroy any sunken obstruction endangering navigation in such waters when it has existed for a period of more than 30 days or when its abandonment can be established legally in a shorter period of time.

        b. In an emergency, such as when a vessel sinks in or otherwise unduly delays the operation of any government lock or canal, or sinks in any navigable water of the United States so as to stop, seriously interfere with, or especially endanger navigation, the District Engineer may take immediate possession in order to remove or destroy the obstruction.

    2. Communications with the US Army Corps of Engineers.

        a. Figure 6-1 is a Memorandum of Agreement (MOA) between the Department of the Army and the Coast Guard establishing a decision process for the consideration of corrective action to be taken by our respective agencies in response to hazards posed by wrecks and other obstructions to navigation. The decision process outlines the factors that influence a determination to mark or remove an obstruction. This, coupled with the delineation of agency chains of command for the resolution of disagreements as to the appropriate corrective action, should result in effective, timely coordination between the Corps of Engineers and the Coast Guard, and greater safety to the users of our nation's waterways.

        b. Upon notification that an obstruction or hazard to navigation exists, the district aids to navigation branch shall consult with the respective USACE District Engineer and propose appropriate corrective action. Any correspondence between the Coast Guard and the owner of a wreck concerning its abandonment shall be forwarded to the USACE District Engineer.

c. If agreement as to the appropriate corrective action cannot be reached, procedures outlined in paragraph 5.d of the MOA shall be followed. The maximum delay after which unresolved issues are forwarded along the chain of command for resolution has not been specified. Normally, however, delays of over thirty days shall be avoided unless progress is being made or is anticipated.

d. Chief, **Visual Navigation Branch (CG-54131)** is the Headquarters-level authority. In addition to forwarding unresolved marking/removal issues to Commandant **(CG-54131)**, the District Commanders shall also keep that office informed of potential disputes. Copies of the dispute documentation, required in paragraph 5.d of the MOA, shall be forwarded to Commandant **(CG-54131)** for information purposes.

C. Liaison with National Ocean Service.

1. General.

    a. District commanders are authorized direct liaison with the Office of Coast Survey within the National Ocean Service/NOAA on matters relating to general day-to-day operations of the districts and National Ocean Service.

    b. District Commanders shall ensure that matters involving a change of procedure with National Ocean Service that would require a service wide change of procedure be forwarded to Commandant **(CG-54131)** for approval of the basic request before it is conveyed to National Ocean Service.

2. Wreck or Submerged Obstruction Data.

    a. The Office of Coast Survey manages the nautical charting and nautical data collection and information programs. The office collects and evaluates marine hydrographic and other navigational data, as well as directing field programs for ship-and shore-based hydrographic survey units and the development of hydrographic survey specifications. Reports of wrecks or obstructions should contain as much information as possible. Information, if available, should include the name of the wrecked vessel, type and size of the wrecked vessel or obstruction, who first initiated the report of the sinking, how the position was determined, and the relative accuracy of the position.

b. Along with issuing proper Local Notice to Mariners and Broadcast Notices to Mariners, District Commanders shall forward other amplifying information on wrecks and submerged obstructions shortly after the data is acquired, for use in assisting the planning of survey operations. Data should be addressed to:

> Director, Office of Coast Guard Survey (N/CS)
> National Ocean Service/NOAA
> 1315 East West Highway STE 1
> Silver Spring, MD 20910-3282

D. Authority of the Coast Guard.

1. Coast Guard Marking Authority.

   a. In general, a sunken wreck is no different than any other submerged danger insofar as Coast Guard Authority is concerned. In any waters in which the Coast Guard has authority to establish aids, it may mark (or elect not to mark) wrecks as required by the needs of safe navigation.

   b. Federal law (33 USC 409) requires the owner of a wreck, sunk in the navigable waters of the United States, to suitably mark it until removed or legally abandoned. Should the owner fail to do so the Coast Guard may mark **the wreck**.

   c. The liability of the owner of a sunken obstruction, for the costs of Coast Guard marking, ends when the obstruction or wreck is either legally abandoned or removed. The District Commander acknowledges receipt but does not "accept" any notice of abandonment provided by the owner. This acknowledgment shall state that it shall in no way be construed as acceptance by the United States of the abandonment of the vessel or other obstruction, nor as a waiver of any right to enforce liability for any damage caused by its sinking, for the cost of removal or for the cost of marking (33 CFR 64.33, 209.170). A copy of all notices of abandonment shall be forwarded to the Corps of Engineers District Engineer. The District Commander should be aware that any purported acceptance of abandonment by the Coast Guard could prejudice the ability of the Corps of Engineers to recover removal costs from the owner of the wreck.

2. Action When Requested By Owner. The marking of a wreck by the Coast Guard is for the protection of navigation and not for the sole benefit of the owner. Therefore, a request by the owner for the Coast Guard to mark it shall be construed to indicate only the owner's inability to do so. Decision to mark or not shall be based on the need of marking for the protection of navigation as determined by the Coast Guard.

3. Adequacy of Marking. Commanding Officers and Officers-in-Charge of Coast Guard units establish markings at the direction of the District Commander. They must exercise extreme caution ensuring that the marking which they establish conforms to the standards set forth herein and the District Commander's instruction.

4. Marking After Abandonment. The legal responsibility of the owner of a sunken wreck to suitably mark it ends when the wreck is legally abandoned. If the wreck is a hazard requiring marking it may be marked by the Coast Guard as long as is necessary for the safety of navigation.

E. Procedures to be Followed by Individual Units.

1. Information Required by Marking Unit. When a unit receives a report of or discovers a wreck, a report shall be made immediately to the District Commander. This information shall be supported with a Hazard to Navigation message to the appropriate **Sector** and info to the District. It shall include as much of the below information as is available:

    a. The name, description, and accurate location of the wreck.

    b. The name and address of the owner or his agent.

    c. The depth of water over the wreck.

    d. The action or intent of the owner to mark the wreck, and when such action will be taken.

    e. The type, description, and location of the marking, if any.

    f. An opinion as to whether or not immediate marking of the wreck by the Coast Guard is necessary for the protection of navigation.

2. Communication with Owner.

    a. If contact is made with the owner or agent, the Commanding Officer/Officer-in-Charge shall provide:

    (1) Information on the owner's legal duty to mark the wreck immediately.

(2) Notice that if the owner fails to do so immediately, and if the District Commander considers the marking of the wreck required for the protection of navigation, the Coast Guard will establish a suitable marking. The charges for the establishment, maintenance and discontinuance of such Coast Guard markings will accrue against the owner until such time as a suitable marking is established by the owner or the wreck is removed or legally abandoned. If practicable, the owner shall be advised of the estimated cost if marking is performed by the Coast Guard. The cost can be determined from Commandant Note 7310.

(3) Information on the duty to make a report to the nearest Coast Guard District Office, setting forth the following:

(a) Name of the wreck and accurate location.

(b) Depth of water over the wreck.

(c) Location and description of marking established or proposed by the owner.

Note: The intent of the Coast Guard to establish a suitable marking upon the owner's failure or inability to comply with their statutory duty, does not relieve the owner of the legal responsibility to do so.

b. Regardless of whether or not the Coast Guard unit first receiving a report of the wreck has been in contact with the owner, the District Commander shall communicate with the owner, or the owner's representative, by the most appropriate means under the circumstances and explain the legal responsibilities and duties with respect to marking the wreck, and ascertain the owner's intent to comply with the regulations. The District Commander shall inform the owner of the charges for Coast Guard marking thus far incurred or pending, if any. All oral communications shall be promptly confirmed in writing.

3. <u>On-Scene Action by Marking Unit</u>.

a. If any doubt exists as to whether or not a wreck/obstruction might be a hazard to navigation, the on-scene unit should request instructions from the District Commander.

b. A complete record of all reports, conversations, correspondence and action taken shall be maintained by the unit.

4. <u>Time Allowed for Markings</u>.

    a. The period of time allowed the owner to suitably mark a wreck before action is taken by the Coast Guard under 33 CFR 64.33 to mark the obstruction shall be determined by the circumstances in each case. Every effort should be made to encourage the owner of a wreck to establish the required markings.

    b. If it becomes necessary for the Coast Guard to mark the wreck on behalf of the owner, every reasonable effort shall be made to minimize expenses.

5. <u>Marking Contractor</u>. The District Commander is authorized to have the marking of a wreck performed by contract when deemed advisable in the interest of expediency or economy.

6. <u>Tender Scheduling</u>. As the cost of tender time generally forms a large part of the total charge for Coast Guard marking, this charge can frequently be reduced by arranging for discontinuance of a wreck marking during a tender's regular itinerary rather than by requiring a separate trip for this purpose.

This Page Intentionally
Left Blank

MEMORANDUM OF AGREEMENT
BETWEEN
THE DEPARTMENT OF ARMY AND THE U.S. COAST GUARD

SUBJECT: Coast Guard and Department of Army Responses to Marking
and Removal of Sunken Vessels and Other Obstructions
to Navigation

1. Purpose. The purpose of this memorandum of agreement (MOA) is to improve the efficiency and effectiveness of the Coast Guard and the Department of Army responses under each agency's respective authorities for the marking and removal of sunken vessels and other obstructions to navigation.

2. Provision of Agreement. This agreement provides procedures on coordination to determine whether an obstruction is a hazard to navigation and procedures to determine the appropriate corrective actions to be taken by both agencies.

3. Definitions. For the purpose of this agreement, the following definitions apply:

a. Obstruction: Anything that restricts, endangers, or interferes with navigation. Obstructions can be authorized man-made structures such as bridges, pier heads, offshore towers, etc., or unexpected interferences which must be assessed as to their effect on navigation.

b. Hazard to Navigation: An obstruction, usually sunken, that presents sufficient danger to navigation so as to require expeditious affirmative action such as marking, removal, or redefinition of a designated waterway to provide for navigational safety.

c. Responsible Field Officers Are:

(1) Department of the Army:

(a) District Engineer, Army Corps of Engineers District, and

(b) Division Engineer, Army Corps of Engineers Pacific Ocean and New England Divisions.

(2) Coast Guard: Chief, Operations Division, Coast Guard District.

4. Objectives.

a. Promote close coordination and cooperation between the Department of Army and the Coast Guard leading to prompt and decisive action in marking or removal of obstructions declared to be hazards to navigation.

Enclosure 6-1

1

b. Provide guidance on the parameters and procedures for making multi-agency decisions for determining when an obstruction should be declared a hazard to navigation.

c. Provide the chain-of command and relationships for resolving differences of opinion between the Department of Army and the Coast Guard as to the appropriate corrective action to initiate for hazards to navigation.

d. Assure timely and effective action to provide safe navigation to the maritime community.

5. Required Actions. Upon receiving reports of sunken vessels or other obstructions to navigation, each agency through its field office will take the following actions:

a. Assess the impact upon navigation of each reported obstruction and expeditiously identify appropriate corrective actions. In emergency situations, the agency first on scene should initiate immediate actions to mitigate the hazardous situation.

b. Decide through joint consultation and agreement between agency field offices if an obstruction is a hazard to navigation, agree upon appropriate corrective action(s) to reduce the danger to navigation to an acceptable level, and decide which agency shall act as lead agency for contacting the owner, if one exists, of the obstruction and executing corrective actions.

(1) Personal Contacts between agency field offices are encouraged to facilitate decision-making.

(2) Timely response dictates that decisions are made at the field office level when possible.

(3) Decisions concerning corrective actions shall be supported by records appropriate to the specific case.

(4) Marking Issues. In every case where an obstruction is declared to be a hazard to navigation, the owner will mark the location immediately. In the event that the owner cannot be identified, refuses to mark the obstruction, inadequately marks the obstruction, or is otherwise unable to properly mark it, the Coast Guard has authority under 14 U.S.C. 86 to take appropriate action. When necessary the Department of Army will assist the Coast Guard in locating and marking hazards to navigation. Marking of an obstruction determined to be a hazard to navigation does not by itself remove the "hazard to navigation" status of the obstruction; however, under sane circumstances it can be an acceptable alternative to other corrective actions.

(5) Removal Issues.

(a) Where an obstruction is declared to be a hazard to navigation and removal is the agreed appropriate corrective action, the respective Army Corps of

Engineers District Engineer may take the initiative in accordance with 33 CFR 209.190 (h) where in removal of an obstruction under the provisions of Section 19 of the River and Harbor Act of 1899 (33 U.S.C. 414) may be undertaken without prior approval of the Chief of Engineers if the obstruction has been in existence over 30 days or its abandonment by the owner can be legally established in a shorter period, the cost of removal will not exceed $100,000 for each incident, and all reasonable efforts to require the owner to remove the wreck himself within a reasonable period have been exhausted. If an emergency condition exists, the district engineer may undertake removal under Section 20 of the River and Harbor Act of 1899 (33 U.S.C. 414), which eliminates the necessity to establish abandonment. The district engineers' authority under Section 20 is limited to those removal incidents costing less than $100,000. For all incidents costing more than $100,000, prior approval from the Chief of Engineers must be obtained under either Section 19 or Section 20.

    (b) The Coast Guard has authority for the alteration or removal of obstructive bridges under 33 CFR 114 and has authority to remove sunken vessels when they create a substantial pollution threat to the public health or welfare under 33 CFR 153.

  c. The Coast Guard has authority to disseminate and maintain navigational safety information pertaining to obstructions and is the lead agency responsible for this type of information. This mission is complemented by related services offered by other sources, including the Army Corps of Engineers. Each agency's field offices will immediately notify their counterpart of any reported obstructions and will maintain close coordination to ensure that navigational safety information is disseminated in a timely and effective manner. Free exchange of information related to obstructions, including owner's name and address, will be made between agencies, subject to the requirements of the Privacy Act, 5 U.S.C. 522a.

  d. Disagreements arising over the resolution of problems raised by hazards to navigation. The district engineer and the Chief of Operations will document the area(s) of disagreement and present them to each other for consideration at least 14 days before forwarding of the issue to higher authority. If resolution cannot be achieved, the problem should be forwarded to the next higher level of authority. At the next higher level, a similar exchange of reviews should be made in the same time frame. If resolution cannot be reached here, a similar referral process should be made until resolution is achieved or the highest referral possible is made. Paragraph 8 delineates the chain-of-command for the purposes of this agreement.

  e. The Coast Guard and Department of Army shall develop individual agency instructions to implant the MDA.

  f. Field level offices of both agencies shall periodically review the status of existing obstructions to determine the adequacy of corrective action(s), to determine if a resurvey of the obstruction's location is necessary, to revise appropriate records, and to update public notification records.

6. Applicability. This agreement applies to the navigable waters of the United States, as defined in Title 33 CFR 2.05-25.

7. Decision-making Guidance.

    a. Options to consider in formulating appropriate action(s):

        (1) No action.

        (2) Charting.

        (3) Broadcasting and publication of navigational safety information.

        (4) Marking.

        (5) Redefinition of navigational area, e.g., channels fairway, anchorage, etc.

        (6) Removal.

        (7) Combination of the above.

    b. Factors (not to be taken as all inclusive) to be considered in determining if a sunken vessel or other obstruction is a hazard to navigation and in determining which course of action(s) listed in paragraph 7.a. is appropriate to increase safety to an acceptable level:

        (1) The degree to which the obstruction restricts, endangers, or interferes with the navigability of a body of water.

            (a) Location with respect to navigational traffic patterns.

            (b) Navigational difficulty at the site of the obstruction.

            (c) Clearance or depth of water over obstruction.

            (d) Fluctuation of water level and other hydraulic characteristics.

        (2) Physical characteristics of the obstruction, including cargo (if any exists).

        (3) Possible movement of the obstruction.

        (4) Marine activity in the vicinity of the obstruction.

            (a) Type of commercial and recreational vessel traffic.

            (b) Density of commercial and recreational vessel traffic.

(c) Trends of waterway use.

(5) Location of obstruction with respect to existing aids to navigation.

(6) Prevailing and historical weather conditions.

(7) Length of time the obstruction has been in existence.

(8) History of vessel accidents involving obstruction.

8. Chain-of-command Relationships for Resolution of Differences.

   a. Chief, Operations Division, Coast Guard District/District Engineer, Army Corps of Engineers District.

   b. District Commander, Coast Guard District/Division Engineer, Army Corps of Engineers Division.

   c. Chief, Office of Navigation, Coast Guard/Director of Civil Works, Office, Chief of Engineers.

9. Amendment, Duration, and Termination.

   a. This MOA may be modified or amended by mutual Consent of the signatories to this agreement or their designees. All such changes will be documented by written agreement.

   b. This MOA is intended to remain in effect for as long as it continues to serve the purpose and objectives defined herein.

   c. Either agency may terminate this MOA six months after giving formal written notice of intent to terminate.

10. Effective Date. This MDA is effective 90 days after execution by the Chief, Office of Navigation, U.S. Coast Guard, and the Director of Civil Works, Department of the Army.

_____   _____

Rear Admiral, U.S. Coast Guard   Major General, USA
Chief, Office of Navigation   Director of Civil Works

        16 OCT 1985   10 OCT 1985
    (Date)   (Date)

Enclosure 6-1

This Page Intentionally
Left Blank

CHAPTER 7 - GENERAL OPERATION INSTRUCTIONS FOR AIDS TO NAVIGATION UNITS.

A. Introduction.

    1. Types of Units.

        a. Watched units are units with resident personnel responsible for continuous attention to the operation of an aid to navigation. Loran stations, though watched, are not discussed in this manual.

        b. Servicing units are responsible for periodic maintenance of unwatched aids to navigation. Details regarding the operation of servicing units are discussed in Chapter 9.

B. General Instructions for Aids to Navigation Units.

    1. Inspection. The term inspection means to view or examine closely and critically the operating features and methods, care and upkeep, administration, and general overall efficiency of an aid to navigation.

        a. Watched aids. The District Commander shall require a thorough general inspection of each watched aid to navigation annually. Inspection check off lists prepared by the district staff shall be used as criteria.

        b. Unwatched aids. Inspection of unwatched aids shall be conducted during routine visits. Required corrective and/or preventive maintenance, which may include items such as replacing retro-reflective material, light and/or fog signals, painting, and recharging shall be accomplished. Inspection of formally watched lights for structural integrity shall be conducted in accordance with the Lighthouse Maintenance Management Manual, COMDTINST M16500.6 (series).

    2. Discrepancy. Failure of an aid to provide advertised light, sound signal, appearance, or position as described in the Light List or on charts is a discrepancy. Whenever a discrepancy or damage to an aid is found by or reported to a Coast Guard unit which cannot immediately effect repairs, the District Commander shall be notified by message. The report shall state the exact nature of the discrepancy and any corrective action taken. If corrective action is beyond the capabilities of the unit, the report shall include this fact. If the damage or destruction is the result of collision and/or vandalism, the reporting unit shall make every reasonable effort to obtain complete information regarding the situation. If available, report the names and addresses of the vessel or persons involved, including witnesses. Consult Chapter 9 for information on action to be taken in correcting various types of aid discrepancies.

3. <u>Tolerance</u>. The maximum allowable tolerance for light or sound signal rhythm characteristic is +/- 6% of the specified value per period, or 3.6 seconds per minute, whichever is smaller. For revolving lights the tolerance is 3.6 seconds per minute. No tolerances can be prescribed for the positioning of buoys that would be applicable in all situations. The preciseness with which a buoy is positioned is determined by many factors but the ultimate test of the adequacy of any buoy's position is: "Does the buoy adequately serve its intended purpose as portrayed on the largest scale chart and in the Coast Guard Light List?" See Volume 5 for detailed information on buoy positioning.

4. <u>Discrepancy Buoys</u>. Discrepancy buoys may be used to temporarily replace damaged or missing buoys or structures until the discrepancy can be corrected. Discrepancy buoys are used to allow a unit to complete scheduled servicing runs or inport routines rather than to immediately respond to discrepancies which may be located many miles from the area then being serviced by the unit. Discrepancy buoys may have less signal capability than the aids they replace. Action should be initiated to restore the damaged or missing aid whenever an ATON unit becomes available in the area of the discrepancy without seriously affecting the vessel's routine schedule. See paragraph C.5 of Chapter 3 for more information on temporary aid changes. The term "discrepancy buoy" also includes any floating aid that provides a signal less than the authorized on-station hull.

5. <u>Unauthorized Changes in Aids</u>. Except in an emergency, each aid shall conform to its current Light List (corrected to date) description. Where deviations from the Light List must be made in emergencies, they shall be reported immediately to the District Commander. Another report shall be made when the aid is restored to its authorized condition.

6. <u>Vandalism</u>. Vandals ruin thousands of dollars worth of aids to navigation equipment each year. Through vandalism, the Coast Guard not only loses valuable equipment but many hours are wasted in repairing damaged and destroyed aids or searching for sunken buoys. In addition to these losses, discrepancies in the aid system caused by vandals could result in injury to mariners as well as damage and loss to vessels and property. Experience and studies have indicated that vandalism is usually centralized in one or more small areas in each district during specific times of the year, i.e. hunting season, school vacation, etc. District, Sector, and local unit commanders shall take vigorous measures to curb vandalism by employing the following:

   a. Where vandalism is centralized, inform the District Intelligence and Law Enforcement Branch of the vandalism, listing the various acts and providing as much information as possible.

b. Conduct a public information effort in the area by providing articles to the local news media with particular attention paid to school newspapers or hunter's digests, etc., stressing the possible harm and definite expense caused by vandals.

c. Post official Coast Guard aid to navigation warning signs throughout the area. Attempts should especially be made to place the signs at boat launching ramps, marinas, sporting goods shops, or other places where potential vandals or witnesses to vandalism might congregate.

d. **These warning signs should stress the penalties that could result from the theft, moving, damaging, defacing, destroying, or interfering with aids as provided in 14 USC 84; 18 USC 641, 1361, and 1363; and 33 USC 411. Depending upon the statute and the nature of the violation, the maximum penalties upon conviction are up to 20 years of imprisonment and as much as $2,500 fine per day for each violation. Also stress the financial rewards payable to persons providing information leading to a conviction, each of whom may be entitled to a portion of up to one half of the assessed fine (see 33 USC 411, 33 CFR Part 70).**

C. Servicing Policy.

The servicing interval will be the lowest result after calculating service interval for the components. In addition the unit commander should also consider any history of vandalism, excessive guano, or any other problem that suggests the aid should be visited more frequently than every 36 months. The service interval should be coordinated in such a manner as to maximize efficiencies of each service visit. During the annual waterway visit by a qualified Coast Guard ATON member from the primary servicing unit (paragraph 7.C.2.f), the condition of the aids should be reviewed to determine if servicing should occur before the next scheduled service.

1. Frequency of Relief of Buoys.

a. Steel Buoys. Six years is the minimum on-station period of all steel buoys except where earlier relief is dictated by unusual circumstances. **Relief intervals should be extended where possible.** See Aids to Navigation Manual – Technical, COMDTINST M16500.3 (series) for detailed maintenance instructions.

b. Plastic and foam buoys. Plastic and foam buoys shall remain on-station as long as they can be maintained by a servicing unit and serve as an effective aid to navigation. They should not be relieved or returned to a base unless they are damaged beyond a servicing unit's ability to patch, paint or repair them. See Aids to Navigation Manual – Technical, COMDTINST M16500.3 (series) for detailed maintenance instructions.

2. Frequency of Routine Visits.

    a. Lighted Aids on Fixed Structures. Routine visits to lighted aids on fixed structures, other than those listed in paragraph e. below, shall be scheduled as determined by the servicing unit using the ATON Servicing Interval Flowchart (ATON SIF) provided in this chapter. Routine servicing intervals shall not exceed three years. A variation of up to three months to coordinate servicing trips is allowed. Inspection of the aid shall be the purpose of the visit. During each visit to an ATON structure, the servicing unit shall also perform the Field Unit Maintenance Inspection described in Aids to Navigation Manual - Structures, COMDTINST M16500.25 (series).

    b. Unlighted Aids on Fixed Structures. Routine visits to unlighted aids on fixed structures shall be scheduled as determined by the servicing unit using the ATON SIF provided in this chapter. Routine servicing intervals shall not exceed five years. A variation of up to three months to coordinate servicing trips is allowed. Inspection of the aid shall be the purpose of the visit. During each visit to an ATON structure, the servicing unit shall also perform the Field Unit Maintenance Inspection described in Aids to Navigation Manual – Structures, COMDTINST M16500.25 (series).

    c. Buoys.

        (1) Routine visits to buoys shall be scheduled as determined by the servicing unit using the ATON SIF provided in this chapter. Routine servicing intervals shall not exceed three years. A variation of up to three months to coordinate servicing trips is allowed. These visits will be for the purpose of inspection.

        (2) A buoy's position shall be checked each time it is visited and an on/off station determination made in accordance with the Aids to Navigation Manual – Positioning, COMDTINST M16500.1 (series).

        (3) Battery recharging cycles shall coincide with inspection visits, mooring inspections, or reliefs to the maximum extent possible. The effective use of vessel operating time, however, has priority over the economics of using all power available from batteries. The Aids to Navigation Manual – Technical, COMDTINST M16500.3 (series) Chapter 9 shall be used as a guide for determining appropriate rated battery discharge times.

        (4) Lifting buoys from the water shall be avoided except as required for inspection of moorings, relocation, relief, recharge, or correction of a discrepancy. Inspection of the underwater portion of buoy hulls shall be accomplished in conjunction with scheduled mooring inspections. Inspections that do not require lifting of buoys should be accomplished,

where feasible, by small units such as Aids to Navigation Teams or by the most economical means available.

d. Mooring Inspection.

   (1) Three years is the normal period between mooring inspections for all buoys. These inspections, to examine the underwater body, mooring, and associated components, should be extended beyond three years where possible. The period will be determined based on the buoy's location and its historical data. However, in known areas of accelerated chain wear, such as areas exposed to the full force of the seas, or a history of the sinker being mudded in exists, inspections will be conducted as frequently as is deemed necessary by the servicing unit.

   (2) When chain is used, greater chain size than ordinarily recommended in the Aids to Navigation Manual – Technical, COMDTINST M16500.3 (series) may be used in the chafe zone when this will allow the mooring to remain on station two years or more. This heavier chain must not materially affect the signal characteristic of the buoy.

   (3) The sinker, or anchor need not be lifted off the bottom unless its condition or the condition of that part of the mooring that touches the bottom is questionable or a history of the sinker being mudded in exists.

e. Fixed Aids with Complex Equipment. Aids with the following complex equipment (refer to Major Aids to Navigation Preventive Maintenance System Guide, COMDTINST M16500.10 (series)) require semiannual servicing:

   (1) Aids using large ATON batteries (Fulmen, Classic, Exide, Sonnenschein, Absolyte IIP)

   (2) Engine generators providing backup power.

   (3) Trickle charged batteries used as a secondary power source to commercial power.

   (4) Category I, II and III solar powered lighthouses and ranges with comparable power systems should be visited semiannually, or more frequently based on lamp life.

   (5) 120 VAC powered sound signals.

f. Waterways.

   (1) Each waterway shall be visited by a qualified Coast Guard ATON member from the primary servicing unit at least once a year. The District Commander may adjust this schedule for special cases. These visits can be in conjunction with the inspections listed previously. Alternate visits should be during nighttime hours. The purpose of these visits is the overall assessment of all the aids to navigation in the waterway, their proper operation, physical condition and their ability to meet the needs of the mariners. All ranges in the waterway shall be run and their Light List advertised values checked. Such a visit will be logged by the servicing unit, whether an afloat or a shore unit, in an appropriate manner.

   (2) When scheduling permits, representatives of the sector commander, the secondary servicing unit and local users should be invited to accompany the servicing unit during the waterway visits.

3. Component Service Period.

   a. All aids to navigation should, ideally, have components which are designed to provide trouble free operation without service or maintenance for three years or longer.

   b. District commanders shall implement a program to extend the service of, or eliminate, as many items of equipment as possible which require routine maintenance more often than once every 36 months.

4. Trends toward More Frequent Visits.

   a. The preceding sections specify scheduling of relief and routine visits to aids to navigation. Aids that cannot meet the servicing intervals prescribed herein may be placed in a schedule corresponding to their expected endurance. Problems causing a trend to more frequent visits than prescribed shall be identified. Solutions to these problems such as relocation, change of aid type, change of equipment, or elimination of the aid station shall be considered before assigning a more frequent visit schedule. The Commandant (**CG-54131**) shall be advised of any trend causing visits to aids more frequently than prescribed and of proposed solutions to the problem.

5. Additional Guidelines.

   a. District (**dpw**) and ATON units should aggressively pursue extending ocean buoy, minor light and beacon servicing intervals, but also must recognize that there are locations where it would not be prudent. District Offices and ATON units are empowered to use their best local judgment in making these determinations, using the ATON SIF as a guide.

b. Following the standardized procedure(s) recommended in the accompanying ATON SIF, each USCG ATON servicing unit shall review and analyze each non-seasonal ocean buoy, day beacon and minor lights assigned. The servicing unit Commanding Officer/Officer-in-Charge shall make a determination, based on the ATON SIF review, and local knowledge and judgment, and assign a routine servicing interval for each aid. A new SIF worksheet must be completed each time a servicing interval is changed. A brief explanation should be entered in the comments section of the SIF whenever a servicing interval shorter than three years is determined. The SIF should be reproduced locally and shall be maintained in the aid file.

c. Scheduled recharges (replacements) for aid batteries should be determined based on the rated battery discharge time (in the case of primary batteries) or maximum service life (in the case of secondary batteries) as published in the Aids to Navigation Technical Manual, COMDTINST M16500.3 (series). All planned recharges shall coincide with the aid's routine servicing interval; batteries lacking sufficient remaining service life to reach the next regular service visit shall be replaced. The cost of discarded remaining battery life is minuscule compared to the cost of a service visit.

d. Whenever possible, ATON inspections and servicing operations should be accomplished by the least expensive available resource.

e. Units shall maintain a hard copy folder of all required information not otherwise assigned to a specific aid station. Units shall maintain the folder in a neat and orderly manner to ensure ease of understanding. The folder shall have separate sections for Verification Reports, Vessel Configurations (to include dates), and any other pertinent information such as positioning system design information.

f. All efforts shall be made to conserve chain to the maximum extent possible. Each mooring has to be evaluated on a case by case basis to determine the best course of action, and accurate record keeping is vital to assist in this process. Further guidance on chain conservation can be found in Chapter 2 Aids to Navigation Manual – Technical, COMDTINST M16500.3 (series).

This Page Intentionally
Left Blank

Aids to Navigation Servicing Interval Flowchart (ATON SIF)

Name of Aid: _____

Aid #: _____

Unit: _____

Decision Date _____

Commanding Officer/Officer-in-Charge _____

     Servicing Interval will be the lowest result after calculating service interval for the optic, dayboard and battery as applicable. In addition, the unit commander should also consider any history of vandalism, excessive guano, or any other problem that suggests the aid should be visited more frequently than every 36 months. The service interval should be coordinated in such a manner as to maximize efficiencies of each service visit. The service interval does not have to be in whole years.

     During the annual waterway visit by a qualified Coast Guard ATON member from the primary servicing unit (paragraph 7.C.2.f) the condition of the aids should be reviewed to determine if servicing should occur before the next scheduled service.

<u>Results:</u>

A. Component   <u>Service Interval result</u>

- ❏ Optic   _____
- ❏ Battery   _____
- ❏ Dayboard   _____

B. Mooring Inspection: <u>Comments:</u>

- ❏ Less than 12 mos   _____
- ❏ 12-24 mos   _____
- ❏ 24-36 mos   _____

C. Servicing Inspection:

- ❏ Less than 12 mos   _____
- ❏ 12-24 mos   _____
- ❏ 24-36 mos   _____
- ❏ Greater than 36 mos   _____
  (daybeacons only)

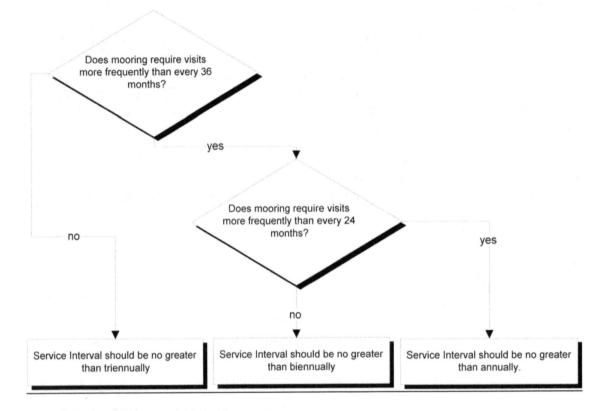

Mooring Interval Determination

Items to consider
Chain wear rate
Chain Balling
Bale/bridle wear rate
Silting/mudding in
History of being found off station

Does mooring require visits more frequently than every 36 months?

yes

Does mooring require visits more frequently than every 24 months?

no

yes

no

Service Interval should be no greater than triennually

Service Interval should be no greater than biennually

Service Interval should be no greater than annually.

Enclosure 7-1

2

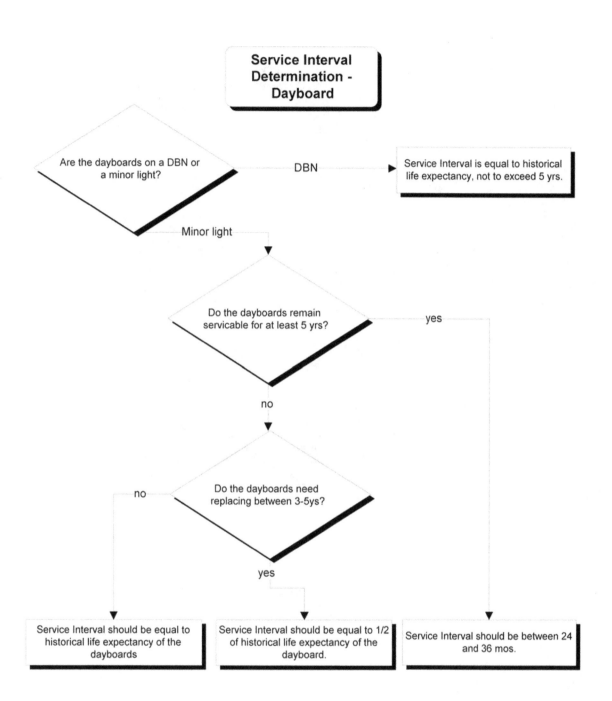

Service Interval Determination - Dayboard

Are the dayboards on a DBN or a minor light?

DBN → Service Interval is equal to historical life expectancy, not to exceed 5 yrs.

Minor light ↓

Do the dayboards remain servicable for at least 5 yrs?

yes →

no ↓

Do the dayboards need replacing between 3-5ys?

no →

yes ↓

Service Interval should be equal to historical life expectancy of the dayboards

Service Interval should be equal to 1/2 of historical life expectancy of the dayboard.

Service Interval should be between 24 and 36 mos.

Enclosure 7-1

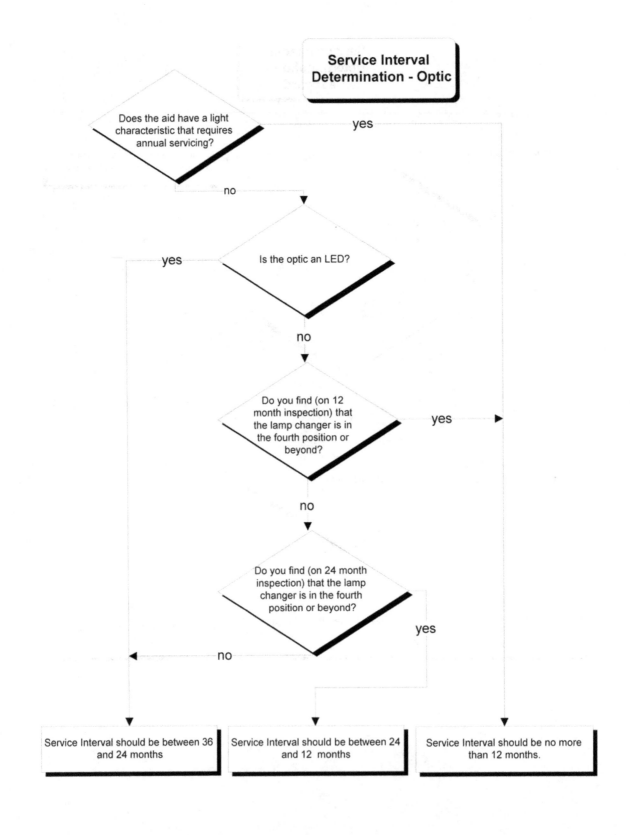

Service Interval Determination - Optic

Does the aid have a light characteristic that requires annual servicing?
— yes →

— no →

Is the optic an LED?
— yes →

— no →

Do you find (on 12 month inspection) that the lamp changer is in the fourth position or beyond?
— yes →

— no →

Do you find (on 24 month inspection) that the lamp changer is in the fourth position or beyond?
— yes →
— no →

Service Interval should be between 36 and 24 months

Service Interval should be between 24 and 12 months

Service Interval should be no more than 12 months.

Enclosure 7-1

4

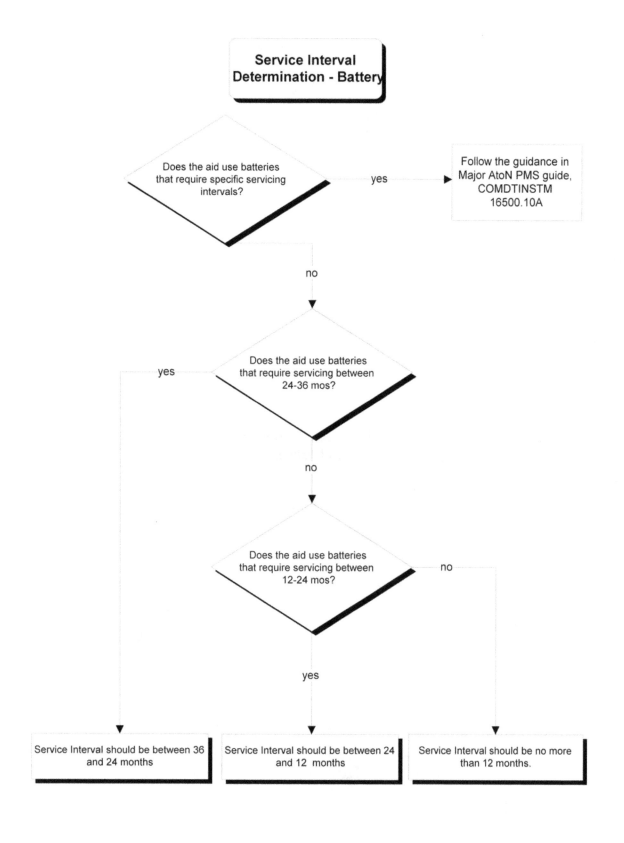

Service Interval
Determination - Battery

Does the aid use batteries that require specific servicing intervals? — yes → Follow the guidance in Major AtoN PMS guide, COMDTINSTM 16500.10A

no

Does the aid use batteries that require servicing between 24-36 mos? — yes

no

Does the aid use batteries that require servicing between 12-24 mos? — no

yes

Service Interval should be between 36 and 24 months

Service Interval should be between 24 and 12 months

Service Interval should be no more than 12 months.

Enclosure 7-1

5

This Page Intentionally
Left Blank

CHAPTER 8 - DUTIES OF AIDS TO NAVIGATION UNITS

A. <u>General</u>.

1. This chapter outlines the general responsibilities of tenders, and other servicing units for aids to navigation. The District Commander assigns servicing responsibility to individual units for particular aids. This assignment is made in the Aid to Navigation Annex to District Operation Plans, Aids to Navigation Assignment Lists or individual Operation Orders. These references will also contain supplementary district instructions concerning the procurement of aids to navigation equipment, inventory control procedures and reports, logistic support functions, and operation schedules.

2. <u>ATON Professionalism</u>. Safety of the crew and the mariner should always be at the forefront while conducting the ATON mission. The standard evolutions and safe seamanship as outlined in Aids to Navigation Manual- Seamanship, COMDTINST M16500.21 (series) and the various manuals published by the Office of Boat Forces must be adhered to. The District Training Teams and National Aids to Navigation Schools should be used to the fullest extent to ensure ATON professionalism is achieved and maintained at all aids to navigation units.

3. <u>Discrepancies</u>. Coast Guard Regulations (33 CFR 62.21(g)) require that all units make every reasonable effort to correct and/or report any discrepancy coming to their attention. Observing all aids in passing regardless of assigned servicing responsibility and stopping to correct observed discrepancies saves overall working time. (See Chapter 9 for actions concerning discrepancies.)

4. <u>Storm Survey</u>. Promptly following a hurricane, seismic sea wave, ice conditions, or other sever storms likely to cause widespread discrepancies; a survey of all aids shall be made to verify their proper operation. The results of this survey shall be reported to the District Commander via the chain of command.

5. <u>Unit Efficiency</u>. When it is necessary to correct discrepancies on an emergency or unscheduled basis, unit commanders will consider the most efficient yet safe method of responding to the discrepancies. Judicious consideration should be given to employing a smaller unit when possible, rather than requiring a larger unit to recall crew and get underway or extend scheduled operations by diverting a unit to a distant operating area.

6. <u>Maintenance Schedule</u>. District Commanders shall ensure that scheduled visits to and relief of aids to navigation are conducted in accordance with the requirements set forth in Chapter 7 of this manual. Units responsible for periodic maintenance of Coast Guard aids shall maintain current Light List(s), charts, Notice to Mariner's file, and records required by I-ATONIS instructions.

7. <u>Marine Accidents</u>. Upon notification of a marine accident, the Commanding Officer or Officer-in-Charge of the nearest unit capable of checking aids to navigation in the vicinity shall immediately ascertain if the aids were on station and working properly. The position of all buoys should be carefully checked and recorded. An Aids Positioning Report (APR) shall be printed with the found data recorded. Any aid found operating improperly shall be restored to correct operation. Buoys found off station should be reset on their assigned positions as soon as possible. Personnel of the unit performing the work should not make any statements to news media or representatives of the parties involved in the accident. Such questions should be referred to the District Commander for response. A report of the results of this check and action taken should be made to the District Commander as soon as possible after the accident. In addition to any supplemental instructions provided by the District Commander, a copy of the signed APR shall be provided to the Chief, **Visual Navigation Division (CG-54131)** within 72 hrs.

8. <u>Remotely Monitored Lights and Sound Signals</u>.

   a. Operating instructions shall be posted in the vicinity of each piece of sound and light signal equipment and control/monitor equipment at units responsible for remotely monitored lights or buoys.

   b. When the remotely monitored light cannot produce or maintain its characteristics as described in the Light List, a log entry shall be made at the unit.

   c. The voltage of the light circuit must be maintained within the voltage limits. They shall be checked on a regular schedule established by the District Commander.

   d. Should a remotely monitored light listed as a primary light by the Light List either lose its main and standby lights or should any of its signals become erratic (unable to control from monitor/control station), the following actions will be taken:

      (1) energize emergency light;

      (2) reduce power on aid if possible; notify District Commander;

      (3) broadcast information, and

      (4) attempt to reach and repair aid.

   e. <u>Sound Signals</u>. Once in operation, the timing and characteristic of the signal shall be checked. This check shall be repeated at the intervals specified per District Commander's instructions on remotely monitored lights.

9. <u>Destroyed or Damaged Aids</u>. District Commanders will ensure that district aids to navigation servicing personnel are made aware of the Coast Guard's responsibility for searching for the remains of destroyed aids and marking them if they can not be immediately removed. Not only is floating debris from a destroyed structure a hazard but submerged stubs of pilings are even more dangerous. If the remnants of the damaged aid to navigation pose a hazard to navigation the wreckage shall be marked similarly to the marking of wrecked vessels and other obstructions.

B. <u>Aid to Navigation Units</u>.

1. Tenders, Aids to Navigation Teams (ANT) and Station Aids to Navigation Teams (STANT)

2. <u>General Duties.</u>

   a. Tenders are used primarily for servicing operations that require hoisting buoys and their appendages or construction of aids to navigation. They are designed specially to operate in different environments such as: exposed areas offshore; semi-exposed areas or large bays and harbors; and protected or river areas. The primary duty of ANTs and STANTs is the servicing of assigned lights, daybeacon, buoys and correcting discrepancies on assigned aids.

   b. In addition to servicing floating and fixed aids to navigation, units may be used to transport personnel, supplies, water and fuel. They may also be employed in carrying construction material, as well as working parties, to points where normal maintenance operations are in progress or where new aids to navigation are under construction.

   c. When servicing aids to navigation, the information regarding the aid, as published in the **Light List,** shall be verified.

   d. ATON units shall verify the information contained in I-ATONIS, the Light List (corrected up to date from Notice to Mariners), Coast Pilot and nautical charts, every time an aid to navigation is serviced. Errors and omissions should be brought to the attention of the District **(dpw)** staff.

3. <u>Servicing Buoys and Fixed Structures.</u>

   a. In the performance of routine servicing, units shall operate on a definite schedule consisting of servicing trips to specific areas. These servicing trips can be categorized under one or more of the following basic purposes:

      (1) Component Inspection

      (2) Signal Check

(3) Relief

(4) Recharge

(5) Mooring Inspection

(6) Accomplishment of district ATON order

(7) Seasonal Changes, or

(8) Position Check

b. Tenders may also be utilized for the correction of a discrepancy (such as resetting or replacing a buoy on station) where it is not possible to correct the discrepancy using a unit with lesser capability or by the use of a discrepancy buoy.

c. In actual practice, one or more of the tasks of paragraphs a. and b. above may be carried out in the course of a single trip. Whenever a visit is made to an aid, for any purpose, personnel shall ensure that the aid is on assigned position and signal characteristics are as advertised.

4. Removing Buoys under Ice Conditions.

a. On waters where ice interrupts or prevents navigation during the winter, provisions must be made for the temporary removal and replacement of buoys. At least a skeleton system of aids should be kept on station until the last practicable moment to assist late traffic, bearing in mind that the complete removal of floating aids is a task requiring many days.

b. The restoration of the floating aids in the spring of the year should substantially be a reversal of the removal procedure. At the end of the ice season tenders may occasionally be used in searches for larger, expensive buoys and the recovery of those buoys reported driven ashore at various points. However, since employing tenders in this manner is costly, most buoy search and recovery operations shall be conducted by shore parties and/or small craft.

c. In coastal rivers and bays where ice accumulates sufficiently to damage buoyage, certain larger lighted buoys subject to ice damage may be removed from station where endangered. In order that such aid stations may not be entirely unmarked, ice buoys may be employed. An ice buoy may be any type less likely than the principal buoy to be damaged.

C. Integrated Support Commands (ISC) / Bases.

1. Functions. The chief function of Industrial Support Activities or Detachments, assigned to Integrated Support Commands, which are large industrial facilities, is to provide a central point accessible to servicing vessels, where buoy repair, ATON supplies and storage facilities are located.

2. Facilities.

   a. Facilities vary with type and number of aids and units that they serve. Many have equipment and space for the repair of buoys, and for the repair and fabrication of the various structures and solar power components in use throughout the district.

   b. ISC/Bases may carry a supply of spare parts for all the apparatus used in the area. They also may have space for the storage of maintenance relief hulls and boats. They usually have facilities for the repair and maintenance of small boats.

   c. Tools, equipment, and supplies in transit may also be held there for transportation to units by trucks and tenders.

   d. ISC/Bases may prefabricate structures for minor lights and daybeacons and miscellaneous fittings for aids to navigation equipment. ISC/Bases may also serve as an assembly and storage point for new equipment for field construction.

3. Repairs to Aids.

   a. Major repairs to steel buoys will be carried out at bases or contract facilities. Although steel buoys may receive minor repairs and be repainted on-station, complete overhaul and painting require a considerable amount of space. All buoys brought in from station, after the preliminary scraping given on board the tender, will be thoroughly cleaned and painted in accordance with applicable instructions. The repairs may consist merely of straightening parts or bumping out dents, or may involve more extensive work such as renewal of plates or the substitution of new superstructures. While extensive repairs are being made to lighted buoys, all lighting apparatus and batteries will be removed. See Chapter 2 of Aids to Navigation Manual – Technical, COMDTINST M16500.3 (series) for guidance on steel buoy repair.

b. Plastic and foam buoys are designed to require minimal or no servicing while on station. They should be relieved and disposed of when deterioration or damage to the metal hardware, foam hull, or plastic hull adversely impacts the operational performance or safe handling of the buoy. There is generally no shoreside overhaul required for these buoys, although minor repairs or replacement of components may be performed as needed. See chapter 2, Aids to Navigation Manual – Technical, COMDTINST M16500.3 (series) for specific servicing criteria.

c. In dealing with either plastic, or foam buoys, the greatest economy of operation is obtained when buoys are allowed to remain on station as long as possible or until their signal characteristics become affected beyond the ability of a tender to make sufficient repairs. Buoys will be returned to base for overhaul only when the conditions presented in Chapter 7 are met.

D. Depots.

1. Depots support aids to navigation servicing by providing storage, maintenance, and repair facilities for ATON equipment. They also may serve as a mooring facility for one or more buoy tenders.

2. A typical depot consists of piers, buoy slab, sandblasting and painting sheds for buoys, shops, offices, and storage areas. They provide a link in the "Engineering" level of the maintenance chain as outlined in the Engineering Support Program.

CHAPTER 9 - CORRECTION OF AIDS TO NAVIGATION DISCREPANCIES.

A. General.

1. Discrepancy. A discrepancy is defined as the failure of an aid to navigation to display its characteristics as described in the Light List, or to be on its assigned position.

2. Background.

   a. The purpose of the Coast Guard SRA program is to provide practicable, useful, consistent and dependable service to the mariner. Dependability of aids in most geographic areas has been excellent due to high quality equipment and the dedication of ATON personnel to maintain the aids through routine servicing and rapid response to discrepancies

   b. Coast Guard policy regarding unit response to reported discrepancies has changed considerably over the years. Historically buoy tenders spent most of their inport time in BRAVO-2 status. At that time, any aid discrepancy, regardless of its nature, was responded to within two hours. While this policy provided an extremely high level of service to the mariner and greatly enhanced Service image, its drawbacks became unacceptable - it was not cost effective and it placed an undue hardship on personnel.

   c. ANNEX A to the 1972 edition of the Aids to Navigation Manual – Administration (CG-222-1) specifically stated that ATON units should not be placed in a standby status requiring higher readiness than BRAVO-24 solely for the purpose of correcting aids to navigation discrepancies. Three levels of discrepancy response were developed and defined as:

   Priority - Correct within 24 hours.
   Routine - Correct within 48 hours.
   Deferred - Correct when servicing unit next in area.

   Many criteria were offered to help assign a response level, however the determination was subjective. Consequently, in the absence of objectivity, consistency was lacking in this area. Also, with the stated policy that units should not be placed on a readiness status higher than BRAVO-24 strictly for discrepancy response, this meant that the correction requirement for a priority response often couldn't be met and was contradictory.

d. In June of 1979, ANNEX A to the 1972 edition of CG-222-1 was superseded by ALDIST 311/79, the purpose of which was to provide interim guidance pending a forthcoming change to the manual. Specific levels of discrepancy response (including time criteria for correction) were abolished and all decisions regarding response were left entirely to the field commanders. The basic provisions of ANNEX A were still to be used as guidance in determining proper response to discrepancies.

e. Shortly after promulgation of ALDIST 311/79, experienced and knowledgeable personnel set out to establish objective criteria for determination of discrepancy response levels. The factors discussed in the ALDIST as well as ANNEX A were summarized, expanded and molded into a thorough, easily-useable framework providing a consistent and objective methodology for determining the proper level of response. A "DISCREPANCY RESPONSE **FACTOR** DECISION GUIDE" is presented in section B of this chapter.

3. Detecting and Reporting Discrepancies. Statistics indicate that few marine casualties result from aid discrepancies. However, in those marine casualties related to aid discrepancies, extensive losses have occurred. Therefore, particular attention must be given to checking aid position and characteristics, especially in areas of heavy marine traffic. Simple observation of aids by all Coast Guard units while on routine missions is of the highest importance.

4. Evaluating Information and Efficient Response.

a. Once a report of discrepancy has been received by any USCG unit, it is the responsibility of the Commanding Officer/Officer in Charge to evaluate the validity and accuracy of the information received.

b. It is also the responsibility of the Commanding Officer/Officer in Charge to determine the most efficient response to the discrepancy. If the Commanding Officer/Officer in Charge feels that the information received is less than accurate, he may choose to dispatch a small boat to confirm/repair the discrepancy or else he may contact other ships, in the area of the discrepancy, for confirmation. If the report cannot be confirmed, or if confirmation will take an excessive amount of time, the Commanding Officer/Officer in Charge shall respond according to the guidelines of this chapter.

5. Dissemination of Information. District Commanders shall ensure that information relating to discrepancies is promptly and accurately disseminated through Broadcast and/or Local Notice to Mariners in accordance with Chapter 12.

B. Determination of Discrepancy Response Level.

1. <u>Discrepancy Response levels</u>. When an aid discrepancy is reported, a response level for correction of the discrepancy must be determined. The Discrepancy Response Factor (DRF) is defined as a numerical indicator of the criticality of the discrepancy. Once determined, the proper level of response can then be assigned. The higher the DRF, the more critical the discrepancy and, hence, the higher the priority for correction. The five response levels are:

DRF	RESPONSE LEVEL
600 and up	IMMEDIATE: Servicing unit shall respond as soon after notification as weather and resource constraints permit.
450 to 599	HIGH: Servicing unit shall respond within 18 hours after receipt of discrepancy report or as soon thereafter as weather and resources permit.
275 to 449	PRIORITY: Servicing unit shall respond within 36 hours after receipt of discrepancy report or as soon thereafter as weather and resources permit.
150 to 274	ROUTINE: Servicing unit shall respond within 72 hours after receipt of discrepancy report or as soon thereafter as weather and resources permit.
1 to 149	DECISION/DEFERRED: As soon as is practical after receipt of a discrepancy report, the primary servicing unit shall advise district of future plans to correct the discrepancy. If a long period of time will elapse before the primary servicing unit can make the correction, district should coordinate available servicing facilities in order to correct the discrepancy.

2. <u>Discrepancy Response **Factor** Decision Guide</u>.

a. Figure 9-1 contains Part I of the Discrepancy Response **Factor** Decision Guide (DRG). Figure 9-2 contains Part II of the Discrepancy Response **Factor Decision** Guide, final Discrepancy Response Factor (DRF) and a listing of the discrepancy response levels. Figures 9-1 and 9-2 can be reproduced locally. Copies of the completed Part I must be kept on file with the district office, the primary servicing unit, and with Sector offices having operational control of ATON units. Once a discrepancy is reported, Part II can be completed and DRF determined. The discrepancy response level is then assigned and coordination between district and unit begins.

b. Part I needs to be completed only once for each aid to navigation. Part I will require some subjective determinations and shall be completed by the primary servicing unit. Completion will require the exercise of general ATON experience and familiarity with the aid to navigation, the waterway it serves, and the function of the aid. It shall be the responsibility of the District Commander to ensure that Part I is completed properly for each aid.

c. Part I value for each aid shall be reviewed at each servicing interval. This review is to ensure that the Part I is updated in the event of changes in waterway or aid function considerations for the aid.

d. How to use the Discrepancy Response **Factor** Decision Guide:

Part I - In sections A and B, determine the correct response to each question. Then circle the X directly to the right of that response. Add up the number of X's in each column, multiply by the weighting factor provided for the column, and fill in the blank. Add the sum of the products from each column and enter the total for Part I in the box.

Part II- This part can be completed only after the discrepancy has occurred. Complete Part II for the appropriate aid in the same manner as Part I.

Discrepancy Response Factor - Multiply the Part I total by the Part II total. This product is the DRF.

Discrepancy Response Level - Place the DRF in the appropriate numerical range (see pg 9-3) and assign a discrepancy response level. Initiate necessary action.

e. The value derived from the completion of Part I will place each aid into one of the following categories:

CATEGORY 1 Above 50
CATEGORY 2 46 - 50
CATEGORY 3 41 - 45
CATEGORY 4 36 - 40
CATEGORY 5 Below 36

These categories will enable easy identification of the importance of an aid as well as providing a tool for facilities management. The importance of an aid might also be useful in unusual circumstances, i.e. ice season, assessing storm damage, etc.

C. Discrepancy Response Policy.

1. **The date and time at which a unit completes temporary corrective action to a discrepancy but does not completely restore the aid to watching properly status shall be entered in I-ATONIS in the Temp Response DTG field. Some examples of temp action are setting a temporary buoy installation of new optic with reduced intensity, etc.**

2. It is the responsibility of the District Commander to prescribe the specific discrepancy response policy for his district, assuring response times fall within the time frames specified herein. A copy of any supplementary instructions issued to implement policy of this chapter shall be forwarded to Commandant **(CG-5413).**

3. Due to the complexity of aid systems and differences in such things as local geography and specific purpose of a certain aid, a small number of aids may require a set response, determined without the use of the Decision Guide. For example, an especially critical range may be pre-assigned to the immediate category, regardless of the nature of the discrepancy because degradation of its function has a high probability of rendering an entire aid system inadequate.

4. Districts having waterways affected by ice formation shall develop a specific policy for responding to discrepancies during ice conditions. The categories from Part I (B.2.d.) should prove useful and should be utilized in developing such a policy.

5. District and Sector Commanders exercising operational control over aids to navigation servicing units shall review records of outstanding discrepancies on a weekly basis, in conjunction with the LNM, to ensure that corrective action is being taken in accordance with the provisions of this chapter.

6. Commander, Eighth Coast Guard District, while receiving guidance from this chapter, shall develop an independent discrepancy response plan suited particularly to the Western Rivers and forward to Commandant (**CG-5413**).

Part I

Circle the applicable X's and add total points.

A. WATERWAYS CONSIDERATION

	A	B	C	D
1. Is the waterway relatively narrow? W/B is the ratio of the waterway width to beam of the largest user.				
a. a. W/B 10-20		X		
b. b. W/B 1-9				X
2. Is the waterway used by merchant vessels?				
a. Infrequently	X			
b. Regularly with harbor pilot aboard		X		
c. Regularly without harbor pilot				X
3. Is the waterway used by large vessels?				
a. 100 – 400 ft		X		
b. 401 – 650 ft			X	
c. 651 ft or greater				X
4. Is the waterway used to transport hazardous cargo?				X
5. Is the bottom other than soft?				X
6. Is two-way commercial traffic frequent?			X	
7. Is nighttime traffic frequent?			X	
8. Are other aids to navigation available				
a. Many	X			
b. Few		X		
c. None			X	
d. None; but marks turn, shoal or obstruction				X
9. Is visibility often restricted				
a. To 5nm or less		X		
b. To 2nm or less			X	
10. Is the surrounding area especially environmentally sensitive?				X

B. AID FUNCTION CONSIDERATIONS

	A	B	C	D
1. Is the aid lighted?				
a. Yes, nominal range 1-4nm		X		
b. Yes, nominal range 5-14nm			X	
c. Yes, it is part of a terrestrial range				X
2. Is a Racon provided?		X		
3. Does aid have an especially critical function? (entrance, approach, obstruction or turn)				
a. Is it charted as such			X	
b. Uncharted (temporary or new since last edition of chart)				X
Sum of X's				
	x1	x3	x4	x6

Total of Part I   ___ + ___ + ___ + ___ = _____

PART I Category _____

Commanding Officer/Officer-in-Charge _____ Date: _____

Figure 9-1

DISCREPANCY RESPONSE FACTOR DECISION GUIDE

Part II

Circle the applicable X's and add total points.

C. DISCREPANCIES	A	B	C	D	E
1. Buoy:					
a. Sinking					X
b. Off station, adrift or missing				X	
c. Damaged		X			
2. Fixed Structure:					
a. Damaged		X			
b. Destroyed or missing				X	
3. Light:					
a. Extinguished or improper characteristics				X	
b. Reduced intensity		X			
c. Night only light operating during daylight hours	X				
4. Sound signal:					
a. Inoperative or improper characteristics			X		
b. Reduced intensity		X			
5. Daymark damaged, missing, or improper characteristics			X		
6. RACON (Radar Beacon) inoperative/improper characteristics			X		
7. Discrepant ATON produces a misleading signal					X
8. Discrepant ATON poses a hazard to navigation					X
9. Other discrepant ATON in the area elevates the criticality of this discrepancy.				X	
Sum of X's					
	x1	x3	x4	x6	x8

Total of Part II   ___ + ___ + ___ + ___ + ___ = _____

Discrepancy Response Factor

DRF = Product of Parts I and II = ____ x ____ = _____

Commanding Officer/Officer in Charge _____ Date: _____

DRF	RESPONSE LEVEL
600 and up	**IMMEDIATE:** Servicing unit shall respond as soon after notification as weather and resource constraints permit.
450 to 599	**HIGH:** Servicing unit shall respond within 18 hours after receipt of discrepancy report or as soon thereafter as weather and resources permit.
275 to 449	**PRIORITY:** Servicing unit shall respond within 36 hours after receipt of discrepancy report or as soon thereafter as weather and resources permit.
150 to 274	**ROUTINE:** Servicing unit shall respond within 72 hours after receipt of discrepancy report or as soon thereafter as weather and resources permit.
1 to 149	**DECISION/DEFERRED:** As soon as is practical after receipt of a discrepancy report, the primary servicing unit shall advise district of future plans to correct the discrepancy. If a long period of time will elapse before the primary servicing unit can make the correction, district should coordinate available servicing facilities in order to correct the discrepancy.

Figure 9 - 2

This Page Intentionally
Left Blank

CHAPTER 10 - TRAINING

A. <u>National Aids to Navigation (NATON) School</u>.

1. <u>General</u>. In order to maintain and develop a professional service force, all officers and enlisted personnel in the Aids to Navigation field must continuously participate in training. On the job training has been, and should continue to be, a key source of unit/district specific technical training. A variety of resident courses are provided by the NATON School to meet fleet needs. All courses are updated regularly to reflect administrative and/or technical advances. Unit Commanding Officers shall ensure that all ATON-related training is captured in either Direct Access or the Training Management Tool (TMT) in accordance with Mandatory Use of the Training Management Tool, COMDTINST 5270.2.

2. <u>Use of The National Aids to Navigation School</u>.

   a. **Quotas for aids to navigation training are managed through The National Aids to Navigation School with support from the program manager at Coast Guard Headquarters, Visual Navigation Branch (CG-54131).**

   b. District, Sector, and individual unit Commanders shall attempt to use every training quota offered, and where applicable, shall impress the need for formal training upon each Commanding Officer or Officer-in-Charge. Temporary operational demands should not be allowed to overshadow the need for maintaining an adequate level of trained personnel.

   c. Training requests for NATON courses should be sent following the guidance on the Training Quota Management Center Website.

   d. District, Sector, and Unit Commanders shall ensure the correct personnel are sent to the correct course. Resources should not be expended on training either "short timers" or personnel whose ratings or duties rarely involve the type of advanced training provided by the school. Following training, personnel should be assigned to aids to navigation duties commensurate with their training, as a good portion of their training can only be fully understood and maintained after its application on the job.

   e. Exportable training has been developed to provide training to a large number of personnel with minimum disruption to a unit's operations. NATON provides exportable training through opportunities such as tender roundups or district seminars. The benefits to be considered include the cost advantage of sending instructors to the students, the training environment in the field versus the classroom, and the number of people who can be trained in short periods of time. Requests for exportable training must originate from the District Aids to Navigation Office.

f. <u>Technical Advisor</u>. A technical advisor has been assigned to the NATON School for the express purpose of gathering and dispersing timely information regarding ATON servicing equipment and procedures. The technical advisor maintains a liaison with affiliated commercial representatives, headquarters staff, and operational units in an effort to stay abreast of the latest technological and operational developments in the ATON field.

   (1) Queries regarding minor ATON equipment and/or servicing procedures should be addressed to the technical advisor.

   (2) Requests for the technical advisor to perform specific training as a solution to a unique problem must be submitted to your District Aids to Navigation Office.

3. <u>Officer Attendance Requirements</u>.

   a. Officers involved in aids to navigation servicing work or management of the Short Range Aids to Navigation program shall receive training at the NATON School.

   b. Officers in receipt of orders to one of the following assignments shall attend either the Officer Advanced (ANC-OA) or Basic (ANC-OB) Aids to Navigation Course, as detailed in Cutter Training and Qualification Manual, COMDTINST M3502.4 (series).

      (1) Tender - Commanding Officer, Executive Officer, Operations Officer, and First Lieutenant, and DWOs.

      (2) Sector Aids to Navigation Officers.

      (3) District **Waterways Management** Branch - Chief and Assistant Chief

      (4) Certain MLC, CEU and FDCC personnel whose duties are directly related to aids to navigation systems engineering and management.

      (5) Commandant **(CG-54131)** personnel.

4. <u>Petty Officer Attendance Requirements</u>.

   a. Petty officers involved in aids to navigation servicing work shall receive training at the NATON School.

   b. Chief petty officers and petty officers assigned as ATON deck supervisors on tenders are required to attend the Minor Aids Maintenance Aids to Navigation Servicing Technician Course (ANC-MAM) and the ATON Deck Supervisor Course (ANC-ADS) if they have not attended the course within the past five years.

   c. Chief petty officers or petty officers assigned as officers-in-charge of aids to navigation teams shall attend the Officer-in Charge Aids to Navigation Team Course (ANC-ANT).

5. <u>Mandatory Pipeline Training Requirements</u>.

   a. Personnel shall consult the Cutter Training and Qualification Manual, COMDTINST M3502.4 (series) prior to executing permanent change of station orders.

   b. Training should be scheduled as soon as possible after receipt of orders, and in some cases prior to receiving orders, to reduce or eliminate course conflicts and to allow maximum flexibility in scheduling personnel

   c. Transferring members must coordinate all training requests with their present and prospective command to minimize adverse impacts.

B. <u>Aids to Navigation Courses</u>.

1. <u>General</u>. The following sections contain brief descriptions of the courses available at the NATON School at Training Center Yorktown. More information and qualifications for students is contained in COMDTNOTE 1540 (series) or at NATON School website, http://www.uscg.mil/tcyorktown/ops/naton/default.asp

2. Minor Aids Section.

    a. Minor Aids Maintenance, Aids to Navigation Servicing Technician (ANC-MAM)

    Designed for enlisted and civilian personnel assigned to aids to navigation servicing units. Topics: Entry level training in installation, maintenance, trouble shooting, and repair of selected minor ATON lighting equipment, and safety precautions. Students are required to have been assigned to their ATON unit for no less than three months prior to attending this course.

    Prerequisites: Three months at an ATON unit.

    b. Advanced Course Minor Aids to Navigation Servicing Technician (ANC-AC)

    Designed for supervisory enlisted personnel (E4-E9) and civilians of an equivalent supervisory level. Entry level training in safety precautions involved in maintenance and repair of AC powered minor aids to navigation equipment, principles of operation, preventative maintenance, and trouble shooting procedures for minor aids to navigation.

    Prerequisites: ANC-MAM or District Training Team MAM Road Course

    c. Training Team Seminar (ANC-TT)

    This course provides an annual technical update on ATON hardware, changes in procedures and philosophies, and an overview of training techniques. The following topics are covered: ATON hardware, research and development of new ATON equipment, ATON projects, training team projects, training team courses, training team techniques, ATON school quota utilization, and equipment problems and failures.

    Prerequisites: CG personnel serving on ATON Training Teams

3. Major Aids Section.

    a. Videograph B Fog Detector (ANC-FD)

    This course provides training in the operation, installation, and corrective and preventative maintenance of the Videograph B Fog Detector and an overview of the VM-100.

    Prerequisites: Have a background in basic electricity and basic electronics, ability to read and interpret basic electrical, electronic and digital schematics, and diagrams.

b. Auto Aids Lighthouse (ANC-LT)

This course provides training in the proper operation, corrective and preventative maintenance of selected standard equipment found in category I through IV automated lighthouses. The following topics are covered: AVC/NAV-AID, Power System Controller, Light-main/emergency, Sound Signals-main/emergency, Batteries and Battery Chargers, Halon Fire Extinguishing Systems, Engine Generator System, Drytank assembly ACMS, and Environmental Control System.

Prerequisites: A background in basic electricity and basic electronics, completion of the CG Electrician's Mate or Electronics Technician A School and is an EM or ET. E-4 through E-9. Also will accept CG civilians with equivalent standards. Completion of the Basic and Advance Aids to Navigation course is highly recommended.

c. Solar Powered Major Aids to Navigation Course (ANC-SP)

This course is designed to provide training in the proper operation, preventive and corrective maintenance of the equipment found in solar powered major aids to navigation and low energy ACMS. All standard equipment will be covered, with the exception of solar range light controller (S-RLC). The S-RLC will be added to the curriculum at a later date if enough units are installed in the field to justify resident training support.

Prerequisites: A background in basic electricity and basic electronics, completion of the CG Electrician's Mate or Electronics Technician A School and is an EM or ET. E-4 through E-9. Also will accept CG civilians with equivalent standards. Also will accept CG civilians with equivalent standards. Completion of the Basic and Advance Aids to Navigation course is highly recommended.

d. Differential Broadcast Site Maintenance (ANC-DB)

This course provides training in the proper configuration of a differential broadcast (DGPS) site. The instruction will include the following: site equipment configuration, preventative and corrective and alignment for the DGPS equipment rack, and differential transmitter.

Prerequisites: ET, E-4 and above, and civilian employed by the Coast Guard or other government agencies.

4. Operations Courses.

  a. Aids to Navigation Management (ANC-OB)

    This is an entry-level course providing commissioned officers (O-1 through O-3), warrant officers, and senior petty officers training in theoretical and practical aids to navigation. Material covered includes: minor aid hardware, power systems, buoy tender operations, aids system theory and design, aids positioning, legal aspects and responsibilities, administration, safety, visual signaling, waterways analysis and management, and ATON mishap prevention.

    Prerequisites: Assignment to an ATON supervisory billet.

  b. Officer Advanced ATON (ANC-OA)

    This course provides theoretical and practical training in the design, administration, legal ramification and supervision of the Coast Guard's Aids to Navigation Mission, as well as a review of Aids to Navigation vessel mishaps. The program of instruction includes: All areas listed under Officer Operations (ANC-OB) and principles and interrelations of higher echelons in administration.

    Prerequisites: Aids to Navigation Management (ANC-OB). Prospective Commanding Officers, Executive Officers, Officers in Charge, and Executive Petty Officers of ATON Cutters.

  c. Officer in Charge Aids to Navigation Team (ANC-ANT)

    This course covers operation, installation, and overview of 12-volt (DC) 120 volt (AC) Aids to Navigation equipment, boat procedures, deck operations, positioning, and various administrative topics.

    Prerequisites: OICs and XPOs of ANTs. E-5 and above.

  d. Aid Positioning (ANC-AP)

    This course trains petty officers to serve in aid positioning responsible billets afloat and on Aids to Navigation teams. The training consists of classroom lectures and laboratories involving maintenance of positioning equipment, determining positioning standards, maintaining aid files, I-ATONIS, AAPS and differential Global Positioning System (DGPS), ATON Administration, Legal Issues, and Computer Maintenance.

    Prerequisites: Designated E3's through E-9 and directly responsible for positioning Aids to Navigation.

5. Exportable Training and Standardization.

   a. Buoy Deck Training Team (BDTT)

   The BDTT Course is designed to provide training to 225' WLBs and 175' WLMs in weight handling equipment and standard buoy deck operation per the Aids to Navigation Manual – Seamanship, COMDTINST M16500.21 (series) and the Buoy Deck Interactive Courseware for WLBs and WLMs. Emphasis will be placed on readiness and standardization as a daily process, with operational commanders continually aware of factors that limit the ability to safely operate as designed. The BDTT will evaluate the material condition of weight handling equipment and ensure unit compliance with preventive maintenance requirements, evaluate the effectiveness of the unit's buoy deck crew training program, evaluate buoy deck crew performance skills essential to safe operations, and provide ready for operations evaluation guidance to the Operational Commander. Buoy Deck Training Team assessments shall be conducted on a 24 month schedule for each WLB and WLM.

   b. 49' BUSL Standardization Team

   The BUSL shall conduct Readiness and Standardization assessments per 49' Buoy Utility Stern Loading (BUSL) Boat Operator's Handbook, COMDTINST 16114.22 (series). Emphasis will be placed on readiness and standardization as a daily process with Operational Commanders continually aware of factors that limit the ability of their boats to safely operate at design limits. The STAN Team will evaluate the material condition of standard boats and ensure unit compliance with preventive maintenance and configuration management requirements, evaluate the effectiveness of the unit's boat crew training program, evaluate boat crew performance skills essential to safe operations, and provide ready for operations evaluation guidance to the operation commander. STAN Team assessments shall be conducted on a biennial schedule to each unit assigned a 49' BUSL.

   c. ATON Deck Supervisor

   This course is designed to train petty officers, chief petty officers, and chief warrant officers assigned as deck supervisors and safety supervisors aboard aids to navigation vessels. Topics include: safety procedures; maintenance, inspection, and usage of wire rope, chain, synthetic lines; rigging theory and principles; and buoy deck evolutions/operations.

   Prerequisites: Chief Warrant Officers, Chief Petty Officers, and Petty Officers assigned to aids to navigation vessels, having a minimum of 6 months ATON deck experience and qualified as a deck rigger. District/Sector personnel responsible for Ready for Operations Inspections may attend.

d. River Tender Course (ANC-RIV)

This course is designed for deck supervisors serving on WLRs. Topics include crane operation, buoy deck evolutions, structure construction, wire rope maintenance, rigging safety, Oxy-acetylene use, and chain saw safety.

Prerequisites: Currently stationed on or ordered to a CG River Tender.

e. Construction Tender (ANC-C)

This course provides technical training on deck procedures on WLICs and the operation and maintenance of associated equipment. The following topics are covered: WLIC fleet overview, wire rope rigging, Braden winches, CG 300 Oceanmaster crane and rigging, Delmag D6 pile driving hammer, Minor aids to navigation materials, structures, servicing, Oxy-acetylene use, and chain saw safety.

Prerequisites: Chief Warrant Officers and Coast Guard enlisted E-4 and above, who serve as COs/OICs/XPOs and construction deck supervisors on WLICs.

f. Construction Tender for MKs (ANC-C-MK)

This course provides manufacturer training on CG 300 Oceanmaster crane, Braden winches, and Delmag D6 hammers on WLICs. The following topics are covered: disassembly/reassemble/PMS of diesel pile driving hammer, complete disassembly/assembly of brake system of Branden winch, basic hydraulic theory, operation of Branden winch, and PMS/inspections of CG 300 Oceanmaster crane.

Prerequisites: CG enlisted Machinery Technicians E-4 and above assigned to WLIC class tenders

C. District Aids to Navigation Training.

1. General. Completion of one or more of the aids to navigation courses offered at the National Aids to Navigation School greatly improves the qualifications of aids to navigation servicing personnel. However, a continuing need exists for updating the knowledge of field personnel based on improvements and new techniques, dissemination of information peculiar to individual operating areas, and for on-the-job observation and assistance by trained aids to navigation instructors. Hence the need exists for a comprehensive district aids to navigation training program. Billets have been allocated to districts specifically for aids to navigation training to meet this need.

2. Aids to Navigation Training Teams.

   a. Each district that is allocated training team billets will maintain at least one mobile training team composed of one or more enlisted personnel well qualified for such duties by virtue of training and field experience.

   b. Personnel selected for training teams should have considerable aids to navigation field experience at various types of units and be graduates of the Advance and Minor Aids Courses at the National Aids to Navigation School within the last three years or six months upon arrival. Instructor Development Course training is mandatory. A current knowledge of hardware and servicing techniques is a prerequisite. Candidates for this assignment should be screened for ability to get necessary points across to field personnel, while at the same time establishing a good rapport and basis of understanding, functioning primarily as counselors, not inspectors.

   c. Training teams are normally required to visit all aids to navigation units within a district at least semi-annually. The length of the visit may vary in accordance with the expertise of the personnel attached. Visits should be scheduled to coincide with normal unit operations, and the team should participate in the unit's scheduled aids to navigation work.

   d. Training Teams emphasize daily, on-the-job training, determining problem areas and correcting them on the spot. Training teams should perform the following specific tasks:

      (1) Conduct Minor Aids Maintenance (MAM) training as outlined by NATON to meet requirements for NE qualification code as per Enlisted Qualification Manual COMDTINST M1414.9 (series) and introduce new aid equipment to field personnel as necessary. Training should be held at the unit or central location.

      (2) Assist and monitor units in developing and conducting an aids to navigation training program.

      (3) Provide guidance in the installation and maintenance of both AC and DC powered aids.

      (4) Consult with the unit Commanding Officer or Officer-in-Charge on the current status of the unit's library of manufacturers' publications and Coast Guard aids to navigation directives and publications.

      (5) Discuss unit aids to navigation material allowance, supply and ordering information for navigation equipment making recommendations for changes as required.

(6) Observe the unit servicing aids to navigation within the unit's operating area and tailor additional training and feedback to the unit to meet the unit's training needs.

(7) Provide feedback to the Commanding Officer or Officer-in-Charge, and NATON School on problems found or specific areas needing improvement at the units visit.

e. The Training Team operates independently of the *unit's* chain of command. Recommendation and advice serve only as suggestion to the unit command and are not considered as requirements unless the requirement is specified in program guidance.

f. Training Teams are to supplement, not replace, unit training programs and the use of the National Aids to Navigation School. Additionally, to standardize training methods and material, one team member will be required to attend the annual training team seminar at the National Aids to Navigation School. Additional team members are encouraged to attend at District expense.

g. The number of Training Team members needed may vary among Districts, depending on the number of District aids to navigation units, amount of travel necessary to visit units, and District use of the National Aids to Navigation School.

h. Training Teams should be molded to best suit district needs while accomplishing the ultimate goal of upgrading overall professionalism in the aids to navigation program.

i. Review maintenance of unit battery log, ATON battery tracking system, and unit rigging log.

D. <u>District Aids to Navigation Seminars</u>.

1. The purpose of the District seminar is to provide for the exchange of information between district and field personnel. Participation in these seminars results in better methods of handling equipment, identification of problem areas and solutions, development and promulgation of new techniques, and discontinuance of erroneous practices.

2. A District-wide seminar for district aids to navigation unit Commanding Officers, Officers-in-Charge and senior Sector aids to navigation personnel should be conducted at least annually. In addition to the District wide seminar each Sector or combination of adjoining Sectors will hold a seminar for Sector aids to navigation unit Officers-in-Charge or their representatives, at least once every year. In addition to aids to navigation operating and servicing personnel, civilian employees and industrial managers should attend.

3. A team from the district and the Civil Engineering Unit shall conduct the seminars. Minutes of each seminar shall be distributed to all units in the district having any aids to navigation servicing responsibility with copies to Commandant **(CG-54131), (CG-45)** and **(CG-443)** plus each District Commander **(dpw)**, and the National Aids to Navigation School. In this respect each seminar will benefit all district aids to navigation units, and not just those attending a specific seminar, while also providing another avenue for inter-district communications.

E. Training Team Coordinator.

1. The Training Team Coordinator billet is assigned to the National Aids to Navigation School. This person is the contact point with the school and provides for the gathering and dissemination of information to the training teams.

2. The Training Team Coordinator serves as the liaison with the district training teams regarding enlisted quotas for NATON School courses. Queries regarding training requirements, quota availability, course scheduling, etc. should be addressed directly to the Training Team Coordinator.

3. A primary function of the Coordinator is assisting district training teams. The Training Team Coordinator will review courses taught by training teams and can be made available to visit district training teams upon request.

4. The Training Team Coordinator will gather information from the district training teams on a monthly basis and ensure courses completed by the training team are entered in the training management database.

F. Unit Training.

1. Personnel assigned to an aids to navigation unit must be familiar with the basic aspects of aids to navigation equipment operation and maintenance when their duties are directly related to aids to navigation. In this regard the following minimum training requirements are established:

    a. Every ATON unit shall ensure that adequate "all hands" training is conducted in safety precautions. At least one "all hands" safety training session will be held semi annually.

    b. Drills, lectures, and instructions found in appropriate publications and instructions.

    c. Guidance on climber safety training is provided in Aids to Navigation Manual – Structures, COMDTINST M16500.25 (series).

d. Lesson plans for various aspects of aids to navigation training can be found in The Unit Training Manual Afloat, Volume VI, COMDTINST M3502.7 (series).

2. Recent graduates from the National Aids to Navigation School should be used as much as possible in planning and conducting unit training. This not only aids in keeping information current but also boosts the individual's prestige, thereby aiding overall unit morale.

G. Annual Senior Officer Aids to Navigation Conference.

1. Headquarters, **Visual** Navigation **Branch (CG-54131)**, Civil Engineering Division **(CG-43)**, and the National Aids to Navigation School will conduct an annual conference for all district **waterways management** branch chiefs and appropriate Maintenance and Logistics Command engineering and real property representatives. The attendees will review common areas of aids to navigation interest and will be briefed by cognizant headquarters personnel on current or projected trends, problems, or developments in aids to navigation.

H. Aids to Navigation Bulletin.

1. The Aids to Navigation Bulletin is published for information purposes only and is intended to:

   a. Provide another vehicle of communications between Headquarters, field and staff organizations.

   b. Increase professionalism and professional knowledge of all aids to navigation personnel.

   c. Improve the esprit de corps of Coast Guard aids to navigation personnel.

2. Articles relevant to aids to navigation work are appreciated and solicited from anyone. Commanding Officers and Officers-in-Charge are encouraged to use these articles as training aids.

3. Forwarding Articles. Forward articles to the Editor, Aids to Navigation Bulletin, c/o National Aids to Navigation School, Training Center Yorktown, Yorktown, VA 23690-5000. Material intended for the Bulletin does not have to be routed through the chain of command; it may be submitted directly to the editor.

4. Distribution. Commanding Officers and Officers-in-Charge shall make the bulletin available to all hands. Although not required, it is recommended that a file of Bulletins be maintained for future reference

CHAPTER 11 - EXTERNAL RELATIONS

A. <u>Public Relations</u>.

   1. <u>General</u>.

      a. Coast Guard personnel at all levels often receive some requests and questions from the public concerning aids to navigation. When this happens, it is of primary importance to remember that the purpose of the Coast Guard in this field is to serve the public. Members of the Coast Guard must exercise tact and courtesy in dealing with questions and requests, and should see that prompt response is made in each case. To avoid delay, response to the public should be made at the lowest level where proper authority exists.

      b. Care must be exercised to avoid making statements which are beyond the authority of the speaker. For example, while the District Commander has the authority to make many permanent changes in the aids to navigation system, other major changes must be approved by the Commandant. Requests and suggestions for such changes therefore must be handled with some care to avoid making commitments which cannot be carried out or which might be contrary to the District Commander's or Commandant's policy. Cases have arisen where the statements of the Officer-in-Charge of a small unit have been quoted as supporting a proposed change in correspondence from members of Congress and others before the proposal reached Headquarters for approval. Such cases can put the Commandant in the embarrassing position of having to disapprove, for budgetary or other reasons; changes, which a member of the Coast Guard has publicly stated, are necessary.

      c. Another aspect to the problem is that the Coast Guard has the duty of choosing the specific means of meeting aids to navigation requirement. A member in the field cannot always be sure that the specific aid proposed by the requester is the best method of meeting that need, and should not, in effect, commit the Coast Guard in any particular way.

      d. Proper action for the member in a field unit is to ask the requester to write to the District Commander concerning the request and to give amplifying information as to the reasons for the request. Such information should include items such as the volume of traffic and the particular navigation problem that gives rise to the request. Title 33, Code of Federal Regulations Subpart 62.63, specifically shows the information that should accompany public requests for changes in aids. Chapter 3 also contains information useful in dealing with requests for aids to navigation

e. Well-considered recommendations from field units concerning changes to the aids to navigation system are encouraged. These recommendations may well be the result of inquiries from the public, but discussion of such recommendations with the public should emphasize that the recommendations do not become official Coast Guard policy until approved by the Commandant or District Commander, as applicable.

2. Public Access to Aids to Navigation Facilities.

   a. Correspondence received at Headquarters requesting visiting privileges at Coast Guard units in previously unpopulated seashore or lake side locations is an indication of growing importance of recreational areas and the growing number of people who use them. Most numerous are inquires from government, recreational, or park authorities interested in opening unmanned lighthouses to the public.

   b. In response to these requests visitors may be allowed aboard units in accordance with paragraph 7-1-3 of Coast Guard Regulations, COMDTINST M5000.3 (series).

      (1) Floating units: In accordance with District policy and at the discretion of the Commanding Officer.

      (2) Manned Shore Stations: Public visitation at shore units is a long established practice. It is encouraged to the extent that there are sufficient personnel to escort or supervise the movement of visitors on station grounds so as not to interfere with the unit's operation. It is recognized that denying or restricting visitation without justification would result in public complaint. However, indiscriminate visitation should not be permitted. Consistent with operational requirements, Sector Commanders are encouraged to establish visiting hours for units under their commands, ensuring that adequate control of visitors is possible, and areas off-limits to visitors are posted.

      (3) Unmanned Stations: Visiting of unmanned Coast Guard Light Stations is not allowed unless the station is of special architectural or historical significance, i.e., it is the only one of its kind or the only structure of its type in the general area, and it is located in a centrally accessible area of a park or other well visited public area.

c. The light tower at many stations is the major point of interest. However, the extended climb up narrow winding steps, with low overhead openings (trap doors) at one or more landings, and the limited walkway space in the lantern room are potential hazards. The constant maintenance of safety standards and adequate control of visitors is therefore essential. Commanding Officers and Officers-in-Charge of units with light towers open to the public shall review the conditions at these structures and ensure that:

(1) All practicable safety measures have been taken; i.e., sufficient and proper warning signs and markings on steps, landings, and approaches to trap doors; sturdy and secure trap door latches; and chains at trap doors; and non-slip walk surfaces.

(2) Escort is provided for visitors, or personnel are stationed at key points, such as the lantern room.

(3) Children under 12 years of age are accompanied by an adult.

(4) The rules are not relaxed to accommodate too large a number of visitors.

(5) Any necessary restriction on visitation that may be imposed is brought to the attention of the unit's immediate commander who will, as appropriate, advise the District Commander.

d. Closing-Off Property. When it is necessary to fence off a property to which the public has traditionally had access while disposal action is in progress, the effect on public relations should be considered. In such cases, a sign stressing the temporary nature of the closing and the reasons for such action may forestall much correspondence.

B. Historic Aids to Navigation Structures.

1. Introduction. This section is provided to briefly acquaint aids to navigation personnel with information so that they will be able to recognize situations in which Executive Order (E.O.) 11593, the National Historic Preservation Act of 1966 (NHPA), and the National Environmental Policy Act (NEPA) of 1969 and their applicable regulations apply.

2. National Historic Preservation Act and Executive Order 11593 Requirements.

   a. The National Historic Preservation Act of 1966, 16 U.S.C. 470 Section110, and E.O. 11593 impose specific responsibilities upon the Coast Guard regarding its historic resources. In accordance with Section 110 and E.O. 11593, the Coast Guard is required to establish a program to locate, inventory, and nominate properties that appear to meet the criteria of historic significance (criteria are listed at 36 CFR Part 60) to the National Register of Historic Places (National Register). Properties under the jurisdiction or control of the Coast Guard that are listed in or may be eligible for the National Register must be managed and maintained in a way that considers the preservation of their historic, archaeological, architectural, and cultural values in compliance with Section 106 of the NHPA and must give special consideration to the preservation of such values in the case of properties designated as having National significance. Failure to identify properties that meet National Register criteria does not exempt the USCG from its responsibilities under NHPA. Regulations promulgated by the National Park Service at 36 CFR Part 60, 63, and 65 pertain to Coast Guard responsibilities under Section 110 of NHPA.

   b. NHPA Section 106 requires the Coast Guard to take into account the effects of its undertakings on historic properties. Regulations promulgated by the Advisory Council on Historic Preservation (ACHP) under 36 CFR Part 800 implement Executive Order 11593 and, Section 106 of NHPA and establish the procedures to be followed any time a Federal "undertaking" (project, action) will have an "effect" on a structure which is eligible for or listed on the National Register. The Coast Guard has sole responsibility for identifying its historical, cultural, architectural, and archeological properties that are listed, or eligible, for listing in the National Register. This must be accomplished before undertaking any projects or actions that might affect such properties. It is important to note that Section 106 applies to our proposed actions on an eligible property regardless of whether the property is actually listed on the Register. For the purposes of compliance with Section 106, properties that are just eligible or may be eligible must be treated in the same manner under Section 106 as a property that is actually listed.

   c. Aids to navigation properties that may be eligible for the National Register. Aid to Navigation sites, buildings, structures, and objects that are 50 years old and possess significance in American history, architecture, archeology, engineering, and culture and that possess integrity of location, design, setting, materials, workmanship, feeling, and association and:

      (1) that are associated with events that have made a significant contribution to the broad patterns of our history; or

      (2) that are associated with the lives of persons significant in our past; or

(3) that embody the distinctive characteristics of a type, period, or method of construction, or that represent the work of a master, or that possess high artistic values, or that represent a significant and distinguishable entity whose components may lack individual distinction; or

(4) that has yielded, or may be likely to yield, information important in prehistory or history. As a general rule, if the aid to navigation is a lighthouse or light station which is 50 years old or older it is probably either eligible or listed on the National Register. However, any aid to navigation structure, site, etc. that is 50 years old and meets the above criteria could be eligible for or listed on the National Register including day marks, skeletal towers, light poles, etc. Additionally, while resources that are less than 50 years old are not normally eligible for listing, if the resource is less than 50 years old and is exceptionally significant under the criteria above it is then eligible for listing. Determinations of whether an aid to navigation property is eligible or listed on the National Register should be made with the assistance of environmental staff in the CEU or MLC and ultimately through appropriate compliance with Section 106 and 110 processes.

3. Aids to Navigation Projects Affecting a Historic Property.

a. An aid to navigation project is considered to have an "effect" on a historic aid to navigation property if the project causes or may cause any change, beneficial or adverse, in the quality of the historical, architectural, archeological, or cultural character that qualifies or might qualify the property for the National Register of Historic Places. Routine maintenance of an aid does not generally fall into this category. Lack of maintenance resulting in deterioration or destruction of a historic property is considered to have an "adverse effect" on the property and is subject to 36 CFR Part 800 requirements. Examples of actions which can either affect or adversely affect an historic aid include the following: interior renovations, removing and replacing windows and/or doors, putting up solar panels, disestablishing a light, removing a Fresnel lens, painting the interior or exterior, doing major additions, alterations, or renovations, demolishing buildings or structures, doing extensive soil disturbance, installing antennas, installing fences, installing new modern aids, etc. Generally, "adverse effects" occur under conditions which include but are not limited to:

(1) Destruction or alteration of all or part of a property;

(2) Isolation from or alteration of its surrounding environment;

(3) Introduction of visual, audible, or atmospheric elements that are out of character with the property or alter its setting;

(4) Transfer or sale of a federally owned property without adequate conditions or restrictions regarding preservation, maintenance or use; and

(5) Neglect of a property resulting in its deterioration or destruction.

b. When it is determined that an aid to navigation undertaking may have an "effect" on a historic property under the ACHP guidelines set fourth in 36 CFR Part 800, the State Historic Preservation Officer (SHPO) and any interested parties (the public) must be consulted so that the Coast Guard can make a determination of whether or not the property is in fact historic, whether there is an effect, and whether the effect is adverse. Aids to navigation personnel who are aware of a proposed action or project that could impact a possibly historic aid to navigation should contact Headquarters G-SEC-3, or their servicing MLC and or CEU environmental staff (as appropriate) for assistance prior to implementing the project or action. Since a project cannot be carried out until the requirements of 36 CFR Part 800 has been satisfied, it is beneficial to notify the MLC or CEU as early in the planning stage as possible. If the USCG, in consultation with SHPO and any other consulting parties, determines that there are "no historic properties affected," the 36 CFR Part 800 requirements have been satisfied and the project or action can proceed. If it is found that the action will have effects but that they are not adverse or that the ACHP criteria of "adverse effect" applies to the project in consultation with the SHPO, Aids to Navigation personnel will work with their environmental staff in Headquarters **CG-43**, the CEU or MLC as appropriate to provide technical information and program direction to environmental staff as needed to complete appropriate compliance under Section 106 prior to project implementation. Coast Guard policy on compliance with Section 110 and Section 106 of the NHPA is contained in Chapter 2 of National Environmental Policy Act Implementing Procedures and Policy for Consideration of Environmental Impacts COMDTINST M16475.1 (series).

c. Coast Guard aids to navigation property for which there is no further operational requirement should be declared excess to the needs of the Coast Guard (see Real Property Management Manual, COMDTINST M11011.9 (series), for excessing procedures). The excessing process may be long and cumbersome if there is no other agency or organization ready to take control of the property. Licensing and leasing agreements may provide a solution until the property can be excessed. Licensing and leasing historic aids to navigation triggers the requirements of Section 106 which should be completed prior to approval of the license or award of the lease; however, individual section 106 compliance may be avoided for each lease or license by complying with the USCG Programmatic Agreement Regarding Out granting of Historic Lighthouse Properties, 1996 and its 2003 Amendment (Appendix).

4. National Environmental Policy Act Requirements.

   a. Aid to navigation actions or projects that may or will affect an historic aid, also trigger the requirements of the National Environmental Policy Act (NEPA), 42 U.S.C. 4321, *et seq.*) NEPA declares that it is Federal government policy to use all practical means to improve and coordinate Federal plans, functions, programs, and resources to achieve the preservation of important historic, cultural, and natural aspects of the national heritage. NEPA also states that the Federal government will utilize an interdisciplinary approach that will insure the integrated use of the natural and social sciences and the environmental design arts in planning and decision-making. Regulations for compliance with NEPA can be found at 36 CFR Part 1500-1508. Coast Guard policy on NEPA is contained in National Environmental Policy Act Implementing Procedures and Policy for Considering Environmental Impacts, COMDTINST M16475.1 (series). If you plan to take actions that will or may affect historic aids to navigation, contact Commandant **(CG-43)**, or your servicing MLC and or CEU, as appropriate, as early as possible for assistance.

C. Relations with User and Public Interest Groups.

   1. User Participation in Aid System Design.

      a. Although the authority granted under 14 USC 81 is discretionary, the Coast Guard's policy in regard to establishing or changing aids to navigation is to rely substantially on the recommendation of knowledgeable users. Moreover, the policy includes soliciting the opinions and recommendations of users regularly in evaluations of aids to navigation systems. Despite being an essential part of our procedures, announcements of proposed changes in Local Notices to Mariners providing "opportunities for mariners to comment" are not enough. As a continuing process to distinguish between valid needs and costly excesses, the District Commander shall promote user participation to the greatest extent practicable. Normally, this will require regular daytime and nighttime travels on waterways by Coast Guard short range aids to navigation personnel in company with users.

      b. With few exceptions, it is not possible for key district staff personnel to deal directly with all user groups on a regular basis. Field-unit Commanding Officers generally must be assigned part of this responsibility. For each discrete waterway used for commercial navigation, the District Commander should assign a field unit Commanding Officer to deal with affected user groups in a continuous critical evaluation of aids to navigation effectiveness.

c. As problems, deficiencies or excesses are identified; field units generally have several courses of action depending upon the procedures promulgated by the District Commander. Local solutions, such as correcting discrepancies or making temporary aid changes, should be considered first. Occasionally, however, changing traffic patterns or vessel types will necessitate extensive analysis and redesign. Here, the field unit and the District aids to navigation branch must coordinate solutions with other field units and users. Permanent changes in aids to navigation signals or aid systems require either District or Headquarters approval, depending on the extent of the change.

d. Changes should be presented graphically to interested parties using charts, photographs, drawings or simulation before being advertised in Local Notices to Mariners where changes are often misconceived as irrevocable. Although traditional system design procedures are useful in forming tentative solutions, the opinions of knowledgeable users shall weigh heavily in the decision-making process and be reflected in final recommendations.

e. The method and extent of user participation should evolve naturally in reaction to the initiatives of the unit to which preliminary critical evaluation responsibility has been assigned. Nominal quarterly travels on cognizant waterways with authorized user group representatives may be adequate in some cases, but on more important waterways, frequent transits, both day and night, in good visibility and bad, will be necessary. Regular participation in meetings of local navigation councils and other forums for review of aids to navigation should be perpetuated by successive Commanding Officers, reacting responsibly to and encouraging user recommendations while extending the contacts established by their predecessors or by District personnel

2. <u>Public Participation in Aids to Navigation Projects</u>.

a. User groups include pilots, masters, mates, and boat operators. Maritime interests include vessel owners, owner associations, maritime trade associations, the Coast Guard Auxiliary, the U.S. Power Squadron, the Corps of Engineers, and port authorities. Public interest groups include Federal, state and local governments, local/regional waterways management committees, and diverse citizen associations that are concerned with or that might be affected by improvements to waterways. When dealing with any group, it is important to deal only with the group's authorized representative(s) and not with an individual member whose opinion may not reflect the official position of the group.

b. Aids to navigation improvement projects generally are of little concern to public interest groups. Dredging projects quite often do not affect public interests outside the maritime city, interaction with the public normally being accomplished by the Corps of Engineers in consultation with local COTPs. There may be occasions, however, when the Coast Guard, because of its obligation for safe and efficient conduct of maritime commerce (33 USC 1221) should act as lead agency in the comprehensive analysis of appropriate changes for a waterway. For instance, analysis of waterway requirements for accommodating larger vessels, increased vessel traffic or dangerous cargoes, or corrective measures in reaction to a marine tragedy, might affect public as well as maritime interest groups. Public interests, too, should be heard as part of a formal public participation process for deciding appropriate changes to the waterway. In these cases, Federal, State and Local agencies alike would be guided by the outcome of the Coast Guard's analysis as affected through maritime and public participation.

c. Public participation initiated early in the information and opinion gathering stage of the district aids to navigation project should be viewed as an essential part of the decision-making process. Public participation must be encouraged by the Coast Guard as a means of identifying and resolving problems, particularly where movements could be perceived as damaging to some segment of the public. Although in no way a substitute for sound decision-making by the Coast Guard, enlightened participation enhances the public's assurance that all changes made are appropriate and provides a framework for cost-benefit determinations that are a necessary part of any improvement project.

D. Liaison with the U.S. Army Corps of Engineers (**USACE**).

1. General.

   a. District Commanders shall contact district and division Corps of Engineers offices from time to time, inquire as to which plans for improvement or new developments may affect Coast Guard functions, and obtain information on such plans or developments directly.

   b. The Chief of the Corps of Engineers has directed District Engineers to provide the following information directly to District Commanders:

      (1) Advice as to the authorization by Congress of a project involving changes in channel limits, breakwaters, etc., with a copy of the project documents;

      (2) The proposed operations on such projects during the next fiscal year; and

      (3) Blueprints showing the final location of the channel limits, breakwaters, etc., of the work to be undertaken.

2. <u>Cost Estimation for USACE</u>.

   a. The estimated cost of Coast Guard aids to navigation must be included in the USACE determination of the cost-benefit ratio for any river and harbor project. The total investment in the necessary aids to navigation system must include the cost of any additional personnel and supporting facilities as well as that of the aids themselves. In the absence of a favorable cost-benefit ratio, the Corps of Engineers will generally not recommend the project. In marginal situations, however, the District Commander may be asked to review the Coast Guard's estimates with a view toward reducing the overall costs and bringing the project closer to, or within, the limits of the acceptable cost-benefit ratio.

   b. The Coast Guard must not be placed in a position where a revision of the aids to navigation supporting facility requirements disguises the actual overall first cost of the project. The first responsibility of the Coast Guard, in support of river and harbor projects, is to provide accurate estimates of its part of the total Federal investment required for an adequate aid to navigation system. Recurring operating and maintenance costs should also be provided.

3. <u>Relationship of Coast Guard - Corps of Engineers Authorities</u>.

   a. The Coast Guard, when establishing aids to navigation, is exempt from the general obligation to obtain Corps of Engineers approval for the creation of an obstruction to the navigable capacity of the navigable waters of the United States (33 USC 1 and 403).

   b. Accordingly, in the interest of interagency cooperation, it may be beneficial in many cases to inform the Corps of the establishment of aids to navigation or even to discuss with them problems rising out of such an establishment. The discussions should not be on the basis that there is an obligation to obtain Corps permission prior to their establishment except, of course, if the Corps has what might best be called proprietary jurisdiction, as when aids are to be placed on Corps structures such as wing dams, breakwaters, etc.

   c. Corps of Engineers approval is required prior to the establishment of mooring buoys, floats, booms, piers, dolphins, and other devices that are not aids to navigation.

E. <u>International Association of Marine Aids to Navigation and Lighthouse Authorities (IALA).</u>

1. The Coast Guard is a member of the International Association of Marine Aids to Navigation and Lighthouse Authorities (IALA). IALA, a non-governmental organization, seeks to exchange information on the technical aspects of maritime aids to navigation and associated operating techniques. The association publishes a bi-monthly bulletin from its headquarters in Paris and sponsors a conference at four-year intervals.

2. The Coast Guard represents the US as the National member on the IALA Council and assigns personnel to the various technical committees and working groups. The St. Lawrence Seaway Corporation is an associate member and several United States companies that manufacture and service aids to navigation equipment are industrial members.

This Page Intentionally
Left Blank.

CHAPTER 12 - NAVIGATION INFORMATION

A. Navigation Information.

1. Navigation Information is the manner in which the Coast Guard keeps mariners aware of important safety information such as changes to aids to navigation, hazards, channel depths and conditions, and corrective information for charts and publications. Navigation information is primarily disseminated in the form of Local Notices to Mariners (LNM), Light List, and Broadcast Notices to Mariners (BNM).

2. The importance of accurate and timely navigation information cannot be overstated as errors could result in vessel groundings or allisions, which could lead to serious personal injuries, environmental damage and/or extensive suits/expensive torts against the Federal government.

3. The Integrated Aids to Navigation Information System (I-ATONIS) should be utilized in gathering, storing, maintaining, processing, and disseminating navigation information.

B. Local Notice to Mariners.

1. Description.

   a. The Local Notice to Mariners is the primary means for disseminating navigation safety information concerning aids to navigation, hazards to navigation, and other items of interest to mariners navigating the waters of the United States, its territories, and possessions.

   b. Each District shall issue a Local Notice to Mariners each week.

2. Responsibility and Distribution.

   a. Each District Commander is responsible for issuing a Local Notice to Mariners containing information that contributes to navigation safety and maritime security within the boundaries of the District. The District Commander has broad discretion in determining the content of safety and security information in the Local Notices to Mariners. Other important information of wider geographical application, such as changes to Traffic Separation Schemes, may also be published.

   b. Individual issues of the Local Notice to Mariners are available free of charge over the Internet from the Coast Guard Navigation Center (NAVCEN) web site (www.navcen.uscg.gov).

   c. A brief notice concerning the availability of the Local Notice to Mariners from the NAVCEN website shall be included in each issue.

d. NAVCEN's website has a list server capability. Subscriber lists shall be captured once per year by NAVCEN on June 1. The list shall be retained for a minimum of six years at the NAVCEN and then forwarded to the Federal Record Center for the remainder of the retention period (four years).

e. Prior to publishing the Local Notice to Mariners, an electronic copy of chart corrections shall be transmitted to the National Ocean Service/NOAA to conduct a quality control review.

f. Due to their historical and legal significance, Local Notice to Mariners are considered *Permanent Records*. Permanent Records are those that protect Coast Guard interests and that document the accomplishments of the Coast Guard. A complete paper copy of each Local Notice to Mariners shall be retained at the District office for a period of 10 years and then forwarded to the Federal Record Center. For complete guidance on transferring the Local Notice to Mariners to the Federal Records Center, reference the Information and Life Cycle Management Manual, COMDTINST M5212.12 (series). Disregard the authorized disposition of Local Notice to Mariners in Information and Life Cycle Management Manual, COMDTINST M5212.12 (series). Reappraisal is pending and the citation is being revised.

3. <u>Scope</u>. Local Notices to Mariners are primarily used to publish information concerning the establishment of, changes to, and deficiencies in aids to navigation. Local Notices to Mariners can also include, at the District Commander's discretion, any other information pertaining to the navigational safety or maritime security of the waterways within each Coast Guard District. This information potentially includes:

a. Reports of channel conditions, obstructions, hazards to navigation, dangers, anchorages, restricted areas, regattas, and similar items.

b. Information concerning charts covering waters within District boundaries.

c. Changes relating to aeronautical beacons for charting purposes.

d. Establishment, discontinuance, or relocation of any Coast Guard station with search and rescue capabilities as listed in Coast Pilots.

e. Oil, gas, mineral, and related industry information including:

(1) The establishment or removal of drill rigs and vessels.

(2) The proposed construction and establishment of artificial islands, fixed structures, and sub-sea installations.

f. Information on bridges such as:

(1) Public Notices concerning proposed construction of new bridges or modifications to existing bridges. The entire Public Notice shall not be published in the Local Notices to Mariners. A brief summary of the notice and where a copy can be obtained shall be included.

(2) Available clearance after construction or when a modification is actually completed. With few exceptions, a chart correction indicating these changes should also be published. Coordination with NOAA may be necessary to obtain the proper wording and charted clearances.

(3) Changes in clearances, either permanent or temporary, of existing bridges. As stated above, with few exceptions, a chart correction indicating these changes should also be published. Coordination with NOAA may be necessary to obtain the proper wording and charted clearances.

(4) Proposed changes in drawbridge operations or regulations.

(5) Deviations from published drawbridge regulations.

(6) Time and place of public hearings.

4. Special Local Notice to Mariners.

a. The Special Local Notice to Mariners cannot be generated by I-ATONIS. However, a Special Local Notice to Mariners should be compiled on an annual basis outside the I-ATONIS application. Once compiled, the Special Local Notice to Mariners should be posted on the NAVCEN website. The Special Local Notice to Mariners includes the following information:

(1) Selected paragraphs similar in scope to those appearing in National Geospatial-Intelligence Agency (NGA) Notice to Mariners No. 1.

(2) A listing of chart sales agents, particulars on how to report discrepancies in aids to navigation, the phone numbers and the assigned area of aids to navigation units, etc.

(3) A general warning concerning reliance upon aids to navigation. The general warning shall be:

CAUTION TO BE USED IN RELIANCE UPON AIDS TO NAVIGATION.

THE AIDS TO NAVIGATION DEPICTED ON CHARTS COMPRISE A SYSTEM OF FIXED AND FLOATING AIDS TO NAVIGATION WITH VARYING DEGREES OF RELIABILITY. PRUDENT MARINERS WILL NOT RELY SOLELY ON ANY SINGLE AID TO NAVIGATION, PARTICULARLY A FLOATING AID TO NAVIGATION. WITH RESPECT TO BUOYS, THE BUOY SYMBOL IS USED TO INDICATE THE APPROXIMATE POSITION OF THE BUOY BODY AND THE SINKER WHICH SECURES THE BUOY TO THE SEABED. THE APPROXIMATE POSITION IS USED BECAUSE OF THE PRACTICAL LIMITATIONS IN POSITIONING AND MAINTAINING BUOYS AND THEIR SINKERS IN PRECISE GEOGRAPHICAL LOCATIONS. THESE LIMITATIONS INCLUDE, BUT ARE NOT LIMITED TO, INHERENT IMPRECISIONS IN POSITION FIXING METHODS, PREVAILING ATMOSPHERIC AND SEA CONDITIONS, SLOPE OF AND THE MATERIAL MAKING UP THE SEABED, THE FACT THAT BUOYS ARE MOORED TO SINKERS BY VARYING LENGTH OF CHAIN, AND THE FACT THAT THE BUOY BODY AND/OR SINKER POSITIONS ARE NOT UNDER CONTINUOUS SURVEILLANCE, BUT ARE NORMALLY CHECKED ONLY DURING PERIODIC MAINTENANCE VISITS WHICH OFTEN OCCUR MORE THAN A YEAR APART. DUE TO THE FORCES OF NATURE, THE POSITION OF THE BUOY BODY CAN BE EXPECTED TO SHIFT INSIDE AND OUTSIDE THE CHARTED SYMBOL. THE MARINER IS ALSO CAUTIONED THAT BUOYS MAY BE EXTINGUISHED OR SOUND SIGNALS MAY NOT FUNCTION AS THE RESULT OF ICE, RUNNING ICE, OR OTHER NATURAL CAUSES, COLLISIONS, OR OTHER ACCIDENTS. FOR THE FOREGOING REASONS, A PRUDENT MARINER MUST NOT RELY COMPLETELY UPON THE POSITION OR OPERATION OF FLOATING AIDS TO NAVIGATION, BUT WILL ALSO UTILIZE BEARINGS FROM FIXED OBJECTS AND AIDS TO NAVIGATION ON SHORE. FURTHER, A VESSEL ATTEMPTING TO PASS CLOSE ABOARD ALWAYS RISKS COLLISION WITH A YAWING BUOY OR WITH THE OBSTRUCTION THAT THE BUOY MARKS.

b. Generally, this special notice shall be the first Local Notice to Mariners of each new year. Those Districts having a regular and a seasonal/summer boating season may delay publishing the Special Local Notice to Mariners until the start of the boating season.

c. Each District shall mail an electronic copy of the Special Local Notice to each of the other Districts.

C. Format of the Local Notice to Mariners.

1. General.

a. The Coast Guard's Integrated Aids to Navigation Information System (I-ATONIS) shall be used to generate the Local Notice to Mariners.

b. The I-ATONIS system-generated cutoff date for **Light List** information being included in each LNM is midnight Tuesday (Wednesday AM). **LNMs** shall be generated **and dated each Wednesday. Districts shall submit LNM to NAVCEN no later than 1800 (local district time) every Wednesday.**

c. Each notice shall be numbered consecutively during the calendar year.

d. A notice stating that questions or inquiries about the Local Notice to Mariners should be directed to the **District (dpw)** shall be included on the first page.

e. Pages shall be numbered "Page 1 of 6", etc., at the bottom of each page. Enclosures may be numbered separately.

f. Information in the notice shall be arranged in the same geographical sequence as the Light Lists with the exception of the Chart Corrections. This shall apply equally to channel reports, bridges, notice of regattas, reports of obstructions, designation of danger areas, etc.

g. Sketches or reproductions of portions of charts on which information concerning changes in aids to navigation are indicated may be included in Local Notices to Mariners when they will assist the mariner in interpreting the data more easily. Reproduced chart portions must be annotated with the statement "NOT TO BE USED FOR NAVIGATION." They may be prepared and included for, but not limited to, the following:

   (1) When aids to navigation are relocated to facilitate dredging operations.

   (2) When a number of changes are made in a locality at the same time.

2. Abbreviations.

   a. The following standard abbreviations will be used in the Local Notice to Mariners. These abbreviations are consistent with agreements between National Ocean Service (NOS), National Geospatial-Intelligence Agency (NGA), and standards established by the International Hydrographic Organization (IHO) and International Association of Marine Aids to Navigation and Lighthouse Authorities (IALA).

   b. All Local Notice to Mariners items concerning oceanographic data buoys (ODAS)/ (NOAA weather buoys) shall include the notation (ODAS) in the buoy name. The abbreviation (SPM) shall be included in all items concerning lighted single point mooring buoys used by tankers.

EXAMPLES:

Al - Alternating	MHz - Megahertz
bl - blast	Mo - Morse Code
bu - blue	Oc - Occulting
C - Canadian	ODAS - Anchored Oceanographic Data Buoy
Dbn - Daybeacon	Q - Quick
ec - eclipse	R - Red
ev - every	RACON - Radar Transponder Beacon
F - Fixed	Ra ref - Radar reflector
fl - flash	s - seconds
Fl - Flashing	si - silent
G - Green	SPM - Single Point Mooring Buoy
I - Interrupted	SS - Sound Signal
Iso - Isophase	W - White
kHz - Kilohertz	Y - Yellow
Lt - Light	

3. Sequence.

  a. The following sequence of sections shall be used in the Local Notice to Mariners.

   (I)   Special Notices
   (II)   Discrepancies - Discrepancies Corrected
   (III)   Temporary Changes - Temporary Changes Corrected
   (IV)   Chart Corrections
   (V)   Advance Notices
   (VI)   Proposed Changes
   (VII)   General
   (VIII)   Light List Corrections
   Additional Enclosures, including Publication Corrections

  b. Questions on the format should be directed to Commandant **(CG-54131)** or NAVCEN. Headquarters, NAVCEN, and District staffs shall work closely together on this matter.

4. Accuracy.

  a. Accuracy is of prime importance in the positioning of an aid to navigation and the reporting of that position.

   (1) A complete set of charts (digital or paper) for a District's area of responsibility shall be maintained. These charts shall be kept up-to-date from information supplied by units doing the aid to navigation work.

   (2) Prior to advertising a new position, positioning results shall be reviewed by district staffs in accordance with Chapter 4 of Aids to Navigation Manual – Positioning, COMDTINST M16500.1 (series). Coordination between the positioning staff and the marine information staff is essential.

b. Before a notice is issued, all information shall be checked and proofread by someone other than the person preparing it initially.

c. It is imperative that the position of new fixed structures be determined to an accuracy required by its accuracy standard (See section 5.C.1 of Aids to Navigation Manual – Positioning, COMDTINST M16500.1 (series)). When a Local Notice to Mariners is issued for a High Level of Accuracy aid as outlined in the Aids to Navigation Manual – Positioning before a post-construction survey can be completed, the notice shall be based on the best information provided by the reporting unit and shall include "position approximate (PA)." A subsequent notice shall be issued after the survey indicating the accurate position and the PA removed.

d. Chart correction positions shall be listed using degrees, minutes, and seconds to three decimal places (thousandths).

e. The assigned position of an aid to navigation shall be the position specified on the CG-3213 and advertised in the Local Notice to Mariners. Any time an aid to navigation is permanently relocated, the new assigned position must be advertised, regardless of how minor (small) the change.

f. Positions shall be listed in the Light List corrections using degrees, minutes, and seconds to three decimal places (thousands).

g. Any questions that may arise concerning entries or the format of the Local Notice to Mariners shall be referred to NAVCEN or Commandant **(CG-54131)** prior to publication.

5. <u>Purpose and Content of Each Section</u>.

    a. <u>Special Notices</u>.

        (1) The purpose of the Special Notices section is to allow the District the latitude of promulgating information of a special nature that affects the marine environment.

        (2) In this section, reference to Armed Forces gunnery exercises, pyrotechnics drills, night photography, changes in regulations pertaining to pilotage, and other operations affecting marine traffic can be announced.

        (3) The format of the Special Notices should be edited to provide simple, to-the-point, information.

(4) If the information is of a specific nature where geographic positions are required, start the paragraph with the state (island, territory), followed by general location, (offshore, bay, etc.), then the specific location (river, channel), followed by the message. These geographic references immediately alert the user to the general location of the action being taken. If additional positioning information is required for charting purposes, the chart number for the largest scale chart of the area shall be added for ready reference. A chart correction may also be required.

b. <u>Discrepancies - Discrepancies Corrected</u>. This section contains a tabulation of all discrepancies to aids to navigation and those which have been corrected from the last published list. A discrepancy is any change in the status of an aid to navigation that is different than what is charted and/or published in the Light List. Where a corrected discrepancy affects information published on the charts or in the Light List, an appropriate correction must be written.

(1) The BNM reference column under Discrepancies is to be used to list the first time the discrepancy is announced in a BNM. The LNM Start (LNM St) column is used to indicate when the discrepancy was first advertised in the LNM. The LNM End (LNM End) column is not used.

(2) The BNM reference column under Discrepancies Corrected is to be used to list the BNM in which the correction was announced. The LNM Start (LNM St) column is used to indicate when the discrepancy was first advertised in the LNM. The LNM End (LNM End) column is used to indicate the LNM in which the correction was announced.

(3) Only the largest scale chart on which the discrepancy appears on shall be listed.

(4) An aid that is damaged should not be listed as destroyed unless the aid is completely destroyed or is leaning at an angle greater than 45 degrees. An aid that can be repaired without replacing the structure should not be listed as destroyed.

(5) Range lights may create unique circumstances because a structure may serve as a support for two different aid functions. Perhaps the most common example is a range structure that displays an omnidirectional light shown from the range lantern or a separate lantern. If a range light is arranged so that it produces, in addition to the beam on the channel axis, an all-around light of lower intensity, care must be taken when advertising a discrepancy. If the lantern displaying the beam on the channel axis is extinguished, the range should be advertised as operating at reduced intensity on rangeline. If the omnidirectional light is extinguished, the light should be advertised as visible on rangeline only.

EXAMPLES:
DISCREPANCIES

LLNR	Aid Name	Status	Chart No	BNM Ref.	LNM St	LNM End
165	Southwest Pass Light	RACON INOP	11361	1124-03	02-04	
175	Cat Island Pass LWB CI	EXTINGUISHED	11357	51-04	03-04	

LLNR	Aid Name	Status	Chart No	BNM Ref.	LNM St	LNM End
28380	Brownsville Channel Range Front Light	REDUCED INT ON RANGELINE	11123	58-04	04-04	
24055	Baytown Bend Range Front Light	VISIBLE ON RANGELINE ONLY	11328	77-04	05-04	

DISCREPANCIES CORRECTED

LLNR	Aid Name	Status	Chart No	BNM Ref.	LNM St	LNM End
165	Southwest Pass Light	WATCHING PROPERLY	11361	48-04	02-04	06-04
175	Cat Island Pass LWB CI	WATCHING PROPERLY	11357	68-04	03-04	06-04
28380	Brownsville Channel Range Front Light	WATCHING PROPERLY	11123	77-04	04-04	06-04
24055	Baytown Bend Range Front Light	WATCHING PROPERLY	11328	77-04	05-04	06-04

    c. <u>Temporary Changes - Temporary Changes Corrected</u>. This section contains a tabulation of all temporary changes to aids to navigation and those corrected since the last published list. Where aids to navigation are temporarily relocated for dredging, a temporary correction shall be listed in Section IV giving the relocated positions. Where a corrected temporary change affects information published on the charts or in the Light List, an appropriate correction must be written.

    (1) The BNM reference column under Temporary Changes is to be used to list the first time the discrepancy is announced in a BNM. The LNM Start (LNM St) column is used to indicate when the Temporary Change was first advertised in the LNM. The LNM End (LNM End) column is not used.

    (2) The BNM reference column under Temporary Changes Corrected is to be used to list the BNM announcing the correction to the temporary change. The LNM Start (LNM St) column is used to indicate when the temporary change was first advertised in the LNM. The LNM End (LNM End) column is used to indicate the LNM in which the temporary change correction was announced.

    (3) Only the largest scale chart the temporary change appears on shall be listed.

EXAMPLES:
TEMPORARY CHANGES

LLNR	Aid Name	Status	Chart No	BNM Ref.	LNM St	LNM End
4330	Lemon Bay Channel Buoy 19	RELOCATED FOR DREDGING	11470	25-04	2-04	

TEMPORARY CHANGES CORRECTED

LLNR	Aid Name	Status	Chart No	BNM Ref.	LNM St	LNM End
4330	Lemon Bay Channel Buoy 19	RESET ON STATION	11470	152-04	2-04	06-04

d. Chart Corrections.

(1) This section lists all new establishments, deletions, and corrections to federally and privately maintained aids to navigation, as well as chart corrections provided by the National Ocean Service (NOS) and/or the Army Corps of Engineers. Additionally, information received on wrecks and other hazards to navigation as well as reports received from NOS survey vessels shall be listed.

(2) This section is the heart of the Local Notice to Mariners. The information published here is used by mariners to correct their charts, and by the NOS and National Geospatial-Intelligence Agency (NGA) to initiate chart revisions and Coast Pilot corrections. Accuracy is imperative.

(3) An explanation of the format of the Chart Correction Section shall be listed.

EXAMPLE:

This section contains corrections to federally and privately maintained aids to navigation, as well as NOS chart corrections. This section contains corrective action affecting chart(s). Corrections appear numerically by chart number and pertain to that chart only. It is up to the mariner to decide what chart(s) are to be corrected. The following example explains the individual elements of a typical correction.

Chart Number	Chart Edition	Edition Date	Last Local Notice to Mariners	Horizontal Datum Reference	Source of Correction	Current Local Notice to Mariners
|	|	|	|	|	|	|
12200	19th Ed.	08-APR-04	Last LNM: 30/04	NAD 83		35/04

Chart Title: **CHESAPEAKE BAY - CHESAPEAKE CHANNEL**
   Main Panel

CGD05

(Temp)	ADD	Chesapeake Channel Lt 1 Fl G 4 45ft 8M	36-57-57.481N 075-59-30.624W
	|	|	|
	Corrective Action	Object of Corrective Action	Position

(Temp) indicates the chart correction action is temporary in nature. Courses and bearings are given in degrees clockwise from 000 true. Bearings of light sectors are toward the light from seaward. The nominal range of lights is expressed in nautical miles (M), except in the Ninth Coast Guard District where statute miles are used.

The letter (M) immediately following the chart number indicates the correction should be applied to the metric side of the chart only.

(4) Chart corrections shall be listed in the format described above. Five "Corrective Action Verbs" shall be used. They are: Delete, Relocate, Substitute, Change and Add. These corrective action verbs will cover all situations encountered. (See examples.)

(a) The chart number in ascending order, the edition and date of chart, the last Local Notice to Mariners in the district to affect the chart, the source of the correction, and the Local Notice to Mariners the correction appears in shall be listed.

(b) (Temp) shall be listed below the chart number for temporary corrections. Temporary and permanent corrections shall not be listed together under the same correction.

(c) The official title of the NOAA chart, as well as the Panel/KAPP number shall be listed.

(5) The five corrective action verbs shall be listed in the following order.

(a) <u>Delete</u> shall be used when deleting (discontinuing) an aid or when deleting an object from the chart.

EXAMPLES:

13214	12th Ed.	01-JUN-02	Last LNM: 13/03	NAD 83		12/04

Chart Title: **LONG ISLAND SOUND - MILFORD HARBOR**
Main Panel

CGD01
DELETE   Milford Harbor Buoy 12   28-05-08.409N 117-06-35.156W

12245	10th Ed.	10-JUL-02	Last LNM: 23/03	NAD 83		9/04

Chart Title: **HAMPTON ROADS - WILLOUGHBY BAY**
Main Panel

CGD05
DELETE   Willoughby Bay Buoys
1   36-27-49.145N 077-56-47.566W
3   36-27-49.652N 077-56-47.678W
6   36-27-49.356N 077-56-47.677W

12237	14th Ed.	22-AUG-02	Last LNM: 6/04	NAD 83		11/04

Chart Title: **RAPPAHANNOCK RIVER**
Main Panel

CGD05
DELETE   BELL from Rappahannock River Bell Buoy 1   37-34-34.312N 076-11-56.587W

(b) <u>Relocate</u>. Use the verb "Relocate" when something is physically moved. The object being relocated is followed by the former position or "Close", the direction, and the preposition "to." "Close" may be used in lieu of the former position. All changes to the assigned position must be advertised as a chart correction.

EXAMPLE:

11358	18th Ed.	14-FEB-02	Last LNM: 52/03	NAD 83		20/04

Chart Title: **MIAMI HARBOR - SOUTH CHANNEL**
Main Panel

CGD07
RELOCATE   South Channel Buoy 7 from 25-45-36.222N 080-11-19.123W to   25-45-35.432N 080-11-19.456W

(c) <u>Substitute</u>. Use the verb "Substitute" when replacing one item for another. This verb will probably be the least used of the five.

EXAMPLES:

13214	21st Ed.	01-DEC-02	Last LNM: 15/03	NAD 83		35/04

Chart Title: **FISHER ISLAND SOUND - SILVER EEL POND**
Main Panel

CGD01
SUBSTITUTE   Legend "Shoaling Rep 2004" for depth 10 feet in   41-15-49.567N 072-01-58.086W

14843	22nd Ed.	23-JAN-03	LAST LNM: 30/04	NAD 83		35/04

Chart Title: **LAKE ERIE-HURON HARBOR**
Main Panel

CGD09
SUBSTITUTE   Wreck for dangerous wreck in   41-24-16.545N 082-32-38.278W

(d) <u>Change</u> shall be used when something is changed such as the height, color, or nominal range of a light.

EXAMPLES:

13003	38th Ed.	22-FEB-02	Last LNM: 35/03	NAD 83	50/03

Chart Title: **MA – SEACOAST**
    Main Panel

              CGD01

        CHANGE   NOAA Buoy 11003 to yellow, Fl (3) R 20s   56-00-00.023N 148-00-00.000W

18765	17th Ed.	16-MAR-02	Last LNM: 25/03	NAD 83	5/04

Chart Title: **MISSION BAY - MARINERS BASIN**
    Main Panel

              CGD11

        CHANGE   Anchorage Buoys to yellow, Fl Y 4s
                          MB   47-57-30.908N 122-34-29.458W
                          MC   47-55-40.356N 122-30-30.746W

18502	31st Ed.	18-APR-02	Last LNM: 46/02	NAD 83	12/03

Chart Title: **GRAYS HARBOR - WESTHAVEN COVE**
    Main Panel

              CGD13
        CHANGE   Westhaven Cove Buoy 9 to green   38-04-02.225N 122-15-18.478W

12214	29th Ed.	19-MAY-02	Last LNM: 46/03	NAD 83	8/04

Chart Title: **CAPE MAY TO FENWICK ISLAND**
    Main Panel

              CGD05
        CHANGE   Lewes Bay Breakwater LT 6 to Fl R 6s   46-57-28.212N 139-37-48.223W

(e) <u>Add</u> shall be used when adding (establishing) an aid or when adding an object to the chart.

EXAMPLES:

16660	22nd Ed.	22-SEP-02	Last LNM: 28/03	NAD 83	12/04

Chart Title: **COOK INLET - FIRE ISLAND**
    Main Panel

              CGD17
       Add   Race Point Range Front Light, Iso W 6s 176ft   61-09-56.623N 150-13-28.976W
                      Race Point Range Rear Light, F W 252ft   61-10-13.932N 150-12-31.767W
                      Range line extending in a 238° degree direction from
above the rear light, dashed for 2 miles, thence
solid for two miles.

19347	12th Ed.	13-OCT-02	Last LNM: 21/03	WGS 84	11/04

Chart Title: **KALOHI CHANNEL**
    Main Panel

              CGD14
       Add   Visible wreck "Wailua"   32-46-40.812N 118-34-56.947W

11372	13th Ed.	24-NOV-02	Last LNM: 26/03	NAD 83	3/04

Chart Title: **DOG KEYS PASS TO WAVELAND**
    Main Panel

              CGD08
       Add   Square Handkerchief Shoal Lighted Buoy SH
                     Green and Red bands (topmost band green), Fl (2+1) G 6s   29-57-13.721N 80-37-47.674W

12205	17th Ed.	16-DEC-02	Last LNM: 23/03	NAD 83	51/03

Chart Title: **MANTEO - SHALLOWBAG BAY**
    Main Panel

CGD05

Add   Manteo Channel Lighted Anchorage Buoys, yellow
Fl Y 4s (Priv maint)
     A   31-08-08.498N 73-38-29.535W
     B   31-09-00.389N 73-38-29.253W

18645	12th Ed.	14-JAN-03	Last LNM: 32/03	NAD 83	50/03

Chart Title: **SAN FRANCISCO BAY ENT. - POINT BONITA**
    Main Panel

CGD11

Add   Point Bonita Light, Fl 4s 265ft 24M Horn, RACON F (..-.)   33-28-48.467N 77-58-31.848W

12200	19th Ed.	28-FEB-03	Last LNM: 40/03	NAD 83	15/04

Chart Title: **CHESAPEAKE BAY - CHESAPEAKE CHANNEL**
    Main Panel

CGD05

ADD   Chesapeake Channel Buoy 2, Red Nun   34-24-57.481N 075-03-30.624W

12237	14th Ed.	23-MAR-03	Last LNM: 45/03	NAD 83	11/03

Chart Title: **RAPPAHANNOCK RIVER**
    Main Panel

CGD05

ADD   Rappahannock River Flats Daybeacon 19, SG   30-12-34.312N 076-34-56.587W

(f) <u>Names</u>. The proper name of the aid to navigation (i.e., Jones Point Light 10) shall be listed with each correction.

(g) <u>Frequently Relocated Aids</u>. When a chart note indicates aids are not charted due to frequent relocation, districts should still publish relocation information for the mariner.

(h) The following terms shall always appear within parenthesis: (PA), (Priv maint), (Navy maint).

(i) The color of the light shall always be listed, even if the light is white. Do not use Fl 4s to describe Fl W 4s.

(j) When advertising any chart correction, all information concerning any particular item will be published without regard to the scale of chart. It is up to the mariner to determine how much information is placed on the chart.

EXAMPLES: *(Note: The following examples change only the light characteristic.)*

Incorrect:

12214	29th Ed.	20-APR-03	Last LNM: 38/03	NAD 83	18/04

Chart Title: **CAPE MAY TO FENWICK ISLAND**
    Main Panel

CGD05

CHANGE   Lewes Bay Breakwater LT 6 to Fl R 6s   46-57-28.267N 139-37-48.366W

Correct:

12214	29th Ed.	20-APR-03	Last LNM: 38/03	NAD 83	18/04

Chart Title: **CAPE MAY TO FENWICK ISLAND**
    Main Panel

CGD05

CHANGE   Lewes Bay Breakwater LT 6 to Fl R 6s 16FT 4M   46-57-28.267N 139-37-48.366W

(k) <u>Wrecks.</u> A wreck is always written as a permanent notice, even though source material may indicate the wreck is temporary. When wrecks are reported to districts, a correction shall be added along with the name of the wrecked vessel, if known. If an aid to navigation is placed to mark the wreck, the chart correction should indicate whether the aid is permanent or temporary. The wreck will remain on the chart unless a report is received that the wreck has been salvaged. If the wreck is salvaged, then a correction shall be made to delete the wreck. If a wreck is searched for and not found, a correction shall be issued to add the designation (PA) to the previously reported wreck. The legends "ED" (existence doubtful) or "PD" (position doubtful) shall not be used. Never use the expression "non-dangerous wreck". Use either "wreck," "visible wreck," or "dangerous wreck."

EXAMPLES:

11340	12th Ed.	19-MAY-03	Last LNM: 28/03	NAD 83	30/03

Chart Title: **GALVESTON ENT. CHANNEL**
Main Panel

			CGD08
ADD	Dangerous wreck "Barbara D"		32-46-40.125N 118-34-56.236W

11340	12th Ed.	19-MAY-03	Last LNM: 30/03	NAD 83	12/04

Chart Title: **GALVESTON ENT. CHANNEL**
Main Panel

			CGD08
CHANGE	Dangerous wreck "Barbara D" to dangerous wreck (PA)		32-46-40.125N 118-34-56.236W

11340	12th Ed.	19-MAY-03	Last LNM: 12/04	NAD 83	13/04

Chart Title: **GALVESTON ENT. CHANNEL**
Main Panel

			CGD08
DELETE	Dangerous wreck "Barbara D" (PA)		32-46-40.125N 118-34-56.236W

(l) <u>Shoals, Rocks, and Piles.</u> Information on shoals, rocks, and piles shall be reported as received. If a report is received in March 2004 that there is shoaling in a particular area, the district shall publish the correction as "Shoaling Rep Mar 2004", and give the geographic position of the shoal. Rocks and piles should be handled in the same manner. If an aid to navigation is placed to mark the hazard, the chart correction should indicate whether the aid is permanent or temporary.

EXAMPLES:

14860	28th Ed.	16-AUG-03	Last LNM: 31/03	NAD 83	20/04

Chart Title: **STRAITS OF MACKINAW - DETOUR REEF**
Main Panel

			CGD09
Add	Legend - Rocks Rep March 2004		45-57-00.387N 083-54-20.478W
Add	Detour Reef Lighted Buoy WR, Red, Q R		45-57-00.687N 083-54-20.784W

13214	21st Ed.	26-SEP-03	Last LNM: 49/03	NAD 83	15/04

Chart Title: **FISHER ISLAND SOUND - SILVER EEL POND**
Main Panel

			CGD01
Add	Legend - Shoaling to 2 feet Rep Feb 2004		41-15-49.525N 072-01-58.098W

(m) Research buoys. Information on research buoys established for the collection of data and that are temporary in nature should be listed as a Temporary chart correction.

EXAMPLE:

11340	50th Ed.	14-OCT-03	Last LNM: 16/03	NAD 83	40/03

Chart Title: **GULF OF MEXICO**
  Main Panel

CGD08

(Temp)	ADD	LSU Research buoys, yellow, Fl Y 4s	
		A	27-10-01.011N 092-15-02.077W
		B	27-10-03.087N 092-15-04.044W

(n) NOAA survey vessel information. Information received from NOAA survey vessels will be published as received from the NOAA vessel. The legend "reported" will not be used. The source to be listed will be the name of the vessel. No attempt should be made to convert feet to fathoms or vise versa. If the depths are given in fathoms and tenths then those depths shall be used in the LNM.

EXAMPLE:

16476	8th Ed.	13-NOV-03	Last LNM: 24/03	NAD 83	51/03

Chart Title: **ALEUTIAN ISLANDS - ADAK ISLAND**
  Main Panel

NOAA RAINIER

Add	Depths	
	2 fathoms	51-52-16.011N 176-36-23.177W
	1.5 fathoms	51-52-02.925N 176-36-43.299W
	0.5 fathom	51-52-45.736N 176-36-03.355W

(o) Receipt of Positions for Aids to Navigation (via Chart Corrections) from NOS.

    i. Occasionally, NOAA survey vessels or hydrographic field parties will survey the positions of aids to navigation while conducting the hydrographic survey. These positions may be reported directly to the District or they may be reported to NOS. NOS may elect to issue a chart correction.

    ii. If a chart correction containing an updated position for a Federal fixed aid is received, the District shall publish the correction. NOS shall be listed as the source of the chart correction and will be requested to provide documentation, such as the date of survey, for the aid file. NMEA strings are not required for fixed aids. NOS will not provide updates for Federal floating aids.

    iii. If the District has a position on file for a Federal fixed aid that is more recent than the date of the NOAA survey, notify NOS of this fact and do not issue a chart correction. If the aid was never relocated, but the Coast Guard and NOS positions do not agree, the differences need to be resolved and then issue the chart correction as necessary. If the aid was

relocated, use the most recent position and publish a correction if necessary.

iv. **If chart corrections containing updated positions for fixed or floating private aids to navigation are received for NOS, publish the updates and notify the owner of the updated position. The owner will then be required to update the private aids permit information at the next verification cycle as defined in 5.B.3 of COMDTINST M16500-7A). NOAA will be requested to provide documentation, such as the date of survey, for the aid file.**

(p) When a Temporary Notice is made permanent, repeat the Temporary Notice without the identification "(Temp)" and add the annotation (Supersedes LNM/Year) in I-ATONIS in the Chart Correction Remarks screen.

EXAMPLES:

12220	33rd Ed	28-DEC-03	Last LNM: 2/04	NAD 83	16/04

Chart Title: **SEACOAST - CAPE HENRY**
   Main Panel

   CGD05

(Temp)	DELETE	Cape Henry Light Sound Signal	36-55-34.409N 076-00-27.367W

12220	33rd Ed	28-DEC-03	Last LNM: 16/04	NAD 83	19/04

Chart Title: **SEACOAST - CAPE HENRY**
   Main Panel

   CGD05

	DELETE	Cape Henry Light Sound Signal (Supersedes 16/04)	36-55-34.409N 076-00-27.367W

(q) <u>Correcting an error</u>. When previously written notices contained erroneous information, write a subsequent notice using the same subject matter and corrected information, and include the annotation (Supersedes LNM/Year) in the I-ATONIS in the Chart Correction Remarks screen.

EXAMPLES:

12301	15th Ed.	13-JAN-04	Last LNM: 37/03	NAD 83	22/04

Chart Title: **SEACOAST - HEREFORD INLET**
   Main Panel

   CGD01

	ADD	Hereford Inlet Lighted Bell Buoy 8, Red, Fl R 6s	38-44-52.409N 073-05-26.377W

12301	15th Ed.	13-JAN-04	Last LNM: 22/04	NAD 83	24/04

Chart Title: **SEACOAST - HEREFORD INLET**
   Main Panel

   CGD01

	ADD	Hereford Inlet Lighted Bell Buoy 8, Red, Fl R 6s (Supersedes 22/04)	39-44-52.409N 073-05-26.377W

(r) Only charts which contain a correction need to be listed, i.e., when correcting an aid to navigation on an inland waterway, the small scale coastal chart need not be listed unless that inland aid to navigation appears on the coastal chart.

(s) <u>Oil drilling platforms</u>. Platforms should be listed according to the type of rig. Jack-up rigs (JU) are usually temporary in nature; however, they leave a cap or covered well head below the surface. If the well head is left on the bottom, a chart correction shall be made.

EXAMPLES:

11340	50th Ed.	22-FEB-04	Last LNM: 35/03	NAD 83	43/03

Chart Title: **GULF OF MEXICO**
    Main Panel

CGD08

(Temp)	ADD	Drilling platform (JU) "EXXON 123-321"	27-10-00.023N 092-15-00.023W

11340	50th Ed.	22-FEB-04	Last LNM: 43/03	NAD 83	48/03

Chart Title: **GULF OF MEXICO**
    Main Panel

CGD08

DELETE	Drilling platform (JU) "EXXON 123-321" (Supersedes 43/03)	27-10-00.023N 092-15-00.023W
ADD	Well and legend "Covered 10 fms"	27-10-00.023N 092-15-00.023W

(t) <u>Chartlets</u>. Chartlets are supplied by NOS and shall be listed as a chart correction. NOS provides an electronic file for each chartlet. Chartlets should be "enclosed" in the LNM via a hyperlink to the electronic file.

EXAMPLE:

18657	12th ed.	15-MAR-04	Last LNM: 6/03	NAD 83	15/04

Chart Title: **CARQUINEZ STRAIT**
    Main Panel

NOS Silver Spring, MD

ADD	Chartlet, reflecting changes in channel limits, aids to navigation, and hydrography (http://chartlet.nos.sample.gov)	38-03-00.987N 122-05-30.345W

(u) <u>Last LNM</u>. The reference Last LNM, indicating the last LNM a chart correction was issued for a particular chart shall be added.

(v) <u>Current LNM number</u>. The current LNM number shall be listed with each chart correction and should agree with the LNM number that the correction is appearing.

(w) <u>Rip rap</u>. If a light that had rip rap around its structure is discontinued, and the rip rap remains, an obstruction shall be added to the chart.

EXAMPLE:

12214	29th Ed.	21-APR-03	Last LNM: 38/03	NAD 83	18/04

Chart Title: **CAPE MAY TO FENWICK ISLAND**
    Main Panel

CGD05

DELETE	Lewes Bay Channel LT 10	46-57-28.452N 139-37-48.378W
ADD	Submerged Obstruction "Rocks"	46-57-28.442N 139-37-48.396W

(x) <u>Chart/Light List correction</u>. If a change to an aid to navigation affects the chart and the Light List, the corrections shall appear in the same LNM.

(y) <u>RACON characteristic</u>. If adding or changing the Morse code characteristic of a racon, the characteristic, as well as the letter character, shall be listed.

EXAMPLE:

11468	12th Ed.	29-APR-03	Last LNM: 32/03	NAD 83	39/03

Chart Title: **MIAMI HARBOR ENT**
Main Panel

			CGD07
ADD	Racon M (- -) to Miami Entrance Channel Lighted Horn Buoy M		33-28-48.363N 077-58-31.145W

(z) <u>Seasonal corrections</u>. When establishing or discontinuing an aid to navigation that is seasonal, the assigned position of the aid to navigation shall be used. The annotation (Seasonal) should be added to I-ATONIS in the Chart Correction Remarks screen.

EXAMPLES:

18433	4th Ed.	21-JAN-03	Last LNM: 48/03	NAD 83	19/04

Chart Title: **PUGET SOUND - FRIDAY HARBOR**
Main Panel

			CGD13
ADD	Friday Harbor Channel Lighted Buoy 2, Fl R 2.5s (Seasonal)		54-08-44.466N 165-43-34.032W

14860	28th Ed.	13-FEB-03	Last LNM: 43/03	NAD 83	45/03

Chart Title: **STRAITS OF MACKINAW - DETOUR REEF**
Main Panel

			CGD09
DELETE	DeTour Reef Light Racon (Seasonal)		45-57-00.434N 083-54-02.044W

(aa) <u>Federal Register changes</u>. Changes published in the Federal Register for COLREGS, anchorage areas, safety fairways, etc., shall be published as a chart correction. The correction should be added to I-ATONIS in the Chart Correction Remarks screen. If multiple geographic positions are involved, the final LNM should be saved as a .RTF file and the correction reformatted manually.

EXAMPLE:

13229	22th Ed.	11-MAR-03	Last LNM: 02/04	NAD 83	16/04

Chart Title: **SOUTH COAST OF CAPE COD AND BUZZARDS BAY**
Main Panel

		(FR 49123, 1/4/04)
ADD	Magenta lines joining and label: Anchorage Area 110.145	41-38-11.055N 070-54-39.088W
		41-38-13.088N 070-54-28.078W
		41-38-14.054N 070-54-40.023W
		41-38-19.043N 070-54-25.045W

(bb) Each chart a correction appears on must be listed separately. However, more than one correction may be listed under a chart.

EXAMPLES:

| 13214 | 21st Ed. | 28-MAY-03 | Last LNM: 30/03 | NAD 83 | 5/04 |

Chart Title: **FISHER ISLAND SOUND - SILVER EEL POND**
    Main Panel

		CGD01
SUBSTITUTE	Legend "Shoaling Rep 2004" for depth 10 feet in	41-15-49.565N 072-01-58.022W
DELETE	Silver Eel Pond Light 2	41-16-24.456N 072-01-51.033W
ADD	Silver Eel Daybeacon 8, TR	41-16-24.134N 072-01-58.244W

| 13216 | 23rd Ed. | 22-JUN-03 | Last LNM: 42/03 | NAD 83 | 5/04 |

Chart Title: **FISHER ISLAND SOUND - SILVER EEL POND**
    Main Panel

		CGD01
SUBSTITUTE	Legend "Shoaling Rep 2004" for depth 10 feet in	41-15-49.565N 072-01-58.022W

(cc) Also incorporated in this section are the chart corrections received from NOAA. These chart corrections will be uploaded into I-ATONIS directly by NOAA. The correction should be added to I-ATONIS in the Chart Correction Remarks screen. If multiple geographic positions are involved, the final LNM should be saved as a .RTF file and the correction reformatted manually.

EXAMPLE:

| 13229 | 22nd Ed. | 4-JUL-03 | Last LNM: 02/04 | NAD 83 | 16/04 |

Chart Title: **SOUTH COAST OF CAPE COD AND BUZZARDS BAY**
    Main Panel

		NOS Silver Spring, MD
ADD	Magenta dashed lines joining	41-38-11.077N 070-54-39.011W
	and label: Cable Area	41-38-13.011N 070-54-28.022W
		41-38-14.022N 070-54-40.033W
		41-38-19.055N 070-54-25.066W

e. <u>Advance Notices</u>.

(1) This section contains advance notice of approved projects scheduled for a certain date of accomplishment. It may also contain notices of forthcoming temporary changes such as dredging, etc. This section shall be in a free style paragraph format and need not conform to the format of Section IV; however, the charts affected must be listed.

(2) Advance notice of significant changes in aids to navigation used by the mariner engaged in transoceanic trade must be given. The amount of advance notice that should be given in Local Notice to Mariners is:

(a) Four months for major changes to important seacoast aids used in transoceanic trade. Publication of such information shall be repeated monthly for the first two months, and then weekly until the changes are accomplished.

(b) Two months for other important changes. Publication of information of this type shall be repeated every week until the changes are accomplished.

(3) When information is not available to give the advance notice shown above, the information should be repeated at weekly intervals from the time the information is available until the change is accomplished. When information contained in an advance notice is changed in a later notice, the later notice should make reference to the initial notice. However, each notice shall be complete in itself so the reader need not refer to the previous notice.

(4) When a change announced in an advance notice cannot be carried out within one week of the date announced, a postponement notice shall be issued. For important aids, this notice should be issued as a Broadcast Notice to Mariners.

EXAMPLE:

SECTION V - ADVANCE NOTICES

This section contains advance notice of approved projects, changes to aids to navigation, or upcoming temporary changes such as dredging, etc.

Mariners are advised to use caution while transiting these areas.

SUMMARY OF ADVANCED APPROVED PROJECTS

Waterway	Project Date	Ref. LNM
NY/BELLPORT BAY/SHINNECOCK BAY	15 April 2004	04/04
MA/BUZZARDS BAY	31 May 2004	03/04
MA/BUZZARDS BAY	31 May 2004	03/04

NY – HUDSON RIVER – *Revised* The reconstruction of **Hudson River Light 86** (LLNR 38350) has been postponed until the Spring of **2004** and will be advertised in a future Local Notice to Mariners.
Chart(s) 12345 LNM 45/03 (CGD1)

f. Proposed Changes.

(1) This section contains notices of projects conceived and in the planning stage, but which have not been approved or scheduled for accomplishment.

(2) A preliminary statement, worded as below, shall be included:

PERIODICALLY, THE COAST GUARD EVALUATES THE SYSTEM OF AIDS TO NAVIGATION TO DETERMINE WHETHER THE CONDITIONS FOR WHICH THE AIDS TO NAVIGATION WERE ESTABLISHED HAVE CHANGED. WHEN CHANGES OCCUR, THE FEASIBILITY OF IMPROVING, RELOCATING, REPLACING, OR DISCONTINUING THE AID IS CONSIDERED. IN THIS REGARD, THE COAST GUARD IS EVALUATING CHANGES IN AIDS TO NAVIGATION AS NOTED BELOW. COMMENTS ARE REQUESTED, AND SHOULD BE ADDRESSED TO: (fill in).

ALL COMMENTS SUBMITTED SHOULD INCLUDE THE FOLLOWING INFORMATION:

(A) QUANTITY, TYPE, CAPACITY, AND VALUE OF VESSELS INVOLVED, AND THE EXTENT THAT THESE VESSELS TRAVERSE THE AREA UNDER CONSIDERATION SEASONALLY, BY DAY, AND BY NIGHT.

(B) WHERE PRACTICABLE, THE TYPE OF NAVIGATION DEVICES, SUCH AS COMPASSES, RADAR, GPS/DGPS, LORAN, AND SEARCH LIGHTS, WITH WHICH SUCH VESSELS ARE EQUIPPED.

(C) THE NUMBER OF PASSENGERS AND THE TYPE, QUANTITY, AND VALUE OF CARGO INVOLVED.

(D) A CHART SECTION OR SKETCH SHOWING THE ACTION PROPOSED WHEN NECESSARY TO CLEARLY DESCRIBE THE RECOMMENDED IMPROVEMENT.

COMMENTS ARE REQUESTED BY (DATE).

EXAMPLE:

SECTION VI - PROPOSED CHANGES

Periodically, the Coast Guard evaluates its system of aids to navigation to determine whether the conditions for which the aids to navigation were established have changed. When changes occur, the feasibility of improving, relocating, replacing, or discontinuing aids are considered. This section contains notice(s) of non-approved, proposed projects open for comment. **SPECIAL NOTE:** Mariners are requested to respond in writing to the District office unless otherwise noted (see banner page for address).

PROPOSED WATERWAY PROJECTS OPEN FOR PUBLIC COMMENT

Waterway	Closing	Docket No.	Ref. LNM
MA/HYANNIS TO NAUSET	30 Apr 2004	N/A	50/03
MA/MARTHAS VINEYARD AND NANTUCKET HARBOR	30 Apr 2004	N/A	50/03

MA – BUZZARDS BAY – *(REVISED)* The Coast Guard is conducting a Waterway Analysis and Management System (WAMS) review of the east side of Buzzards Bay to include Quisset Harbor, Buzzards Bay East Side, West Falmouth Harbor, Wild Harbor, Megansett Harbor, Southwest Ledge, Pocasset Harbor, and Phinneys Harbor Channel. Mariners and other concerned parties are invited to comment on the aids to navigation in these waterways. Any comments or recommended changes to aids to navigation in these waterways should be received no later than **31 July 2004** to be considered. Send comments to; Commander, U.S. Coast **Guard, Sector Southeastern New England, ATTN: Official Title,** 1 Little Harbor Road, Woods Hole, MA 02543-1012. Chart 13230 LNM 09/04 (CGD1)

---

(3) These notices may be written in the same manner as an advanced notice except for stating it is a proposed change.

g. <u>General</u>.

(1) This section contains information which is of general concern to the mariner and not, in the District Commander's opinion, of such a nature to appear under Special Notice.

(a) Included in this category are new publications, salvage operations, anchorages, restricted areas, bridge information, public notices and hearings, bridge construction plans, regattas, large ship launching or maneuvering, routine gunnery exercises and other items which would not specifically fit into another section of the Local Notice to Mariners. Make reference to any ADDITIONAL ENCLOSURE items of interest. Make sure all the facts are stated for each item. Reference previous Local Notice to Mariners, but put all information pertaining to the item in each Local published.

(b) Information on wrecks and hazards to navigation may be published in this section. However, a chart correction <u>must</u> also be published.

(c) It is not necessary to print the entire public notice, hearing notice, etc., in the LNM. A short note that a public notice has been issued and where copies may be obtained will suffice.

(d) This section shall be in a free style paragraph format and need not conform to the format of Section IV.

EXAMPLE:

SECTION VII - GENERAL

This section contains information of general concern to the Mariners. Mariners are advised to use caution while transiting these areas.

NY/NJ - NEW YORK HARBOR - UPPER BAY - Sediment samples are being conducted in the vicinity of the Jersey Flats off the Global Marine Terminal through **March 20, 2004**. The vessels HACKENSACK, DELAWARE and HAYES are working daily, between 7 am and 4:30 pm. Mariners are advised to transit the area with caution and proceed at a no wake speed. Chart(s) 12327, 12334 LNM 09/04 (CGD1)

h. <u>Light List Corrections.</u>

(1) The Light List corrections shall appear in the same format as the Light List publication.

(a) Place an asterisk (*) in the column to indicate any change.

(b) To add a new aid to navigation, the asterisk (*) is placed under all eight columns.

(c) If the physical appearance of an established aid is changed (i.e., Buoy to Daybeacon) an (*) is only required in columns that have changed. Do not remove the old aid from the Light List simply to change the name.

(d) To delete an aid to navigation, only the Light List Number (Col 1), Aid Name (Col 2), and the phrase "Remove from list." (Col 8) are required. Only the first line of information need be printed. The asterisk (*) is placed in column 8.

(e) If the notice contains Light List corrections, the main heading from the Light List shall appear.

EXAMPLE:

SECTION VIII – LIGHT LIST CORRECTIONS
An Asterisk *, indicates the column in which a correction has been made or new information added.

(1) No.	(2) Name and Location	(3) Position	(4) Characteristic	(5) Height	(6) Range	(7) Structure	(8) Remarks
14423.23	BROWN SHOAL LIGHT	38 55 22.333 N 080 25 00.045 W	Fl W 2.5s	23	7	NB on pile.	
		*			*		12/04

(f) Headings shall be added, deleted, or changed in the following manner. In the following examples, note the type styles and fonts for the action line are all **Bold**.

(g) To Add **Galveston Bay (North)** as a header, insert **Add Heading:** proceeded by an asterisk. On the next line, precede **Galveston Bay (North)** with an asterisk. The aid that immediately follows the heading shall also be listed. This method ensures there will be no confusion as to the location within the Light.

EXAMPLES:

SECTION VIII – LIGHT LIST CORRECTIONS
An Asterisk *, indicates the column in which a correction has been made or new information added.

(1) No.	(2) Name and Location	(3) Position	(4) Characteristic	(5) Height	(6) Range	(7) Structure	(8) Remarks
* Add Heading:							
* Galveston Bay (North)							
14229	- Lighted Buoy 2	32 12 16.515 N 081 17 45.424 W	Fl R 2.5s		3	Red.	

SECTION VIII – LIGHT LIST CORRECTIONS
An Asterisk *, indicates the column in which a correction has been made or new information added.

(1) No.	(2) Name and Location	(3) Position	(4) Characteristic	(5) Height	(6) Range	(7) Structure	(8) Remarks
* Add Heading and Note:							
* DELAWARE BAY (Chart 12304)							
* Delaware Bay (Main Channel)							
* *Buoys located 100 feet outside channel limit.*							
14423.23	BROWN SHOAL LIGHT	38 55 22.333 N 080 25 00.045 W	Fl W 2.5s	3	7	NB on pile.	

(h) To Delete **Delaware Bay** as a header, add a second line above the heading, preceded by an asterisk and the words **Delete Heading:**. On the next line, precede **Delaware Bay** with an asterisk. The aid that immediately follows the heading shall also be listed. This method ensures there will be no confusion as to the location within the Light List.

EXAMPLE:

SECTION VIII – LIGHT LIST CORRECTIONS
An Asterisk *, indicates the column in which a correction has been made or new information added.

(1) No.	(2) Name and Location	(3) Position	(4) Characteristic	(5) Height	(6) Range	(7) Structure	(8) Remarks
* Delete Heading:							
* DELAWARE BAY (Chart 12304)							
14423.23	BROWN SHOAL LIGHT	38 55 36.3 N 075 06 06.6 W	Fl W 2.5s	23	7	NB on pile.	

(i) To change a heading, insert one line above the existing heading preceded with an asterisk and insert the words **Change Heading to Read:**. On the following line, insert the appropriate correction to the heading, preceded with an asterisk. The aid that immediately follows the heading shall also be listed. This method ensures there will be no confusion as to the location within the Light List.

EXAMPLES:

SECTION VIII – LIGHT LIST CORRECTIONS

An Asterisk *, indicates the column in which a correction has been made or new information added.

(1) No.	(2) Name and Location	(3) Position	(4) Characteristic	(5) Height	(6) Range	(7) Structure	(8) Remarks
* Change Heading to Read:							
* Galveston Bay (South)							
14229	- Lighted Buoy 2	32 12 23.591 N 075 06 32.276 W	Fl R 2.5s		3	Red.	

SECTION VIII – LIGHT LIST CORRECTIONS

An Asterisk *, indicates the column in which a correction has been made or new information added.

(1) No.	(2) Name and Location	(3) Position	(4) Characteristic	(5) Height	(6) Range	(7) Structure	(8) Remarks
Wrightsville Channel							
* Change Note to Read:							
* *Due to frequently changing conditions, positions of buoys are not listed.*							
42095	- Buoy 1					Green can.	

SECTION VIII – LIGHT LIST CORRECTIONS

An Asterisk *, indicates the column in which a correction has been made or new information added.

(1) No.	(2) Name and Location	(3) Position	(4) Characteristic	(5) Height	(6) Range	(7) Structure	(8) Remarks
* Page iii: Change Address to Read:							
* SEVENTEENTH	*** P.O. Box 25517**						
	* Juneau, AK 99802-5517						
	* PHONE: DAY 907-463-2245						
	* PHONE: NIGHT 907-463-2000						

SECTION VIII – LIGHT LIST CORRECTIONS

An Asterisk *, indicates the column in which a correction has been made or new information added.

(1) No.	(2) Name and Location	(3) Position	(4) Characteristic	(5) Height	(6) Range	(7) Structure	(8) Remarks
* Pages 66-91: Change Footnote to Read:							

* *Fish net buoys in Chesapeake Bay and tributary waters are not listed; however, they are shown on nautical charts.*

(j) All heading corrections shall conform to the formats listed above. Heading corrections will follow all other Light List corrections.

(k) To change a Light List number, first delete the old entry. The new entry can then be added.

(l) The only corrections allowable in Column (1) include additions, deletions, or changes to the cross reference number.

(m) Abbreviations for Daybeacons, i.e., TR (triangular red), SG (square green), shall be those listed in the introductory chapter of the Light Lists under Daybeacons.

SAMPLE LIGHT LIST CORRECTIONS (Volumes 1, 2, 3, 4, 6, 7)

SECTION VIII – LIGHT LIST CORRECTIONS

An Asterisk *, indicates the column in which a correction has been made or new information added.

(1) No.	(2) Name and Location	(3) Position	(4) Characteristic	(5) Height	(6) Range	(7) Structure	(8) Remarks
42095	- Buoy 1						Green can.
14423.23	*NOAA Environmental Lighted Buoy 46049*	36 44 46.423 N 122 26 34.667 W	**Fl (4) Y** 20s				Yellow disc-shaped buoy.
*	*	*	*	*	*		* (12/04)
455	*Noyo Approach Lighted Whistle Buoy NA*	39 25 45.978 N 123 50 23.091 W	**Mo (A) W**		5		Red and white stripes with red spherical topmark
							* (12/04)
1605	- Buoy 7						Green can.
						*	* (12/04)
1700	HARBOR ISLAND LIGHT	32 43 23.512 N 117 12 45.823 W	**Fl W** 4s	56	8	On top of red roofed building.	
						*	* (12/04)
2436.3	- Bio-structure Buoy C						Remove from list
							* (12/04)
2436.4	- Bio-structure Buoy D						Remove from list
							* (12/04)
3260	*- Lighted Buoy 2*		**Fl R** 2.5s		4		Red.
*	*	*	*	*	*		* (12/04)
3280	- APPROACH RANGE FRONT LIGHT	33 42 12.634 N 118 17 56.045 W	**Fl Y** 2s	61		On red striped post.	Private aid.
		*					* (12/04)
3285	- APPROACH RANGE REAR LIGHT 220 yards, 255 from front light.		**F Y**	86		On red striped post.	Private aid.
		*					* (12/04)
4115	**- Municipal Wharf Fog Signal**	36 57 17.556 N 122 01 10.667 W					HORN: 1 blast ev 15s (2s bl). Maintained from Apr. 1 to Nov. 1. Private aid.
							* (12/04)

SAMPLE LIGHT LIST CORRECTIONS (Volume 5)

SECTION VIII – LIGHT LIST CORRECTIONS
An Asterisk *, indicates the column in which a correction has been made or new information added.

(1) No.	(2) Name and Location	(3) Mile	(4) Bank	(5) Characteristic	(6) Structure/Dayboard Up/Down	(7) Remarks
425	Cypress Creek Upper Daybeacon	169.3	Right			Remove from list. * (12/04)
2008	Belk Corner Lower Daybeacon	153.7	Left			Remove from list. * (12/04)
4117	BIGELOW LIGHT	148.5 *	Right	Fl G 4s	SG SG On piling.	(12/04)
6235	DRYDEN CREEK LIGHT	41.8 *	Right *	Fl W 4s *	SG CG On piling. *	* (12/04)
*	*					
8222	ARKANSAS POWER AND LIGHT COMPANY DOCK LIGHTS (2) Marks intake and discharge.	659.4	Right	F G	On dolphin	Private aids.
*	*	*	*	*	*	* (12/04)
9636	**Greenville Bridge**	531.3				CLEARANCES: Horizontal channel, 800.0 feet vertical main channel 130.1 feet above zero on bridge gage. * (12/04)
11741.5	*** Change Pool Elevation to Read:** **Lock and Dam No. 5**	30.4	Right			LOCK: 360 feet long, 56 feet wide.
	Normal upper pool elevation 756.8 feet MSL, equal to 10.3 feet on upper gage					
	Normal lower pool elevation 745.0 feet MSL, equal to 10.5 feet on lower gage.					
	*					* (12/04)
12345	Pratt Piling Buoy Marks piling off left bank.	61.5	Right	Red nun. *		(12/04)
13529	*McKnight Lighted Buoy*	584.3	Left	Fl (2) R 5s	Red.	Removed during ice season and replaced with an unlighted buoy. * (12/04)

(2) Light List corrections will always appear in Section 8. If there are no Light List corrections the following format will be used.

EXAMPLE:

SECTION VIII – LIGHT LIST CORRECTIONS
An Asterisk *, indicates the column in which a correction has been made or new information added.

(1) No.	(2) Name and Location	(3) Position	(4) Characteristic	(5) Height	(6) Range	(7) Structure	(8) Remarks

NONE

i. <u>Enclosures</u>. Contained here are items such as chartlets, channel depth tabulations, and other preprinted materials.

EXAMPLE:

SUMMARY OF EFFECTIVE DREDGING/CONSTRUCTION OPERATIONS
The following is a listing of marine construction and dredging projects still in effect in the First District. All mariners are advised to use caution in these areas. The LNM REF column refers to the LNM in which the article first appears and where detailed information may be obtained. The dates listed for completion are tentative. An asterisk in the left margin marks new information.

LOCATION	SUBJECT	COMPLETION DATE	LNM REF
NY/EAST ROCKAWAY INLET	Dredging	14 March 2004	07/04
MA/CAPE ANN TO NEW HAMPSHIRE BORDER	Hydrographic survey	15 March 2004	07/04

D. <u>Light List</u>.

1. <u>Description</u>.

a. The Light List describes both Federal and private aids to marine navigation maintained by or under the authority of the United States Government. It is compiled and published by the Coast Guard, **using I-ATONIS data,** in seven volumes, to provide mariners with more complete details regarding aids to navigation than can be found on charts.

b. **Light List corrections are promulgated weekly via the Local Notice to Mariners (LNMs). All volumes of the Light List and LNMS are available to the public through the NAVCEN website.**

c. The following volumes are issued.

   (1) Light List Volume I, Atlantic Coast, COMDTPUB P16502.1, describing aids to navigation in waters of the United States from St. Croix River, Maine to Shrewsbury River, New Jersey (First Coast Guard District).

   (2) Light List Volume II, Atlantic Coast, COMDTPUB P16502.2, describing aids to navigation in waters of the United States from Shrewsbury River, New Jersey to Little River, South Carolina (Fifth Coast Guard District).

   (3) Light List Volume III, Atlantic and Gulf Coasts, COMDTPUB P16502.3, describing aids to navigation in waters of the United States from Little River, South Carolina to Econfina River, Florida and The Greater Antilles (Seventh Coast Guard District).

   (4) Light List Volume IV, Gulf Coast, COMDTPUB P16502.4, describing aids to navigation in waters of the United States from Econfina River, Florida to Rio Grande, Texas (Eighth Coast Guard District).

   (5) Light List Volume V, Mississippi River System, COMDTPUB P16502.5, describing aids to navigation and broadcast facilities on the Mississippi River and adjoining navigable tributaries (Eighth Coast Guard District).

   (6) Light List Volume VI, Pacific Coast and Pacific Islands, COMDTPUB P16502.6, describing aids to navigation in United States waters on the Pacific Coast and outlying Pacific Islands. For the convenience of the mariner, also included are certain aids to navigation on the coast of British Columbia. (Eleventh, Thirteenth, Fourteenth, and Seventeenth Coast Guard Districts).

   (7) Light List Volume VII, Great Lakes, COMDTPUB P16502.7, describing aids to navigation maintained by the United States Coast Guard and the St. Lawrence Seaway Development Corporation on the Great Lakes and the St. Lawrence River, above the St. Regis River. For the convenience of the mariners, also included are certain aids to navigation maintained by Canada. (Ninth Coast Guard District).

d. Arrangement.

   (1) Aids to Navigation are arranged in geographic order as follows.

      (a) Aids to navigation in Volumes I, II, III, and IV are listed from north to south along the Atlantic Coast and from east to west along the Gulf Coast. Seacoast aids to navigation are listed first followed by entrance and harbor aids to navigation listed from seaward to the head of navigation. Intracoastal Waterway aids to navigation are listed from north to south on the Atlantic Coast and south to north and east to west on the Gulf Coast.

(b) Aids to navigation in Volume V are listed in downstream order for those rivers in the Mississippi River System, as shown in the Table of Contents. Each fixed aid bears a number indicating the mileage of the stream at that point, as determined from the latest chart. The mileage of the aid determines its position in the list. The origin (zero), of most rivers is coincident with the river mouth; otherwise, the origin point is named in the heading of each page.

(c) Aids to navigation in Volume VI are listed from south to north along the Pacific Coast, south to north and east to west in Alaska, and east to west in the Pacific Islands. Seacoast aids to navigation are listed first, followed by entrance and harbor aids to navigation listed from seaward to the head of navigation.

(d) Aids to navigation in Volume VII are listed in a westerly and northerly direction on the Great Lakes except Lake Michigan, which is in a southerly direction on the eastern side and a northerly direction on the western side.

e. Format.

(1) Each volume of the Light List is arranged in the following sequence.
- Title page
- Preface
- Table of contents
- General information
- Aids to navigation listing
- Alphabetic index to selected aids to navigation and waterways
- International cross reference

(2) There are four types of headings used in the Aids to Navigation Listing. The headings are used to subdivide the listings into geographical areas and to highlight particular waterways.

(a) Geographical headings (G-header) appear at the top of every page and whenever major geographical boundaries change. Normally, this heading reflects the change from Seacoast to Bays, Rivers, and Harbors; and Bays, Rivers, and Harbors to Intracoastal Waterway. Large or otherwise significant waterways are also listed in this heading (e.g., Long Island Sound, Columbia River, Lake Erie, etc.). These headings appear centered on the page, in bold type, upper case. Certain amplifying information appears in upper/lower case.

EXAMPLES:

(1) No.	(2) Name and Location	(3) Position	(4) Characteristic	(5) Height	(6) Range	(7) Structure	(8) Remarks
			SEACOAST (New Jersey) – Fifth District				

(1) No.	(2) Name and Location	(3) Position	(4) Characteristic	(5) Height	(6) Range	(7) Structure	(8) Remarks
			CHESAPEAKE BAY (Virginia) – Fifth District				

    (b) Chart reference headings (S-header) indicate the best scale chart on which the aids to navigation appear. These headings appear in bold type, upper case. The chart number is listed in parenthesis in upper/lower case. This heading is the name of the chart on which the aids to navigation appear

EXAMPLE:

(1) No.	(2) Name and Location	(3) Position	(4) Characteristic	(5) Height	(6) Range	(7) Structure	(8) Remarks
			CHESAPEAKE BAY (Virginia) – Fifth District				
	CAPE HENRY TO THIMBLE SHOAL LIGHT (Chart 12254)						

    (c) Major waterway headings (U-header) indicate bays, rivers, channels, and harbors. These headings appear in bold type, upper/lower case. Often they are part of the name of the aid to navigation.

EXAMPLE:

(1) No.	(2) Name and Location	(3) Position	(4) Characteristic	(5) Height	(6) Range	(7) Structure	(8) Remarks
			CHESAPEAKE BAY (Virginia) – Fifth District				
	CAPE HENRY TO THIMBLE SHOAL LIGHT (Chart 12254)						
	Thimble Shoal Channel						

    (d) Minor waterway headings (B-header) indicate smaller channels, rivers, marinas, etc., contained within a major waterway heading. These headings appear in bold type, upper/lower case. These headings may be not be distinguishable from the major waterway heading at first glance, but will be apparent if appearing at the top of a page.

EXAMPLE:

(1) No.	(2) Name and Location	(3) Position	(4) Characteristic	(5) Height	(6) Range	(7) Structure	(8) Remarks
			CHESAPEAKE BAY (Virginia) – Fifth District				
	APPROACHES TO BALTIMORE HARBOR (Chart 12278)						
	Patapsco River						
	Bodkin Creek						

(e) Other lines of text, known as preceding lines, are occasionally included before the aids to navigation listing itself, but after the headings. These text lines appear as italic type, upper/lower case and contain amplifying information concerning the entire waterway referenced by the preceding heading. This information usually summarizes what would appear in Columns 2 (Name and Location) or 8 (Remarks) into one entry rather than repeating it for each aid to navigation. **In the I-ATONIS application, preceding lines are named "Waterway Remarks" and can be entered into the I-ATONIS application via the Light List Waterway screens.**

EXAMPLES:

(1) No.	(2) Name and Location	(3) Position	(4) Characteristic	(5) Height	(6) Range	(7) Structure	(8) Remarks
	SEACOAST (North Carolina) – Fifth District						
	CAPE HATTERAS (Chart 11555)						
	Hatteras Inlet						
	Due to frequently changing conditions, positions of buoys are not listed.						

(1) No.	(2) Name and Location	(3) Position	(4) Characteristic	(5) Height	(6) Range	(7) Structure	(8) Remarks
	DELAWARE RIVER (Delaware and New Jersey) – Fifth District						
	SMYRNA RIVER TO WILMINGTON (Chart 12311)						
	Delaware River						
	Liston Range						
	Buoys are located 50 feet outside channel limits.						

(f) Other information is permissible provided it applies evenly to the aids to navigation below the referenced heading.

(3) The Aids to Navigation Listing is divided into eight columns, except for Volume 5 which has seven columns. Each column contains specific information.

(a) Column 1 (Light List Number) - This column contains the Light List number. Aids to Navigation are arranged in geographic order, except in Volume V where aids to navigation are listed by river mileage. All permanent aids to navigation are assigned a Light List number. Light List numbers are normally a whole number such as 5, 250, 345, etc. Decimal numbers are assigned when a whole number is not available (1.1, 141.10, etc.).

i. The number appears on the first line of the entry. Aids to navigation that are listed in the Seacoast Section and the Bays, Rivers, and Harbors Section will be assigned cross-reference numbers. Any cross-reference number will appear in this column, immediately below the Light List number.

ii. To remove decimal numbers, each volume of the Light List will be periodically renumbered, by fives, in its entirety by NAVCEN. Consult NAVCEN to coordinate renumbering upon completion of large projects.

(b) Column 2 (Name and Location) - This column contains the name of the aid to navigation and amplifying information on the location (e.g., "Marks reef.", "50 yards outside channel limits."). No abbreviations are used in the name. The following rules apply:

i. When numbering or lettering an aid to navigation, standard IALA convention will be used. Channels should be numbered and lettered sequentially. Lateral aids are numbered or lettered as consecutively as possible, beginning at the seaward end of the waterway and increasing in the conventional direction of buoyage. When two or more aids have the same number, the number may be suffixed with an identifying letter (e.g., Buoy 2A, Buoy 2B). Preferred Channel, Safewater, Isolated Danger, and Special Marks may be lettered. Wreck buoys shall be prefixed with the letters WR (e.g., Lighted Wreck Buoy WR6). Both Federal and private aids shall follow this standard. For amplifying information on the proper naming, numbering, and lettering of aids to navigation see Chapter 4 of this manual.

ii. The name of lights with a nominal range of 10 nautical miles (NM) or greater (10 statute miles (SM) in the Great Lakes) appear in upper/lower case, boldface type. In addition, racons and sound signal stations are also listed in this format. The name of lights with a nominal range less than 10 NM (10 SM in the Great Lakes), range lights, and privately maintained lights appear in regular type, upper case only.

iii. The name of lighted buoys appears in italics type, upper/lower case.

iv. The name of unlighted buoys and daybeacons appear in regular type, upper/lower case.

v. When four (4) or more aids to navigation contain the same name, a heading (U-header or B-header) is added and the portion of the name is replaced with a hyphen.

EXAMPLES:

(1) No.	(2) Name and Location	(3) Position	(4) Characteristic	(5) Height	(6) Range	(7) Structure	(8) Remarks
		DELAWARE RIVER (Delaware and New Jersey) – Fifth District					
	CAPE HENRY TO CURRITUCK LIGHT (Chart 12207)						
	Duck Sand Research						
22334	- Buoy A	36 22 37.5 N 075 49 47.7 W				Yellow can.	Private aid.
22335	- Buoy B	36 22 37.5 N 075 49 47.6 W				Yellow can.	Private aid.
22336	- Buoy C	36 22 37.4 N 075 49 47.6 W				Yellow can.	Private aid.
22337	- Buoy D	36 22 37.4 N 075 49 47.7 W				Yellow can.	Private aid.

vi. All entries on the second and subsequent lines are indented two spaces.

vii. Amplifying information, if included in the column, starts on a new line and appears in the regular type, upper/lower case. If the name of the aid to navigation describes the hazard, amplifying information shall not be used except to describe additional features not included in the name.

viii. Listings for the rear range light contain amplifying information describing the distance in yards or feet, and the bearing from the front range light. The distance is listed to the nearest whole foot or yard. If the range exceeds 999 feet or yards, a comma is used. The bearing is rounded to the nearest tenth of a degree, using standard mathematical rounding procedures.

ix. In the case of multiple lights contained in a listing, the number of lights is listed in parenthesis at the end of the name.

EXAMPLE:

(1) No.	(2) Name and Location	(3) Position	(4) Characteristic	(5) Height	(6) Range	(7) Structure	(8) Remarks
		CHESAPEAKE BAY (Maryland) – Fifth District					
	APPROACHES TO BALTIMORE HARBOR (Chart 12278)						
	Patapsco River						
6654	- DOCK LIGHTS (3)	38 25 26.326 N 078 48 12.245 W	**FW**	28		On pile.	Private aid.

(c) Column 3 (Position) - This column contains the latitude and longitude of the aid to navigation.

i. **The position will be printed to the thousandth decimal place. When aids to navigation are not charted due to frequently changing conditions, a**

remark in column 8 or a preceding line is used to bring attention to that fact.

    ii. The datum of positions of aids to navigation shall agree with the datum of the chart referenced in the chart reference heading (S-header).

    iii. In the case of multiple lights contained in a listing, the position in I-ATONIS is the one the District Commander determines best describes the structure.

    iv. (Volume 5). Column 3 (Mile) contains the river mile of the aid to navigation.

(d) Column 4 (Characteristic) - If lighted, this column contains the light characteristic of the aid to navigation. (See paragraph 12.C.2 for a listing of abbreviations.) If the light has a sector or sectors, that fact is noted on the second line, in bold type. The bearings of the sector(s) appear in Column 8 (Remarks).

    i. (Volume 5). Column 4 (Bank) - Contains the side of the bank of the river where the aid to navigation is located.

EXAMPLE:

(1) No.	(2) Name and Location	(3) Position	(4) Characteristic	(5) Height	(6) Range	(7) Structure	(8) Remarks
			SEACOAST (Deleware) – Fifth District				
	DELAWARE BAY (Chart 12304)						
	Salem River						
8945	- LIGHT	39 58 59.0 N 080 25 14.6 W	Fl W 4s (R sector)	80	9	White tower.	Red 123-136
8946	- LIGHT 2	39 58 59.1 N 080 25 14.2 W	Fl G 4s	24	4	SG on pile.	
8947	- LIGHT 3	39 58 59.3 N 080 25 14.4 W	Iso R 6s	24	4	TR on pile.	

(e) Column 5 (Height) - For fixed aids to navigation, the focal height (in feet) above water for the aid to navigation is listed here. In the Great Lakes, the height in meters is also listed, below the height in feet, in bold type.

    i. (Volume 5). Column 5 (Characteristic) - If lighted, this column contains the light characteristic of the aid to navigation. (See paragraph 12.C.2 for a listing of abbreviations.)

(f) Column 6 (Range) - The nominal range in nautical miles, for lighted aids to navigation, is listed here. In the case of a light with sectors, the color with the greater range is listed first, with the letter designation of the color. Nominal range is not listed for range lights, directional lights, leading lights, or private aids to navigation.

i. (Volumn 5). Column 6 (Structure/Dayboard Up/Down) – Contains the structural characteristic including dayboard, if any. Up and down dayboards are listed when appropriate. *Up* indicates the dayboard is facing upstream to aid the mariner headed downstream and *Down* indicated the dayboard is facing downstream to aid the mariner headed upstream.

(g) Column 7 (Structure)

i. Lighted buoys will only list the color of the buoy hull. The color of the topmost band of preferred channel buoys shall be listed first.

EXAMPLES:

(1) No.	(2) Name and Location	(3) Position	(4) Characteristic	(5) Height	(6) Range	(7) Structure	(8) Remarks
			CALIFORNIA - Eleventh District				
	ENTRANCE TO SAN FRANCISCO BAY (Chart 18649) **San Francisco Channel**						
3990	- Harbor Entrance Lighted Bell Buoy SF	36 47 56.8 N 121 48 06.7 W	**Mo (A) W**			Red and white stripes with red spherical topmark.	
4240	Four Fathom Bank Lighted Bell Buoy	37 48 42.6 N 122 32 25.4 W	**Fl (2+1) R** 6s			Red and green bands.	
4255	*- Lighted Buoy 2*	37 48 48.4 N 122 28 48.3 W	**Fl R** 4s			Red.	
4256	- Buoy 3	37 48 48.2 N 122 28 48.1 W				Green can.	

(1) No.	(2) Name and Location	(3) Position	(4) Characteristic	(5) Height	(6) Range	(7) Structure	(8) Remarks
			GULF OF MEXICO (Florida) - Seventh District				
	ESTERO BAY TO LEMON BAY (Chart 11426)						
1310 19905	GASPARILLA ISLAND LIGHT	26 44 31.9 N 082 15 48.7 W	**Iso W** 6s **(R sector)**	105	W 12 R 10	White hexagonal pyramidal skeleton	Red from 001° to 045°

CH-1

ii. Unlighted buoys will be listed with the color and shape of the buoy. The color of the topmost band of preferred channel buoys shall be listed first.

EXAMPLE:

(1) No.	(2) Name and Location	(3) Position	(4) Characteristic	(5) Height	(6) Range	(7) Structure	(8) Remarks
			CALIFORNIA - Eleventh District				
	MONTEREY BAY (Chart 18685)						
	Monterey Harbor						
3972	- Junction Buoy A	36 36 30.1 N 121 53 18.2 W				Red and green bands; nun.	
3973	- Main Channel Buoy 2	36 36 24.3 N 121 53 24.4 W				Red nun	
3974	- North Buoy 5	36 36 30.5 N 121 53 18.6 W				Green can	
4330	Pillar Point Approach Buoy PP	37 28 18.7 N 122 30 48.8 W				Red and white stripes, sphere	

iii. Fixed aids to navigation will be identified by daymark and structure type (e.g., pile, skeleton tower, dolphin, spindle, post, etc.). Construction material (steel, wood, etc.) is not listed. Major aids to navigation may contain further descriptions of the structure when necessary.

iv. Height above ground, in feet, **will** appear on a separate line following the description of the structure **for major lights (lights with a nominal range greater than or equal to 10 nautical miles (statute miles for D9)).**

EXAMPLE:

(1) No.	(2) Name and Location	(3) Position	(4) Characteristic	(5) Height	(6) Range	(7) Structure	(8) Remarks
			WEST INDIES (Puerto Rico) – Seventh District				
	BAHIA DE FAJARDO AND APPROACHES (Chart 25667)						
	Bahia de Fajardo						
31155	**Cabo San Juan Light**	18 22 54.6 N 065 37 06.7 W	**Fl W** 15s	260	24	Cylindrical tower on front of white rectangular dwelling; black band around base. 86	
31156	Las Croabas Daybeacon 1	18 21 48.8 N 065 37 18.9 W				SG on pile.	
31158	CABRAS LIGHT	18 28 30.1 N 066 08 24.2 W	**Iso W** 6s	44	9	NR on tower.	
20420	MANGROVE POINT LIGHT 1	26 53 58.3 N 082 07 14.4 W	**Fl G** 4s	27	6	SG on skeleton tower.	

v. (Volumn 5) Column 7 (Remarks) - Remarks are used to provide amplifying information such as bridge clearances and lock information which is not appropriate to any other column. Each separate comment begins on a new line, left flush to the column.

(h) Column 8 (Remarks) - Remarks are used to provide amplifying information not appropriate to any other column. Each separate comment begins on a new line, left flush to the column. References to sound or electronic devices are made by first stating the device (e.g., HORN, BELL, RACON) in upper case, then describing the characteristics of the device. Bearings for sectors are listed as viewed from the observer toward the aid to navigation.

EXAMPLES:

(1) No.	(2) Name and Location	(3) Position	(4) Characteristic	(5) Height	(6) Range	(7) Structure	(8) Remarks
			SEACOAST (Virginia) – Fifth District				
360	**Chesapeake Light**	36 54 17.1 N 075 42 46.2 W	**Fl (2) W** 15s	117	19	Blue tower on white square superstructure on four black piles, CHESAPEAKE on sides.	Emergency light of lower intensity will be displayed when main light is inoperative. RACON: N (– •). HORN: 1 blast ev 30s (3s bl). Operates continuously.
370	**Cape Henry Light**	36 55 35.3 N 076 00 26.4 W	**Mo (U) W** 20s **(R sector)**	164	W 17 R 15	Octagonal pyramidal tower, upper and lower half of each face alternately black and white.	Red from 154° □to 233°, covers shoals outside Cape Charles and Middle Ground inside Bay.

(4) Ranges are pairs of beacons commonly located to define a line down the channel. They are usually, but need not be lighted. If lighted, the light may only be visible on or near the rangeline. As such, it is important to accurately describe the signal.

(a) If the only light is a pencil-beam light produced by a drum optic (i.e., an RL14 or RL24) then, in the Remarks column, specify a value for light visibility each side of rangeline equal to half the beam width. Full-width values for drum lanterns are listed in the Aids to Navigation Manual – Technical.

EXAMPLES:

(1) No.	(2) Name and Location	(3) Position	(4) Characteristic	(5) Height	(6) Range	(7) Structure	(8) Remarks
			MISSISSIPPI - Eighth District				
	PASCAGOULA HARBOR (Chart 11375)						
	Horn Island Pass						
6825	- ENTRANCE RANGE FRONT LIGHT	30 12 48.1 N 088 30 18.2 W	**Q W**	25		KRW on skeleton tower on mud sills.	Visible 1.5° each side of rangeline.
6830	- ENTRANCE RANGE REAR LIGHT 693 yards, 041.1° from front light.		**Iso W** 6s	50		KRW on skeleton tower on pile.	Visible 1.5° each side of rangeline.

(1) No.	(2) Name and Location	(3) Position	(4) Characteristic	(5) Height	(6) Range	(7) Structure	(8) Remarks
			DELAWARE RIVER (Delaware and New Jersey) - Fifth District				
	SMYRNA RIVER TO WILMINGTON (Chart 12311)						
	Delaware River (Main Channel)						
	New Castle Range						
2730	- FRONT LIGHT	39 38 33.2 N 075 35 44.3 W	**Iso G** 2s	56		White skeleton tower.	Visible 0.5° each side of rangeline during the day, and 1.5° at night. Lighted throughout 24 hours.
2735	- REAR LIGHT 777 yards, 334° □from front light.		**F G**	110		White skeleton tower, small white house.	Visible 0.5° each side of rangeline during the day, and 1.5° at night. Lighted throughout 24 hours.

(b) A range light may be so arranged that it produces, in addition to the beam on the channel axis, an all-around light of lower intensity. If separate lanterns with the same characteristic are used and the lanterns are atop one another, the structure should be considered a single aid. This can be accomplished with a single lantern (250mm with a condensing panel) or with two synchronized, collocated lanterns (for example, an RL14 with a synchronized 155mm atop the RL14 range lantern). Such a light is considered an additional feature of the range as long as the characteristic is the same as the range light.

EXAMPLE:

(1) No.	(2) Name and Location	(3) Position	(4) Characteristic	(5) Height	(6) Range	(7) Structure	(8) Remarks
			FLORIDA - Seventh District				
	PENSACOLA BAY ENTRANCE (Chart 11384)						
	Pensacola Bay						
3930	CAUCUS CHANNEL RANGE FRONT LIGHT	30 19 34.7 N 087 18 44.8 W	**Q G** **Q G**	24 26		KRW on skeleton tower on piles	Visible all around; higher intensity 2° each side of rangeline.

(c) In some situations, a green or red light that is omnidirectional with higher intensity in the direction of the rangeline (as described in subparagraph (b) above) functions as both a range light and a *lateral* aid. Whether or not this is accomplished with one or two lanterns, it should be considered one aid, with the name of the range light suffixed with an appropriate number to indicate the dual function of the aid.

EXAMPLE:

(1) No.	(2) Name and Location	(3) Position	(4) Characteristic	(5) Height	(6) Range	(7) Structure	(8) Remarks
			CALIFORNIA – Eleventh District				
	SAN PABLO BAY (Chart 18654)						
	Napa River						
6185	- RANGE FRONT LIGHT 14	38 12 20.3 N 122 18 26.6 W	**Q R**	12		KRW and TR on pile.	Ra ref.

(d) If a structure uses a range lantern to mark the range, and a separate green or red omnidirectional lantern as a *lateral* aid (showing a light characteristic different than the range lantern), then the structure should be considered as two aids.

EXAMPLE:

(1) No.	(2) Name and Location	(3) Position	(4) Characteristic	(5) Height	(6) Range	(7) Structure	(8) Remarks
			FLORIDA - Seventh District				
	ST. JOHNS RIVER (Chart 11492)						
	St. Johns River						
7920	SOLANO POINT LIGHT 31	29 51 48.3 N 081 35 00.0 W	**Fl G** 2.5s	10	3	SG on skeleton tower on piles. On same structure as Tocoi Cut Range Front Light.	
7925	TOCOI CUT RANGE FRONT LIGHT	29 51 48.3 N 081 35 00.0 W	Iso W **6s**	25		KRW on skeleton tower on piles. On same structure as Solano Point Light 31.	Visible 4° each side of rangeline.

(e) If a structure uses a range lantern to mark the range, and a separate omnidirectional lantern (or lanterns) with a different characteristic to mark the aid for the purpose of avoiding an allision; and, if the omnidirectional lantern has no lateral significance, then the omnidirectional light(s) is described as a "passing light." The range light should be described as a front or rear range light and the omnidirectional light should be assigned a different number and described as a passing light.

EXAMPLES:

(1) No.	(2) Name and Location	(3) Position	(4) Characteristic	(5) Height	(6) Range	(7) Structure	(8) Remarks
			ALABAMA - Eighth District				
	MOBILE BAY (Chart 11376)						
	Mobile Channel						
5415	- RANGE FRONT LIGHT	30 36 28.9 N 088 01 59.1 W	**Q G**	25		KRW on skeleton tower on piles.	For downbound traffic. Visible 4° each side of rangeline.
5417	- RANGE FRONT PASSING LIGHT		**Fl W 2.5s**	27	5	On same structure as Mobile Channel Range Front Light.	
5420	- RANGE REAR LIGHT	1,675 yards, 181.7° from front light.	**Iso G 6s**	55		KRW on skeleton tower on piles.	Visible 4° each side of rangeline.
5423	- RANGE REAR PASSING LIGHT		**Fl W 6s**	14	4	On same structure as Mobile Channel Range Rear Light.	

f. Issuance.

(1) **The Light Lists are issued on an annual basis and are updated throughout the year via the Local Notice to Mariners or the weekly updated publication file posted on the Coast Guard's Navigation Center (NAVCEN) website. Additionally, corrections are provided via the National Geospatial-Intelligence Agency (NGA) Weekly Notice to Mariners that are available through the NGA Maritime Safety Information website. A notice advising District Commanders of the availability of new editions** of the Light Lists will be forwarded from NAVCEN for publication in the Local Notice to Mariners.

(2) **Beginning in 2015, the Coast Guard will no longer produce printed copies of the Light List. While the Light Lists will no longer be available in government printed form, commercial reproductions may be available in the future. Light Lists will no longer be issued to units through the Defense Logistics Agency/Mapping Customer Operations automatic distribution system.**

(3) Upon **issuance** of a new edition of the Light List, NAVCEN **will** prepare a Summary of Corrections. **The Summary will be posted on the NAVCEN website.** An Announcement of Availability of the new editions shall be forwarded **to the districts by NAVCEN. Upon receipt, the Announcement** shall be published in the next edition of the Local Notice to Mariners.

g. **Geographic Names.**

(1) The U.S. Board on Geographic Names (BGN) is a Federal body comprised of representatives of several Federal agencies. The Board is responsible for maintaining uniform geographic name usage throughout the Federal government.

(2) A publication titled Decision on Geographic Names in the United States is published quarterly. Commandant **(CG-NAV-1)** has obtained a subscription for this publication for each District. When received, each District shall review the actions of the BGN and make appropriate changes to the Light Lists and charts. Questions should be directed to Commandant **(CG- NAV-1).**

E. Broadcast Notice to Mariners.

1. Description. Broadcast Notice to Mariners is the method by which important navigation safety information is disseminated in the most expedient manner. This information includes, but is not limited to, information regarding aids to navigation maintained by or under the authority of the Commandant, weather, search and rescue (SAR) information, military exercises, marine obstructions, ice reports, changes in channel conditions, and important bridge information. In general, these transmissions will include information vital to the maritime community operating in or approaching the coastal waters of the United States, its territories, and possessions.

2. Responsibility.

   a. Two agencies within the United States, the U.S. Coast Guard and the National Geospatial-Intelligence Agency (NGA) are responsible for broadcasting navigation information. Each agency has a particular geographic area of responsibility.

   b. Commandant (CG-6) is responsible for the dissemination and receipt of maritime safety information by radio. Commandant **(CG-5PW)** acts as NATIONAL COORDINATOR of the Worldwide Navigational Warning Service (WWNWS) and is responsible for compilation of local and coastal navigation information for broadcasts from sources within the United States and its possessions. Commandant **(CG-5PW)** has delegated the responsibility of issuing these broadcasts to the District Commanders. With Commandant approval, this authority may be delegated to district units.

   c. NGA acts as AREA COORDINATOR of the WWNWS and is responsible for compilation of long-range navigation broadcasts from countries within NAVAREA IV and NAVAREA XII. NAVAREA IV covers the Atlantic coast eastward to 35°W. NAVAREA XII covers the waters of the Pacific coast westward to 180°**W.** NGA is responsible for broadcasting navigation information concerning the "HIGH SEAS."

   (f) NGA broadcasts are issued as a NAVAREA, HYDROLANT, HYDROPAC, or SPECIAL WARNING. In general, these broadcasts are geared toward the deep draft mariner. The information disseminated by these broadcasts includes the reporting of derelicts, ice conditions, drifting buoys, floating mines, etc. All reports on these matters addressed to the Coast Guard should be forwarded to NGA **(E-mail:** NavSafety@nga.mil)**, (PLA: NGA NAVSAFETY WASHINGTON DC).**

3. Scope.

    a. Broadcast Notices to Mariners are not intended to be the source of chart corrections, but rather to inform the mariner of important changes that affect the safety of navigation within a District's area of responsibility. Broadcasts are issued via VOICE and NAVTEX. As a general rule, VHF-FM voice broadcasts will contain all information that applies to inland waters and seaward to 20 nautical miles. High frequency (HF) broadcasts will contain all information that applies to waters from the coastline to 200 nautical miles offshore. NGA broadcasts contain information that concerns waters from approximately 150 nautical miles offshore to deep-ocean.

    b. NAVTEX is an international broadcast service designed for the promulgation of navigational and meteorological warnings and forecasts, as well as urgent marine safety information to ships at sea. NAVTEX has been designated to replace CW broadcasts. The information transmitted is relevant to all sizes and types of vessels at sea within approximately 200 nautical miles of shore. A selective message rejection feature ensures mariners can receive safety information broadcasts tailored to their particular needs. NAVTEX transmissions are limited to dedicated forty-minute time slots. For these reasons, broadcasts intended for NAVTEX must be made as clear and concise as possible.

    c. The primary focus of Coast Guard broadcasts is generally directed towards aids to navigation. The establishment, change, discontinuance, or discrepancy of an aid to navigation should always be broadcast.

4. Procedures.

    a. Broadcast Notices are transmitted by Coast Guard or Navy radio stations on the schedules and frequencies set forth in the Coast Guard Radio Frequency Plan, COMDTINST M2400.1 (series). Personnel should be familiar with the provisions on navigation information broadcasts in this manual as they apply to their district. Notice to Mariners information may also be furnished to commercial broadcasting stations if the District Commander considers the additional dissemination necessary and no charges are involved other than for transmission of the message to the stations.

    b. Determining the priority of a Broadcast is the responsibility of the originator. There are three types of broadcasts: Scheduled, Safety, and Urgent. Under normal circumstances, a Scheduled Broadcast will be a routine or priority message and transmitted at the next scheduled broadcast time. A Safety Broadcast will be a priority or immediate message and broadcast upon receipt, then at each scheduled broadcast until canceled. An Urgent Broadcast will be an immediate message and broadcast upon receipt and then at each scheduled broadcast until canceled. NAVTEX uses three terms to describe NAVTEX message priorities: Routine, Important, and Vital. A "routine" NAVTEX message coincides with a Scheduled Broadcast, an "important" NAVTEX message coincides with a Safety Broadcast, and a "vital" NAVTEX message coincides with an Urgent Broadcast. As a general rule, "Vital" will only apply to SAR messages.

    c. A broadcast should be repeated on subsequent scheduled broadcasts as long as the information is significant.

    d. Each broadcast should be consecutively numbered. It is important that broadcasts are confined to the information necessary for the safety of navigation.

    e. It is unlikely small craft will be equipped with NAVTEX capabilities; therefore, broadcasting navigation information pertaining to the Intracoastal Waterway and other inland waters not normally used by ocean going vessels may be broadcast by voice (radiotelephone) only.

    f. Reported defects in aids to navigation should be broadcast immediately without waiting for positive verification. The word "REPORTED" will be used to describe a discrepancy that has not been verified by a Coast Guard unit or other reliable source.

    g. A weekly summary of BNM's in effect shall be issued each Thursday.

    h. The following organizations and units should receive "hard copy" record traffic Broadcasts:

        (1) District units with primary and secondary responsibility for an aid to navigation.

        (2) District units (as necessary for their safe navigation).

(3) Adjacent USCG District Commanders (as deemed necessary).

(4) National Geospatial-Intelligence Agency (NGA), Bethesda, MD (if appropriate).
   PLA: NGA NAVSAFETY BETHESDA MD

(5) Transiting Area and out-of-District units

(6) Commandant **(CG-5413)** for changes to or discrepancies to primary seacoast or lake coast aids, DGPS, LORAN, racons, and reports of wrecks or other obstructions.

5. <u>Message Drafting</u>.

   a. In an effort to incorporate the NAVTEX system as a broadcast alternative, it is necessary to establish more uniformity in Broadcast Notice to Mariners. As a rule, all types of broadcasts should read the same way and those messages should be capable of NAVTEX transmission without the need to re-key the information.

   b. The Coast Guard has developed a computer program to assist the originator. This program has been installed at each Communication Area Master Station (CAMS) and at each Communication Station (COMMSTA) at the Unclassified Message Switch (UMS). The program will automatically place designated messages into the NAVTEX broadcast loop. If NAVTEX dissemination is desired, the originator is responsible for placing the appropriate subject indicator character at the end of the subject line. This character must appear between double slant bars (//A//) for the program to identify the message for NAVTEX routing.

      (1) The following subject lines shall be used:
         SUBJ: SCHEDULED BROADCAST NOTICE TO MARINERS
         SUBJ: SAFETY BROADCAST NOTICE TO MARINERS
         SUBJ: URGENT MARINE INFORMATION BROADCAST

      (2) A sample NAVTEX subject line would read:
         SUBJ: SAFETY BROADCAST NOTICE TO MARINERS//A//

      (3) The following NAVTEX SUBJECT INDICATOR CHARACTERS shall be used:

         A - Navigational Warnings
         B - Meteorological Warnings
         C - Ice Reports
         D - Search and Rescue Information and Pirate Attack Warnings
         E - Meteorological Forecasts
         F - Pilot Service Messages
         G - DECCA Messages
         H - LORAN Messages
         J - SATNAV Messages
         K - Other Electronic Navaid Messages

L - Navigational Warnings (Additional to A)
Z - No message on hand (QRU)

c. <u>TIME given in the text of a broadcast may be LOCAL or UTC</u>. The single letter time zone indicator shall be used to designate the standard of time in use. The term LOCAL or any abbreviation of the word shall not be used.

d. SPECIAL BROADCAST INSTRUCTIONS shall appear on the line following the subject line. Special instructions may include information such as: antenna sites to transmit from, how frequently to broadcast, broadcast until canceled, etc. Special instructions must be separated from the text of the message by two slant bars and a carriage return (//).

e. The text of the message shall follow a consistent format. Line 1 of the text will include the originator of the information and the broadcast number:

CCGD7 BNM 155-03
CCGD13 BNM 56-03
CCGD5 UMIB 23-03

f. Line 2 shall be used to list the geographic location. A hyphen shall be used to separate distinct segments of a message. Blank spaces shall be used only when the added space further helps to clarify the information. For an aid to navigation, the broadcast shall include the complete name of the aid to navigation, Light List number, and geographic position. The following examples apply:

MARYLAND-SEACOAST
RHODE ISLAND-NARRAGANSETT BAY
VIRGINIA-SEACOAST-VA CAPES OPAREA

g. Cancellation of a broadcast shall be handled in one of the following ways.

(1) Include an automatic cancellation Date Time Group as the last line of the message. This line should appear as a separate paragraph and read as follows:

CANCEL AT TIME//020600Z DEC 03//.

(2) Draft a separate message. In this case, the subject line and text shall read:

SUBJ: BROADCAST NOTICE TO MARINERS CANCELLATION
1. CANCEL CCGD11 BNM 1228-03 DTG 280015Z FEB 03

(3) By means of the weekly Broadcast Notice to Mariners summary as described in 4.g of this section. A NAVTEX cancellation shall be drafted with the NAVTEX indicator appearing at the end of the subject line (see D.4). Broadcasts may be canceled after the information appears in the Local Notice to Mariners or one hour after the completion of a scheduled marine event.

(4) The abbreviations in Figure 12-1 are internationally recognized and shall be used in all broadcasts. The complete name of an aid to navigation will be used with the exception of five acceptable abbreviations for lighted buoys.

(5) For aids to navigation, it is not necessary to list the secondary Light List number; however, the International Light List number shall be listed when applicable. The position of an aid to navigation (to the nearest tenth of a minute) shall be listed. When establishing an aid to navigation, the position shall be accurate to the nearest second.

h. Every effort must be made to keep the text of the message clear and concise. See the examples that follow.

EXAMPLES OF BROADCAST CONTENTS

Wordy	Concise
DGPS BNM 215-04 ALBUQUERQUE, NM THE ALBUQUERQUE, NM DGPS BROADCAST SITE IS OPERATING AT REDUCED POWER AS OF 030948Z APR 04 UNTIL FURTHER NOTICE.	DGPS BNM 215-04 ALBUQUERQUE, NM DGPS BROADCAST SITE OPERATING AT REDUCED POWER AS OF 030948Z APR 04 UNTIL FURTHER NOTICE.
A. COMCOGARD **SECTOR** MOBILE AL//*CC*// 070143Z APR 04, BNM 0307-04 MO CCGDEIGHT BNM 0167-04 MS - MISSISSIPPI SOUND - PASCAGOULA SHIP CHANNEL 1. THE COAST GUARD HAS RECEIVED A REPORT OF THE BARGE AB1116 PARTIALLY BLOCKING THE PASCAGOULA SHIP CHANNEL, IN APPROXIMATE POSITION 30-18-39.0N, 088-32-10.0W._MARINERS ARE URGED TO EXERCISE EXTREME CAUTION WHEN TRANSITING THIS AREA. 2. CANCEL AT TIME//211747Z APR 04// 3. COMCOGARD **SECTOR** MOBILE AL CANCEL REF A	A. COMCOGARD **SECTOR** MOBILE AL//*CC*// 070143Z APR 04, BNM 0307-04 MO CCGDEIGHT BNM 0167-04 MS - MISSISSIPPI SOUND - PASCAGOULA SHIP CHAN 1. BARGE AB1116 REP BLOCKING PASCAGOULA SHIP CHAN IN APPROX POS 30-18-39.0N, 088-32-10.0W. MARINERS ARE URGED TO EXERCISE EXTREME CAUTION WHEN TRANSITING THIS AREA. 2. CANCEL AT TIME//211747Z APR 04// 3. COMCOGARD **SECTOR** MOBILE AL CANCEL REF A

A. COMCOGARD **SECTOR** HAMPTON ROADS VA//**CC**// 070505Z APR 04. CCGDFIVE BNM 0168-04 VA – CHESAPEAKE BAY – THIMBLE SHOAL CHANNEL 1. THE COAST GUARD HAS RECEIVED A REPORT OF THREE PARTIALLY SUBMERGED PONTOON TANKS AND AN UNLIT PRIVATELY OWNED BUOY ADRIFT AS OF PM APRIL 6, 2004, BLOCKING THIMBLE SHOAL CHANNEL, IN APPROXIMATE POSITION; 30-14-00.0N, 088-30-00.0W. MARINERS ARE URGED TO EXERCISE EXTREME CAUTION WHEN TRANSITING THIS AREA. 2. CANCEL AT TIME//211816Z APR 04// 3. COMCOGARD **SECTOR** HAMPTON ROADS VA CANCEL REF A.	A. COMCOGARD **SECTOR** HAMPTON ROADS VA//**CC**// 070505Z APR 04. CCGDFIVE BNM 0168-04 VA – CHESAPEAKE BAY – THIMBLE SHOAL CHANNEL 1. THREE PARTIALLY SUBMERGED PONTOON TANKS AND UNLIT PRIV BUOY ARE REP ADRIFT AND BLOCKING THIMBLE SHOAL CHAN IN APPROX POS 30-14-00.0N, 088-30-00.0W. MARINERS ARE URGED TO EXERCISE EXTREME CAUTION. 2. CANCEL AT TIME//211816Z APR 04// 3. COMCOGARD **SECTOR** HAMPTON ROADS VA CANCEL REF A.
CCGDONE BNM 0169-04 MA - BOSTON HARBOR CHANNEL 1. CONTINUING UNTIL APPROXIMATELY JUNE 1, 2004, THE HOPPER DREDGE STUYVESANT WILL BE OPERATING IN THE BOSTON HARBOR CHANNEL. DREDGE MATERIALS WILL BE DEPOSITED IN THE OPEN WATER DISPOSAL AREA SOUTH OF DEER ISLAND. THE DREDGE WILL MONITOR VHF-FM CHANNELS 13 AND 16. MARINERS ARE URGED TO TRANSIT THE AREA AT THEIR SLOWEST SAFE SPEED TO MINIMIZE WAKE AND PROCEED WITH CAUTION AFTER PASSING ARRANGEMENTS HAVE BEEN MADE. 2. CANCEL AT TIME//221500Z APR 04//	CCGDONE BNM 0169-04 MA - BOSTON HARBOR CHANNEL 1. UNTIL ABOUT JUN 1, 2004, THE HOPPER DREDGE STUYVESANT WILL BE OPERATING IN BOSTON HARBOR CHAN. DREDGE MATERIALS DEPOSITED IN OPEN WATER DISPOSAL AREA S OF DEER ISLAND. VHF CHAN 13 AND 16 MONITORED. TRANSIT AT SLOWEST SAFE SPEED TO MINIMIZE WAKE. PROCEED WITH CAUTION AFTER PASSING ARRANGEMENTS HAVE BEEN MADE. 2. CANCEL AT TIME//221500Z APR 04//
CCGDELEVEN BNM 0174-04 CA – SAN FRANCISCO BAY ENTRANCE 1. THE COAST GUARD HAS RECEIVED A REPORT THAT CA ARTIFICIAL FISHING REEF LIGHTED BUOY (LLNR 1198), IN THE ENTRANCE TO SAN FRANCISCO BAY AND ADJACENT TO THE SAN FRANCISCO TRAFFIC SEPERATION SCHEME, IN APPROXIMATE POSITION; 29-08-36.0N, 094-40-48.0W, HAS BEEN REPORTED EXTINGUISHED. MARINERS ARE URGED TO USE EXTREME CAUTION IN THIS AREA. 2. CANCEL AT TIME//222247Z APR 04//	CCGDELEVEN BNM 0174-04 CA – SAN FRANCISCO BAY ENTRANCE 1. CA ARTIFICIAL FISHING REEF LB (LLNR 1198) IN APPROX POS; 29-08-36.0N, 094-40-48.0W HAS BEEN REP EXTINGUISHED. MARINERS ARE URGED TO USE EXTREME CAUTION IN THIS AREA. 2. CANCEL AT TIME//222247Z APR 04//

CCGDSEVEN BNM 178-04 FL - TAMPA BAY – EGMONT KEY 1. THE COAST GUARD HAS RECEIVED A REPORT OF A PRIVATELY OWNED, UNLIT MOORING BUOY HAS BEEN ESTABLISHED IN THE TAMPA BAY AREA, ADJACENT TO THE SAFETY FAIRWAY IN THE FOLLWOING APPROXIMATE POSITION; 30-15-23.0N, 088-03-15.0W. THE BUOY IS DESCRIBED AS WHITE WITH AN ALL AROUND BLUE BAND. MARINERS ARE URGED TO USE EXTREME CAUTION IN THIS AREA. 2. CANCEL AT TIME//232003Z APR 04//	CCGDSEVEN BNM 178-04 FL - TAMPA BAY – EGMONT KEY 1. A PRIV MAINTD UNLIT MOORING BUOY IS REP TO HAVE BEEN ESTAB IN TAMPA BAY, ADJACENT TO THE SAFETY FAIRWAY IN APPROX POS; 30-15-23.0N, 088-03-15.0W. THE BUOY IS DESCRIBED AS W WITH AN ALL AROUND BU BAND. MARINERS ARE URGED TO USE EXTREME CAUTION IN THIS AREA. 2. CANCEL AT TIME//232003Z APR 04//
CCGDEIGHT BNM 0185-04 LA - MISSISSIPPI RIVER - SOUTH WEST PASS 1. CONTINUING UNTIL APPROXIMATELY APRIL 28, 2004, THE U. S. GOVERNMENT CONTRACT HOPPER WHEELER WILL BE OPERATING IN THE SOUTHWEST PASS OF THE MISSISSIPPI RIVER. THE DREDGE WILL BE INITIALLY WORKING IN THE VICINITY OF MILE 11.0, BHP. FURTHER ASSIGNMENTS FOR THE DREDGE COULD ALSO INCLUDE OTHER REACHES OF SOUTHWEST PASS FROM HEAD OF PASSES, MILE 0.0, TO THE LOWER JETTY AND BAR CHANNEL AND THE MISSISSIPPI RIVER FROM HEAD OF PASSES, MILE 0.0, TO CUBITS GAP, MILE 3.5 AHP. THE DREDGE WILL WORK 24 HOURS A DAY, 7 DAYS A WEEK, AND WILL MONITOR VHF-FM CHANNELS 16, OR 67. MARINERS ARE URGED TO TRANSIT AT THEIR SLOWEST SAFE SPEED TO MINIMIZE WAKE AND PROCEED WITH CAUTION AFTER PASSING ARRANGEMENTS HAVE BEEN MADE. 2. CANCEL AT TIME//281351Z APR 04//	CCGDEIGHT BNM 0185-04 LA - MS RIVER - SW PASS 1. UNTIL ABOUT APRIL 28, 2004 THE DREDGE HOOPER WHEELER WILL BE OPERATING IN SW PASS IN THE VICINITY OF MILE 11.0 BHP AND FROM HEAD OF PASSES, MILE O.O, TO THE LOWER JETTY AND BAR CHAN AND FROM HEAD OF PASSES, MILE 0.0, TO CUBITS GAP, MILE 3.5 AHP. THE DREDGE WILL WORK 24 HR A DAY, 7 DAYS A WEEK, AND MONITORS VHF-FM CHAN 16 OR 67. MARINERS ARE URGED TO TRANSIT AT SLOWEST SAFE SPEED TO MINIMIZE WAKE AND PROCEED WITH CAUTION AFTER PASSING ARRANGEMENTS HAVE BEEN MADE. 2. CANCEL AT TIME//281351Z APR 04//

STANDARD ABBREVIATIONS FOR BROADCASTS

Word(s)	Abbrev	Word(s)	Abbrev
Light Characteristics		**Aids to Navigation (cont)**	
Alternating	AL	Light List Number	LLNR
Characteristic CHAR		Light	LT
Composite Group-Flashing	FL(2+1)	Lighted Bell Buoy	LBB
Composite Group-Occulting	OC(2+1)	Lighted Buoy	LB
Continuous Quick-Flashing	Q	Lighted Gong Buoy	LGB
Fixed and Flashing	FFL	Lighted Horn Buoy	LHB
Fixed	F	Lighted Whistle Buoy	LWB
Group-Flashing FL(3)		Ocean Data Acquisition System	ODAS
Group-Occulting OC(2)		Privately Maintained PRIV	MAINTD
Interrupted Quick-Flashing	IQ	Radar Reflector	RA REF
Isophase	ISO	Radar responder beacon	RACON
Morse Code	MO(A	Temporarily Replaced by Lighted Buoy	TRLB
Occulting	OC	Temporarily Replaced by Unlighted Buoy	TRUB
Single-Flashing FL		Whistle	WHIS
Color[1]		**Organizations**	
Black	B	Commander, Coast Guard District	CCGD(#)
Blue BU		Coast Guard	CG
Green	G	Corps of Engineers	COE
Orange OR		National Geospatial-Intelligence Agency NGA	
Red	R	National Ocean Service	NOS
White	W	National Weather Service	NWS
Yellow Y			
Aids to Navigation		**Vessels**	
Aeronautical radiobeacon	AERO RBN	Aircraft	A/C
Destroyed DESTR		Fishing Vessel	F/V
Differential GPS	DGPS	Liquefied Natural Gas Carrier	LNG
Discontinued DISCONTD		Motor Vessel[2] M/V	
Established ESTAB		Pleasure Craft	P/C
Exposed Location Buoy	ELB	Research Vessel	R/V
Fog signal station	FOG SIG	Sailing Vessel	S/V

Figure 12-1

---

[1] Color refers to light characteristics of aids to navigation only
[2] M/V includes: Steam Ship, Container Vessel, Cargo Vessel, etc.

Compass Directions		Various (cont.)	
North N		Diameter	DIA
South S		Edition	ED
East E		Effect/Effective	EFF
West W		Entrance	ENTR
Northeast	NE	Explosive Anchorage	EXPLOS ANCH
Northwest NW		Fathom(s)	FM(S)
Southeast SE		Foot/Feet	FT
Southwest SW		Harbor	HBR
Months		Height HT	
January JAN		Hertz	HZ
February FEB		Horizontal clearance	HOR CL
March MAR		Hour	HR
April	APR	International Regulations for Preventing Collisions at Sea	COLREGS
May MAY		Kilohertz	KHZ
June JUN		Kilometer	KM
July JUL		Knot(s)	KT(S)
August	AUG	Minute (time; geo pos)	MIN
September SEP		Moderate	MOD
October OCT		Mountain, Mount	MT
November NOV		Nautical Mile(s)	NM
December	DEC	Notice to Mariners	NTM
Days of the Week		Obstruction OBST	R
Monday MON		Occasion/Occasionally	OCCASION
Tuesday TUE		Operating Area	OPAREA
Wednesday WED		Pacific	PAC
Thursday THU		Point(s)	PT(S)
Friday FRI		Position	**PSN**
Saturday SAT		Position Approximate	PA
Sunday SUN		Pressure	PRES
Various		Private, Privately	PRIV
Anchorage ANCH		Prohibited	PROHIB
Anchorage prohibited	ANCH PROHIB	Publication	PUB
Approximate APPROX		Range	RGE
Atlantic	**ATLC**	Reported	REP
Authorized AUTH		Restricted	RESTR
Average AVG		Rock	RK
Bearing BRG		Saint	ST
Breakwater	BKW	Second (time; geo pos)	SEC
Broadcast Notice to Mariners	BNM	Signal station	SIG STA
Channel CHAN		Station	STA
Code of Federal Regulations CFR		Statute Mile(s)	SM
Continue	CONT	Storm signal station	S SIG STA
Degrees (temp; geo pos)	DEG	Temporary	TEMP

Various (cont.)		Countries and States (cont.)	
Thunderstorm	**TSTM**	Maryland	MD
Through THRU		Marshall Islands	MH
True T		Massachusetts	MA
Uncovers; Dries	UNCOV	Missouri	MO
Universal Coordinate Time	UTC	Mississippi	MS
Urgent Marine Information Broadcast	UMIB	Mexico	MX
Velocity VEL		Michigan	MI
Vertical clearance	VERT CL	Minnesota	MN
Visibility	**VSBY**	Montana	MT
Yard(s) YD		Nebraska	NE
Warning WARN		Nevada	NV
Weather WX		New Hampshire	NH
Wreck WK		New Jersey	NJ
Countries and States		New Mexico	NM
Alabama AL		New York	NY
Alaska AK		North Carolina	NC
American Samoa	AS	North Dakota	ND
Arizona	AZ	Northern Marianas	MP
Arkansas AR		Ohio	OH
California CA		Oklahoma	OK
Canada CN		Oregon OR	
Colorado CO		Pennsylvania	PA
Connecticut CT		Puerto Rico	PR
Delaware DE		Rhode Island	RI
District of Columbia	DC	South Carolina	SC
Florida FL		South Dakota	SD
Georgia GA		Tennessee	TN
Guam GU		Texas	TX
Hawaii	HI	United States	US
Idaho ID		Utah	UT
Illinois IL		Vermont	VT
Indiana IN		Virgin Islands	VI
Iowa IA		Virginia	VA
Kansas KS		Washington	WA
Kentucky KY		West Virginia	WV
Louisiana LA		Wisconsin	WI
Maine ME		Wyoming	WY

Figure 12-1

6. Distress Alerts follow an internationally accepted format.

EXAMPLES OF DISTRESS ALERT CONTENTS

Marine Broadcast Text

DISTRESS ALERT WAS TRANSMITTED IN POSITION XX-XXN, XXX-XXX. MARINERS TRANSITING THROUGH THIS AREA ARE REQUESTED TO KEEP A SHARP LOOKOUT AND MAKE FURTHER REPORTS TO RCC NORFOLK. RCC NORFOLK: PHONE 757-398-6231, FAX: 757-398-6392, INM-C 581 OR 584 430370670. TELEX 127775, MF/HF DSC GROUP IDENTITY 003669999.//

Cancellation Text

THE M/V SUNFISH DISABLED AT POSITION XX-XXN, XXX-XX HAS BEEN ASSISTED AND NO LONGER REQUIRES ASSISTANCE. CANCEL RCC NORFOLK

F. Special Warnings.

1. Responsibility and Scope.

   a. The Special Warning messages system provides for the expeditious handling and dissemination of government (both U.S. and foreign) proclamations and decrees to all U.S. ships throughout the world.

   b. The content of Special Warnings is the responsibility of the Department of State (Maritime Affairs).

   c. Special Warnings are promulgated by National Geospatial-Intelligence Agency (NGA) and broadcast in the same manner and on the same Address Indicating Groups (AIG's) as NAVAREA IV/HYDROLANT, NAVAREA XII/HYDROPAC messages. An additional AIG is used to send such messages to home offices of U.S. steamship companies. Special Warnings incorporate the expression "Special Warning" and a serial number early in the text. Special Warnings differ from NAVAREA IV/HYDROLANT and NAVAREA XII/HYDROPAC messages in that the content is political in nature rather than having to do with marine information.

   d. Further dissemination of Special Warnings is achieved by NGA publishing them in the Notice to Mariners and Daily Memorandum. An annual listing of the texts of all Special Warnings in effect is published in January each year in Notice to Mariners No. 1.

   e. In addition to the AIG of a NAVAREA IV/HYDROLANT, NAVAREA XII/HYDROPAC, NGA adds selected addressees for Special Warnings, e.g., Chief of Naval Operations and Secretary of State. NGA also includes Commander, Atlantic Area and Commander, Pacific Area as action addressees of Special Warning messages.

2. Coast Guard Procedures.

   a. In as much as Special Warnings are issued to the NAVAREA IV/HYDROLANT and NAVAREA XII/HYDROPAC AIGs, District Commanders under the OPCON of COMLANTAREA should ensure they are listed on the NAVAREA IV/HYDROLANT AIG (currently AIG 4501) and District Commanders under the OPCON of COMPACAREA should ensure they are listed on the NAVAREA XII/HYDROPAC AIG (currently AIG 4557).

   b. Upon issuing a Special Warning on the AIGs described above, NGA will originate a separate message, action to the District Commander, information to the Commandant. The message is to "flag" the Special Warning message. Upon receipt of a Special Warning message, coastal District Commanders should broadcast it in a manner similar to issuing a Broadcast Notice to Mariners.

   c. The Special Warning should be broadcast upon receipt and at least during the next two scheduled broadcasts unless otherwise directed by the Area Commander. Special Warnings are not broadcast by VHF-FM stations. The Special Warning broadcast should be identified exclusively by its assigned number and must not be replaced with or supplemented by a district Notice to Mariners number.

   d. In addition to the radio broadcast, the Special Warning should be published at least once in the Local Notice to Mariners.

   e. Depending on the content of a Special Warning, NGA may or may not include CCGDNINE as an addressee on the "flag" message. A Special Warning not "flagged" by NGA may be radio broadcast at the discretion of the commands. CCGDNINE should publish a Special Warning at least once in the Local Notice to Mariners whether they issued a Broadcast Notice to Mariners or not.

   f. In order to ensure the receipt of Special Warning messages in critical areas, NGA includes in the dissemination message, (but not as part of the Special Warning) the following: "All U.S. Flag Merchant Ships (in general area of incident) acknowledge receipt of this message to NGA through U.S. Government radio facilities." The responses to this message, compared with the AMVER database, enables NGA to ensure receipt of the Special Warning by all vessels in the critical area. All Coast Guard radio facilities must be prepared to accept and forward Special Warning receipt messages addressed to NGA.

This Page Intentionally
Left Blank

CHAPTER 13 - LIGHTHOUSES

A. <u>Introduction</u>.

1. <u>History of Lighthouse Unmanning</u>. The Coast Guard has been in the process of unmanning lighthouses ever since the responsibility for operating 503 lighthouses was assumed with the transfer of the Lighthouse Service in 1939. Due to the high cost of maintaining isolated manned units, lighthouses have been converted to unattended operation. Because of the distinctive character of each lighthouse, the efforts required for automation varied significantly. The simplest and least costly conversions were accomplished first. These conversions often consisted of nothing more than electrification and unmanning of the lighthouse. In the 1960s it became apparent that the remaining lighthouses had high power requirements and were either: (a) in a remote location which presented a problem in monitoring the aid, (b) in a populous area and subject to a high incidence of vandalism, or (c) of a historically sensitive nature. The solution to these problems was the Lighthouse Automation and Modernization Project (LAMP). LAMP provided for reliable power at isolated sites, monitoring of remote units, centrally supported standard equipment, and, more recently, structural preservation.

2. <u>Problems Resulting from the Process of Unmanning</u>. Although lighthouse unmanning is economically attractive, many associated maintenance problems have been encountered subsequent to the removal of lighthouse personnel. This chapter will provide a framework for efforts to resolve these problems.

   a. Unsightliness and deterioration of lighthouses are major problems, not only from the image an unsightly facility reflects on the responsible unit or Coast Guard, but also to the safety of servicing personnel and the capital investment in the buildings. The causes of these problems are not quite so obvious. The failure to complete a maintenance plan is the main reason for the decline in the condition of a particular lighthouse.

      (1) Typical misconceptions include:

         (a) The Aid to Navigation Team's (ANT) belief that its responsibility is only for the lighthouse's signal and not for the cleanliness and general maintenance of the structure.

         (b) The Sector Commander's assumption that the lighthouses are no longer a responsibility after the removal of personnel.

         (c) The belief that a preventive maintenance plan can be deferred with minimal effect.

(d) That lighthouse maintenance can be deferred because they are not active units.

(e) That the responsibility for structural maintenance will end if the lighthouse is leased or licensed.

b. Unreliability of signals is another problem, with a different cause. Servicing personnel repair proficiency is not high because (a) mockups for regular review and practice are distant, (b) actual visits to lights are infrequent and intimate equipment familiarity is not maintained. Servicing personnel fatigue after a long and tiring small boat ride to a remote light also diminishes efficiency. Despite our best training efforts, the proficiency of maintenance personnel is cyclical. Individuals arrive with little automated aid experience. Their proficiency improves through training and on-the-job experience until the transfer cycle begins again.

B. Lighthouse Maintenance Strategy.

1. Maintenance Goals.

a. Equipment Maintenance. Each lighthouse equipment suite is provided with maintenance intervals which shall be followed. See Major Aids to Navigation Preventive Maintenance System Guide, COMDTIST M16500.10 (series), for more details. Inactive equipment or assemblies should be removed.

b. Facility Maintenance. Each lighthouse serves as a shelter and support for the equipment. Additional considerations of historical preservation may also be needed. Lack of facility maintenance has come under close public and congressional scrutiny. Each lighthouse should provide an enclosure for the signal equipment, a safe workplace, and reflect a favorable appearance for the Coast Guard. This maintenance is the job of the servicing Civil Engineering Unit (CEU).

(1) Foundation or structural flaws should be identified and their maintenance programmed through the shore maintenance system.

(2) Structures should be weatherproof. Adequate ventilation should be provided.

(3) Structures should be vandal resistant to a high degree.

(4) There should be virtually no rust or structural deterioration.

(5) Structures should be completely safe for servicing personnel. Overnight facilities, where necessary, should be kept clean and habitable.

c. Elimination of Unnecessary Structures. In the past, lighthouse maintenance had been accomplished by light keepers, bases, M&R detachments, and tenders. These forces have diminished through lighthouse automations, personnel reductions, reorganizations, and an overall reduction in personnel and facilities. The existing buildings were then divided among the remaining aids to navigation servicing forces. In order to reduce this workload to conform to the capabilities of the servicing forces, every effort shall be made to eliminate unnecessary structures and appurtenances to reduce the need for structural maintenance. Any demolition or other action that may have a detrimental effect on a potentially historic, or historic, site or structure must first go through the Section 106 process and the State Historical Preservation Officer (SHPO) must be consulted. Consultation for any action impacting an eligible or historic property through the SHPO is handled by the appropriate servicing environmental staff at the Maintenance and Logistics Commands (MLCs), or the Civil Engineering Units (CEUs). Often, the SHPO will recognize the difficulties in maintaining isolated structures. In some cases, a thematic program can be established. As an example, demolition of a keeper's quarters at inaccessible stations may not raise as many objections from the SHPO, if similar quarters are accessible and are being maintained. Consider the following actions to reduce the need for structural maintenance:

(1) Demolish or excess outbuildings at formerly manned lighthouses.

(2) Use standard volume fiberglass containers for signal and power equipment whenever practicable to eliminate the need for retaining outbuildings that require extensive structural maintenance.

(3) Remove unnecessary chimneys, stanchions, awnings, fences, catwalks, and unused equipment whenever practicable.

(4) Replace light towers with low-maintenance structures wherever there is no longer a need for a major daymark.

(5) Report as excess the properties which contain buildings no longer required for operational aids. Ensure required easements are retained for visibility of signals and access.

d. Inhabitation. One of the primary goals of LAMP has been the elimination of light keeper billets, a scarce and costly resource. Unfortunately, this goal is not realistic in every case because of vandalism or an extremely harsh environment. In these situations, re-inhabitation of formerly manned lighthouses may be necessary. The following methods of providing a presence at lighthouses are listed in order of preference:

(1) Use light keeper's dwelling for housing of USCG personnel attached to nearby units.

(2) Work with the servicing Civil Engineering Unit (CEU) and Real Property Office to declare the property excess to facilitate transfer under the National Historic Lighthouse Preservation Act (NHLPA).

(3) Assign a military caretaker to maintain the structures and grounds.

2. Maintenance Standards.

   a. Daymark. Every lighthouse is a daymark, unless specifically disestablished. The distinctive shape and colors identify the aid in the same way that numbers or letters identify minor aids. The navigational significance of the daymark has reduced since they were originally built. For those that are still navigationally significant it is imperative that these characteristics be maintained as advertised in the Light List.

   b. Cosmetics. Lighthouses represent the Coast Guard. The public often views nearby lighthouses as part of their local heritage and resents any deterioration. The Coast Guard has a mandate to maintain lighthouses and the public expects compliance. It is not a duty that can be neglected without arousing considerable public concern.

   c. Signal Support and Equipment Shelter. One of the main functions of a lighthouse is to support an optic at a height commensurate with the required geographic range. An associated function at many lights is to provide shelter for power and control equipment. Alternatively, power and control hardware may be housed in adjacent buildings or standard volume containers. Structural maintenance goals must provide clean, dry spaces for electrical and electronic equipment and a sturdy tower for support of and access to the main and emergency signals.

   d. Safety and Cleanliness. Maintenance must also include preservation of safety equipment and devices installed or required at lighthouses. Lighthouses over twenty feet tall pose a safety hazard from falls. Safety railings around exterior walkways and galleries, as well as handrails along spiral ladders, shall be maintained in an effective condition. Docks and access ladders must be safe for boat landings at offshore lights. Safety inspections shall be conducted in conjunction with routine District, CEU, and Sector inspections to ensure compliance with standard safety procedures for working around engines, batteries, and electrical equipment. Lighthouse interiors shall be kept clean, free of debris, expended batteries, oil, obsolete equipment and refuse. Overnight facilities, where necessary, should be kept clean and habitable. The Sector Commander, during inspections, should examine the living spaces.

e. <u>Historicity</u>. Lighthouses and outbuildings that are listed, nominated, or eligible for listing in the National Register of Historic Places shall be maintained in a manner befitting their historical significance. See Section 11.B. of this manual.

3. <u>Maintenance Policy</u>.

   a. <u>Levels of Maintenance</u>. The following levels apply to all aspects of lighthouse maintenance and servicing. Preventive and corrective maintenance actions shall be accomplished by the lowest level that has the capability for any particular required work. Deficiencies detected by lower levels that are incapable of performing the required maintenance shall be reported to the next higher level using established reporting procedures.

      (1) <u>Organizational Maintenance</u>. This is the routine preventive maintenance that is performed by the primary servicing unit (usually ANTs, stations and small vessels) at nominal quarterly intervals. It relates to the manned unit's regular upkeep of its own facilities and equipment. On an unmanned lighthouse this level of maintenance generally consists of cleaning, servicing, lubricating, making minor repairs, testing of systems, (i.e. run, take readings, adjust), housekeeping, and painting. Repairs must often be slated for accomplishment at a higher level of maintenance. However, it is the responsibility of organizational-level maintenance units to communicate all structural discrepancies using the Shore Station Maintenance Report (SSMR.) Without this line of communication, assistance cannot be assured and the primary servicing unit would soon be overburdened with constantly increasing workloads. The remote nature of lighthouses dictates complete documentation of structural conditions to keep Sector, District and Engineering Support Commanders apprised of the status of the facilities and to eliminate the need for unscheduled visits to lights.

      (2) <u>Intermediate Maintenance</u>. The second level of maintenance is generally a non-routine, corrective nature performed by units having a variety of specialized technicians. This maintenance usually consists of more difficult or extensive work performed at the lighthouse. Specific tasks may include equipment calibration, replacement of major components, major troubleshooting and repairs, fabrication of parts, large-scale painting, structural or masonry repairs, welding, specification writing or technical guidance. District, Sector, buoy tender, construction tender, ISC, ISD, MLC, CEU, and Headquarters staff personnel and contractors perform this level of maintenance.

(3) Depot Maintenance. This type of maintenance is performed by shore commands or commercial repair facilities that have the capability for repair or complete overhaul of even the largest and most complex equipment assemblies and parts. Depot level support may be obtained within the Coast Guard from the Yard, the ELC, C2CEN, TISCOM, Integrated Support Actvities Commands, or Industrial Support Detachments (ISDs). These facilities maintain extensive inventories, replacement parts and spare systems. They employ a wide variety of technicians and specialists. Initiating such maintenance is a responsibility of the Sector Commander, although the initial request for assistance may come from the primary servicing unit or unit performing intermediate maintenance that requires depot-level support.

C. Lighthouse Maintenance Responsibilities.

1. Headquarters.

   a. Chief, **Visual Navigation Branch (CG-54131)** is responsible for managing the U.S. system of Short Range Aids to Navigation, which includes lighthouses (but not radionavigational aids). The responsibility with respect to lighthouses involves:

   (1) Maintaining documents and reports required for planning, programming and budgeting.

   (2) Initiating, reviewing and approving plans for establishment, disestablishment or change of lighthouse and associated equipment.

   (3) Developing planning criteria and operational requirements.

   (4) Establishing operational procedures, staffing standards and training requirements for maintenance personnel.

   (5) Monitoring the effectiveness of lighthouse signals.

   (6) Initiating requests to support managers for improving performance or efficiency.

   (7) Maintaining liaison with international, Federal, state, and municipal agencies in carrying out the above responsibilities.

   (8) Obtaining and administering funds for organizational-level maintenance.

   b. Chief, **Electronic Navigation Branch (CG-54132)** manages radionavigational aids collocated with lighthouses.

c. Chief, Office of Civil Engineering **(CG-43)** provides policy for the guidance of the MLC, Civil Engineering Unit (CEU), Facilities Design and Construction Centers (FD&CC), and facility engineering organizations in delivery of the civil engineering, environmental management, and facility management support programs within the Coast Guard. That includes:

   (1) Management and oversight of engineering support for the aids to navigation program and technical guidance to assist program managers in development of documentation to support their sponsorship of shore facility requirements resulting from new or expanded mission requirements.

   (2) Formulate and publish policies governing real property acquisition, disposal and management, and administer the HQ and interagency aspects of the National Historic Lighthouse Preservation of 2000.

2. <u>District Commanders</u>. The District Commander is responsible for coordinating the activities of district aids to navigation servicing units and Sector staffs, and to communicate support needs to the Maintenance and Logistic Command to ensure effective lighthouse maintenance is accomplished at all levels.

   a. Chief, **Waterways Management** Branch **(dpw)** shall ensure that lighthouses are maintained to established standards and that discrepancies are corrected in a timely manner. Specific responsibilities include:

      (1) Training of maintenance team personnel.

      (2) Identifying required personnel qualifications.

      (3) Organization and operation of servicing units.

      (4) Cognizant staff officers shall be actively aware of the condition of all district lighthouses by means of SSMRs, CASREPs, aid discrepancy reports, photography and inspection reports.

      (5) Providing administrative guidance. Specific instructions that supplement or amplify the provisions of this chapter should be included in the District OPLAN or appropriate directorate. Maintenance responsibilities and assignments shall be promulgated for all organizational, intermediate and depot level activities. Mere duplication of the information contained herein shall be avoided.

3. <u>Sector Commanders</u>. The Sector Commander is responsible for coordinating and monitoring the establishment, disestablishment, servicing and maintenance of all lighthouses and their associated aids to navigation signals within the Sector. The appearance and reliability of lighthouses is a functional gauge of the Commander

in meeting these responsibilities. The responsibility may not be delegated to subordinate units although specific maintenance assignments should be made and documented in writing. A Sector Aids to Navigation Officer shall be assigned to assist the Sector Commander in carrying out these responsibilities, either as a primary or collateral duty, depending upon the number and categories of aids to navigation within the Sector. Sector responsibilities include:

a. Administrative guidance, coordination and support of all assigned Sector aids to navigation servicing units.

b. Direct control over major aid servicing teams and structural maintenance teams that are part of the Sector.

c. Conducting inspection and training programs that include regular visits to automated lighthouses. Experience has shown that the direct involvement of the Sector Commander in this responsibility has a positive effect on lighthouse maintenance.

d. Ensuring that appropriate qualification codes are assigned to billets involved with major aids to navigation maintenance and that qualified personnel are assigned.

e. Maintenance of a master SSMR file for all lighthouses within the Sector area of responsibility except those specifically assigned to another unit.

f. Arranging for intermediate or depot-level maintenance in support of Sector units.

g. Where lighthouse maintenance can be more effectively conducted at the Sector level, an OPFAC modifier should be established for a Sector Lighthouse Maintenance Team. The team's duties would be the same as those specified below for ANTs.

4. Aid to Navigation Teams. An ANT is normally assigned primary responsibility for organizational maintenance of unmanned lighthouses. This in no way relieves the Sector Commander of the overall responsibility for the condition of all assigned lighthouses, both manned and unmanned. The ANT Officer-in-Charge is responsible to ensure the continuous availability of all signals, the proper functioning of power and control systems, and the upkeep of all assigned structures and grounds. ANTs are not intended to be capable of all types of lighthouse maintenance and repair work. They are required to communicate (i.e., submit SSMRs) all deficiencies that are beyond their capabilities and to inform the Sector Commander of priority maintenance projects that affect the safety of personnel or the structural integrity of the lighthouse and associated outbuildings.

5. Buoy Tenders and Construction Tenders. Buoy tenders and Construction tenders have been highly effective as intermediate-level maintenance forces and are particularly suited to lighthouse maintenance work. They have experienced technicians, a wide variety of maintenance equipment, planning and management skills and the capability for sustained operations at remote sites. However, their schedules dictate that such work is assigned by tender-order. Because of the specific training required to maintain an automated light system, tender maintenance normally will not include signal or equipment. Sector, ISC/ISA/ISD or ANT support is usually required in procuring equipment and scheduling supply deliveries. Additional technical experts in lighthouse renovation techniques may also be obtained from a Sector, District, Integrated Support Command, or Civil Engineering Unit.

6. Stations. Stations may be assigned organizational level responsibility for lighthouses, especially where the housing units are used for station personnel. In such cases, duties will be the same as for ANTs.

7. Maintenance and Logistic Command Organization.

   a. MLC Commanders. The MLC Commander has the overall responsibility for the structural integrity of lighthouse structures. The MLC coordinates engineering, real property activities, and construction contracts at lighthouses and other aids to navigation facilities.

      (1) Civil Engineering Division. Provides depot level maintenance, (inspections, management of the SSMR program, designs alterations, and provides technical information for organizational maintenance where necessary. Establishes maintenance guidelines for organizational maintenance. Ensures compliance of standards through inspections. Supervises the Civil Engineering Units.

         (a) Civil Engineering Units. The CEU designs alterations, provides technical information for organizational maintenance where necessary. **They** conduct triennial inspections of lighthouses to determine structural conditions, and provide project priority input to the MLC for scheduling projects.

      (2) Finance Division. The Real Property Section arranges leases and licenses at lighthouses, providing copies to District **(dpw)** and Sectors, which inspect for compliance with all lease or license provisions; maintains property records and historical files on lighthouse property; and provides required reviews of property use. The Accounting Section provides AFC30 funds for organizational maintenance beyond the ability of the ANT or Sector, and ensures lighthouse maintenance projects receive an equitable share of AFC30 shore maintenance funding based on Resource Change Proposals and AC&I follow-on funding.

(3) Industrial Support Commands (ISC). The Support Command is a depot level maintenance activity that may be called upon to provide technical assistance or skilled personnel in support of lighthouses. Technicians from these units may also augment organizational-level maintenance teams whenever adequately trained or skilled personnel are not available.

D. Inspections.

1. Servicing Unit. Lighthouse inspections shall be carried out by primary servicing units during all scheduled and emergency servicing visits. Structural, mechanical, and electrical deficiencies that cannot be repaired during these visits shall be reported to the Sector Commander, who will arrange for remedial action by a higher level maintenance force.

2. Sector. Sector Commanders shall personally inspect all manned lighthouses and at least a representative sampling of unmanned lighthouses annually. Sector Engineers and/or Sector Aids to Navigation Officers shall inspect those lighthouses not inspected by the Sector Commander. Inspections shall ensure structural integrity, general cleanliness, safe working conditions, and proper functioning of equipment.

3. District. The Chief, Aids to Navigation Branch shall personally inspect a representative number of lighthouses within the district on an annual basis. To reduce travel complications this should be in conjunction with Sector Commanders visits, and therefore will provide an excellent opportunity for the two most involved managers to discuss lighthouse management.

4. Civil Engineering Units. The CEU conducts the triennial civil engineering inspections required by the Civil Engineering Manual. Copies of this inspection should be provided to the Sector Commander with a copy to the District Aids to Navigation and Waterways Management Branch. Deficiencies in the facility maintenance should be addressed, as well as the organization responsible for discrepancy correction.

E. Required Reports.

1. SSMRs. The Shore Station Maintenance Program is the established system of scheduling, assuring, and controlling the maintenance of shore facilities. This system applies to all shore facilities, including manned and unmanned lighthouses. A thorough explanation of the responsibilities for managing this system is included in the Civil Engineering Manual. ANTs and Sectors are the primary initiators of lighthouse related SSMRs which in turn develop engineering projects. Major recurring items beyond the scope of organizational-level or depot-level maintenance abilities should be submitted on SSMRs to be included on the backlog of projects.

2. <u>CASREPs and Discrepancy Reports</u>. District SOPs contain instructions for completing CASREPs and Discrepancy Reports. ANTs and Sectors should also be aware of any trend in equipment deficiencies which result in an increase of casualties. Identifiable trends should be discussed with the District Training Team and the Technical Advisor at the NATON School for service-wide dissemination.

F. <u>National Historic Lighthouse Preservation Act</u>.

1. <u>Introduction</u>. The National Historic Lighthouse Preservation Act of 2000 (NHLPA) was passed to allow the Coast Guard to transfer ownership of historical lighthouses to preservation groups. The Coast Guard does not have the funding or the personnel required to maintain lighthouses to historical standards required under the National Historic Preservation Act, and the NHLPA was designed by Congress to help facilitate the preservation of these historic landmarks.

2. <u>Transfer Process</u>. The transfer process of a lighthouse is not a quick or easy process. Part of the process requires that the Coast Guard declare the structure and associated buildings as excess property. The fact that the shape and color of a lighthouse is considered its daymark, the lighthouse tower cannot be transferred until the daymark is disestablished. In order to facilitate the process, use the following steps.

   a. Civil Engineering Units or Real Property Offices should work closely with District offices in determining which lighthouses are ready to be declared as excess property. At this time, the District Commander should make the CEU or Real Property office aware of any aspects of the lighthouse that may indicate it is not the best candidate for the NHLPA process (e.g., whole first floor contains batteries that cannot be moved, or power cables or electric equipment in the open creates a safety problem for public access, security concerns, etc.). The District Commander should be aware of any lighthouse that is being considered for excess before the declaration is made.

   b. Upon being informed that a lighthouse is being considered as excess, the district must make a determination of how important the aid is. If the aid is vital and the daymark could not be **discontinued**, that lighthouse cannot be declared as excess. If the daymark could be disestablished, or both the daymark and the light could be **discontinued**, the process to declare the lighthouse as excess can be started by the CEU or Real Property Office. Upon making this determination, the District Commander needs to inform Commandant **(CG-5413)** in order to streamline the HQ concurrent clearance process.

   c. Upon approval by Commandant **(CG-43)** and DHS the Report of Excess will be delivered to GSA. When it reaches GSA, the NHLPA process begins.

Once a recipient has been identified, Commandant **(CG-5413)** will notify the appropriate District that a recipient has been identified.

d. Upon receipt of the notification of recipient, the District Commander will produce Local Notice to Mariners advertising the plans for the lighthouse in the following manner.

(1) For a lighthouse where the light is required as a Federal aid to navigation.

"The daymark on (aid name, LLNR #) will be disestablished on or about (date). (Aid name) and associated buildings will be transferred under the National Historic Lighthouse Preservation Act. The light will continue to be operated as a Federal aid to navigation."

(2) For a lighthouse where the entire aid is not required as a Federal aid to navigation.

"The (aid name, LLNR #) will be disestablished on or about (date). The lighthouse and associated buildings will be transferred under the National Historic Lighthouse Preservation Act."

e. On the date listed in the Local Notice to Mariners, the District Commander will do one of two things based on the notice that was sent out.

(1) Disestablish the daymark and publish a correction to the Light List to remove the description of the tower or structure from the aid in question.

(2) Disestablish the entire aid and remove it from the Light List.

f. After the daymark, or daymark and light, is disestablished, the lighthouse will be transferred to the receiving group. As appropriate, the District Commander shall process the recipient's private aid to navigation application.

g. If the recipient applies for private aid to navigation, the daymark will be created as a separate private aid with its own light list number. If the recipient does not apply for a private aid to navigation the remarks column in the light list shall include "Structure maintained by entity outside the U.S. Coast Guard."

CHAPTER 14 - BUOY INVENTORY MANAGEMENT

A. Purpose.

  1. This chapter describes the Buoy Management Program and provides policy and guidelines for the funding, procurement, and management of Coast Guard ocean buoys. The Buoy Management Program provides the basis for determining annual buoy demand by monitoring buoy inventories and changes to authorized stations. The Buoy Body Transaction Report (BBTR) is the official document used to manage the Coast Guard's ocean buoy inventory and is discussed in detail in Paragraph F of this chapter.

B. Roles and Responsibilities.

  1. There are several Coast Guard activities involved in carrying out the Buoy Management Program. A brief description of their roles and responsibilities is given below. For the BBTR and buoy inventory to remain accurate, it is essential that all parties communicate with each other on a regular basis.

  2. Commandant **(CG-5413)**. Commandant **(CG-5413)** approves Waterways projects **as prescribed in Chapter 2.B.2.b of this manual**.

  3. Commandant **(CG-432)**. Commandant **(CG-432)** purchases both AC&I and OE buoys for the Districts. In addition, Commandant **(CG-432)** is responsible for the Coast Guard buoy inventory database and the BBTR.

  4. Commandant **(CG-483)**. Commandant **(CG-483)** manages the OE and AC&I Waterways accounts and coordinates the transfer of funds.

  5. District **(dpw)**. Districts identify the need for OE and waterways projects. In addition, they are responsible for managing all the hulls assigned to their districts. They are required to send quarterly BBTR update letters to Commandant **(CG-432)** detailing any changes to their buoy inventory. Based on their inventory shortages (if any), Districts provide their annual requirement for new buoy hulls to Commandant **(CG-432).**

C. Required Submittals.

  1. The Buoy Management Program requires the submission of a number of documents throughout the fiscal year by the District to Commandant **(CG-54131)** and Commandant **(CG-432).** These **documents** are summarized below, and are discussed in detail in various sections of this chapter.

2. AC&I waterways projects are submitted by Districts to Commandant **(CG-5413),** which in turn forwards them to Commandant **(CG-432)** when they have been approved for funding and added to the fiscal year's Planned Obligation Prioritization (POP) list.

3. OE projects are submitted by Districts directly to Commandant **(CG-432).**

4. Quarterly BBTR update letters from each District to Commandant **(CG-432)** are required by 31 January, 30 April, 31 July and 31 October. The update letter should document all buoys surveyed, buoys lost/missing, buoys transferred into and out of the District, new buoys received, District-authorized station changes, and buoys previously reported lost/missing but subsequently recovered.

5. Quarterly BBTR. Update letters from Commandant **(CG-432)** to each District are sent by 30 November, 28 February, 31 May and 31 August. These should be reviewed by the District and any discrepancies should be reported to Commandant **(CG-432).**

6. Districts are required to submit their annual Buoy and Chain Prioritized Requirements List to Commandant **(CG-432)** by 31 August. Buoys reported on the list that are not documented as a shortage on the BBTR will not be funded. It is not to be inferred that all items requested will necessarily be funded during the year. Only those items which fall within funding capability will actually be ordered.

D. Funding.

Funding for new buoy procurement comes from both the Coast Guard OE and AC&I appropriations. Commandant **(CG-432)** oversees these funds and manages the buoy procurements.

E. Procurement Process.

1. The procurement of OE and AC&I buoys is executed through contracts with commercial sources managed by Commandant **(CG-432).**

2. OE Funds. OE funds for ATON hardware are allocated at the start of the Fiscal Year. It is essential that Commandant **(CG-432)** receive the District's Buoy and Chain Prioritized Requirements List by 31 August to review and distribute the OE funds in a timely manner. After receipt of these letters from all the Districts, Commandant **(CG-432)** calculates the total cost of the requests and verifies that the requests reflect actual shortages on the BBTR. Funds are allocated based on documented shortages and District operational priorities.

3. <u>AC&I Funds</u>. AC&I funds for ATON hardware are allocated after Commandant **(CG-432)** receives a copy of the Waterways Planned Obligation Prioritization (POP) list from Commandant **(CG-54131)**.

F. <u>Inventory Management</u>.

1. The Buoy Body Transaction Report (BBTR) is the official document which Commandant **(CG-432)** uses to manage the Coast Guard-wide ocean buoy inventory. The BBTR tracks all 3rd class and larger ocean buoy hulls, authorized buoy stations, and authorized maintenance relief hulls for each District. The CFO Act of 1990 required all Government agencies to more accurately manage and account for their assets. Over the years, the buoy quantities shown on the BBTR had become unreliable, and the CFO Act meant that an improvement was required to better control and manage the inventory. In 1995, Commandant **(CG-432)** requested all Districts to provide the serial numbers of their buoy hulls so they could be placed in a database to better track the buoy inventory. The database is designed to store the serial numbers of all 3rd class and larger buoys as they enter and leave a District, but it is not concerned about the buoys' actual physical location within the District. With this improved inventory management system in place, the serial number of each buoy in a specific buoy class can now be tabulated for each District and directly transferred to the BBTR for an accurate count. This new system enables us to validate the BBTR against the Districts' buoy inventories and allocate funds to purchase ATON hardware more effectively.

2. <u>BBTR</u>. The BBTR documents the buoy inventory of each District by standard buoy classes. Buoys approved for manufacture are designated as standard. This is explained in Chapter 2 of the Aids to Navigation Manual - Technical, COMDTINST M16500.3A (series). The BBTR includes the following categories:

   a. <u>Authorized Stations</u>: Stations listed in the Light List or approved by a Form CG-3213 as a <u>permanent</u> aid to navigation. Also included are annual winter marks.

   b. <u>Authorized Maintenance Reliefs</u>: Number of maintenance relief hulls authorized for a particular buoy type.

   c. <u>Total Authorized</u>: This is the sum of the Authorized Stations and the Authorized Reliefs.

   d. <u>Buoys in District</u>: Actual number of non-surveyed buoys that are in the District, including those that are on station and reliefs. Each buoy's serial number is documented in the Coast Guard's Buoy Inventory Database.

e. <u>On Order</u>: Buoys that are on order for the District, but have not been delivered.

f. <u>Short/Excess</u>: The difference between the Total Authorized and the sum of buoys in District and on order.

3. Below is an example of a BBTR for an 8X26LR buoy. This District has 210 Authorized Stations and 32 Authorized Reliefs for a Total Authorized **amount** of 242 buoys. They show only 239 buoys in the District with no buoys on order, resulting in a shortage of 3 hulls.

Buoy Class	Station Auth	Relief Auth	Total Auth	Buoys in Dist	On Order	-Short +Excess	Remarks
8X26LR	209	32	241	235	0	-6	Data Base (15% Relief)
						7	7 FY00 OE Order TCB040
	1		1			-1	Auth District Station Change (7-00-07) 03 Nov 99
				7	-7	0	Delivery of 00 OE Order TCB040 (5/31/00)
				-5		-5	Survey BBTR Update Ltr 28 Aug 00 (9/1/00)
-2			-2			2	Auth Station Change 07-00-29 BBTR Update Ltr 28 Aug 00 (9/1/00)
	2		2		2	0	AC&I Project 07-00-28, FY00 Order EC0026 (9/1/00)
				2	-2	0	Delivery of FY00 Order EC0026 (9/1/00)
8X26LR	210	32	242	239	0	-3	**Total for Manufactured Buoy**

4. <u>Changes to the BBTR</u>. Additions and subtractions to the BBTR occur on a continual basis for all the categories. Descriptions of authorized changes to the BBTR are described below:

a. <u>Authorized Stations</u>. A District's Authorized Stations can be changed in one of the following ways:

(1) <u>AC&I Projects</u>. Station changes to the BBTR for AC&I projects will occur only when the project is approved for funding by Commandant **(CG-54131)**.

(2) <u>OE Projects</u>. Station changes to the BBTR for OE projects will occur when the approved copy of the Form CG-3213 has been received by Commandant **(CG-432)**.

b. <u>Authorized Maintenance Reliefs</u>. Authorized Maintenance Reliefs will constantly be updated as the Authorized Stations of a buoy class changes. A 15% allowance is considered the maximum for Authorized Maintenance Reliefs of a buoy class. Requests for an allowance greater then 15% should be quantitatively justified and forwarded to Commandant **(CG-54131)** for approval.

c. <u>Buoys in District</u>. As previously noted, it is not intended for the BBTR and buoy inventory database to account for the exact location of a buoy in the District, but rather to only monitor the movement of buoys into and out of a District. Buoys may enter or leave a District in one of the following ways:

(1) <u>New Buoy Shipments</u>. New buoys are delivered to each District from the commercial buoy manufacturers. Buoy delivery information should be consolidated by the District and forwarded to Commandant **(CG-432)** via the Quarterly BBTR Update Letter.

(2) <u>Lost from Station</u>. Buoys lost while occupying a station. District Commanders will be aware of these losses through message traffic or reports they require of their units. This information should be consolidated by the District and forwarded to Commandant **(CG-432)** via the Quarterly BBTR Update Letter.

(3) <u>Surveyed buoys</u>. When a buoy cannot be economically repaired and upgraded within the guidelines of Chapter 2 of the Aids to Navigation Manual - Technical, COMDTINST M16500.3A (series), it shall be surveyed. This information should be consolidated by the District and forwarded to Commandant **(CG-432)** via the Quarterly BBTR Update Letter.

(4) <u>Inter-district Transfer</u>. A less frequent source of buoys into or out of a District is through inter-District transfers. This information should be consolidated by the District and forwarded to Commandant **(CG-432)** via the Quarterly BBTR Update Letter.

(5) <u>Recovered Buoys</u>. Buoys recovered after having been reported as lost from station. This information should be consolidated by the District and forwarded to the Commandant **(CG-432)** via the Quarterly BBTR Update Letter.

This Page Intentionally
Left Blank

CPSIA information can be obtained
at www.ICGtesting.com
Printed in the USA
LVHW060352210222
711600LV00006B/39